40-0

EDUCATING THE VIRTUES

EDUCATING
THE VIRTUES

An essay on the philosophical
psychology of moral development
and education

David Carr

London and New York

First published 1991
by Routledge
11 New Fetter Lane, London EC4P 4EE

Simultaneously published in the USA and Canada
by Routledge
a division of Routledge, Chapman and Hall, Inc.
29 West 35th Street, New York, NY 10001

Typeset in 10/12 Palatino by
Florencetype Ltd, Kewstoke, Avon
Printed and bound in Great Britain by
T J Press (Padstow) Ltd, Padstow, Cornwall

British Library Cataloguing in Publication Data
Carr, David
Educating the virtues: an essay on the philosophical
psychology of moral development and education.
1. Moral education
I. Title
370.114

ISBN 0-415-05746-9

Library of Congress Cataloging in Publication Data
Carr, David.
Educating the virtues: an essay on the philosophical psychology
of moral development and education / David Carr.
p.   cm.
Includes bibliographical references.
ISBN 0-415-05746-9
1. Moral education.   2. Moral development.   3. Virtue.   I. Title.
LC268.C257   1990
370.11'4—dc20   90-35707
CIP

To the memory of
Alderman Alfred Carr J.P. 1893–1960.

CONTENTS

PREFACE

Two of my previously published papers were in fact the survivors of an abortive attempt in late 1982 to compose a full length work on moral education focused on the nature of the virtues. The first of these, which was published in *Educational Philosophy and Theory* (1983) under the title 'Three approaches to moral education', led to further work on moral education – in particular, to a paper 'Aristotle and Durkheim on moral education' which I was invited to read at a conference on moral education and character organised by the US Department of Education in Washington during the summer of 1987. I am grateful to the US Department of Educational Research for allowing me to use parts of that paper for the writing of chapters 5 and 11 of the present work.

The second paper which survived the debacle of my 1982 project was presented to a London meeting of the Aristotelian Society in the autumn of 1984 and subsequently published in the *Proceedings* under the title 'Two kinds of virtue'. Again, I am very grateful for permission to use much of that paper (© The Aristotelian Society 1984, reprinted by courtesy of the editor) as the basis of chapter 9 of this work. I have also drawn in this work on ideas from several other previously published papers on moral philosophy and education written in the wake of these two earlier ones, of course, but in this respect I am particularly indebted to the Philosophy of Education Society and their publishers Carfax for permission to reproduce parts of my 1985 article 'The free child and the spoiled child' in chapter 6.

The present work, then is the product of a renewed attempt, in response to a publisher's invitation, to accomplish what

I started out but failed to do almost a decade ago. During the eighteen months or so I have spent on this task I have, of course, benefited from the co-operation, inspiration and assistance of very many people. First of all, I am most grateful to Principal Gordon Kirk and the Research and Development Committee of Moray House College for their enthusiastic response to my request for time for writing and research and also to my many colleagues who shared and bore the burden of my administrative and teaching duties during a term of sabbatical leave I was kindly granted for the autumn of 1988. I am also profoundly grateful to the Department of Moral Philosophy at the University of St Andrews for their kind and most unexpected offer of hospitality during that term as a research fellow in their Centre for Philosophy and Public Affairs. In particular, I am indebted to Dr John Haldane, then director of the Centre, for his constant support and encouragement of my work, then and since, and for his eleventh hour advice on a final title for this book.

My time at the St Andrews' Centre also provided me, via several kind invitations to speak in various Scottish Universities, with valuable opportunities to test out some of the more controversial ideas aired in Section III of this work. Chapter 10, then, is a remote and several times revised descendant of a calamitous paper on moral motivation which I presented to the Dundee philosophers in early autumn and they are due both my apologies for such a poor show and my thanks for the courteous way in which they gave me the benefit of the doubt. Chapter 11, however, is more closely related to a much happier and more successful presentation on virtue and wisdom which I gave to the philosophers in the University of Aberdeen in December and once again I am grateful both for the splendid critical response and – especially to Dr Nigel Dower – for the hospitality I received at that time.

During the winter and spring of 1988–9, I was also privileged to come to know two other St Andrews' Centre fellows – Professor Richard Brook of Bloomsburg, PA, and Professor Rick Werner of Hamilton College, NY – to whom I also owe an immense debt of gratitude for their moral support, their encouragement of my work and, above all, their friendship. I am extremely grateful for all the critical responses of those who have been exposed to the ideas and reflections which have contributed to the making of this book but especially to my friend and erstwhile colleague Dr Ieuan Williams of University College Swansea who kindly and patiently read through the entire typescript of this work. Last but not least I am profoundly indebted to Sheila, Claire, Gladys and other members of the office staff in Moray House College at Cramond for their meticulous, tireless and uncomplaining secretarial assistance with respect to the transcription of this work during a very busy term. Finally, it goes without saying that the final responsibility for any confusions and mistakes in this work lies entirely with me.

David Carr   Moray House College,
December 1989

INTRODUCTION

It is hardly an exaggeration to say that we do not live in an age of moral certainty. In the so-called multi-cultural and pluralist societies which characterise much of the modern world it has become standard practice to submit traditional moral, religious and social beliefs or values to rigorous scrutiny; a particular attitude of rational scepticism appears to have become the order of the day. It is also sensible to concede, moreover, that there is much about this modern scepticism which is reasonable enough and that we should be foolish to regret the passing of precisely some of the moral certainties of earlier human societies and epochs. The cruel and oppressive fanaticisms which, it will be said, have stained the childhood and adolescence of human evolution with the blood of innocents and martyrs are no longer to be tolerated at the coming of age of civilised man. Thus a degree – even a large degree – of healthy scepticism about traditional moral, religious and social beliefs is the most valuable weapon we have in the fight against the exploitation, injustice and oppression that some of those beliefs have endorsed.

But it is also clear – from the history of philosophy for example – that scepticism can be taken too far, to extremes that are themselves not just irrational but dangerous. So whereas it was largely the aim of past great moral philosophers up until the early modern period (let us here regard Kant as the high water mark) to give an account of the conceptual or epistemological basis not just of our moral disagreements but also of our moral *agreements*, it seems to have been the aim of some of the moral sages of middle and late modernity (the first crucial figure here, I suppose, is Nietzsche) to drill out the very foundations of our ordinary moral thinking by arguing that all our basic beliefs and

1

values are in principle suspect or susceptible of revision. This more radical scepticism concerning the possibility of any objective basis for our common moral values, practices and judgements has, especially when reinforced with the modern encounter with cultural diversity, gradually filtered down in modern times not only into the work of academic moral philosophers but into the attitudes and beliefs of ordinary popular consciousness.[1]

But whilst it seems to be a reasonable enough human procedure to question traditional moral values, beliefs and practices wherever they may seem to be suspect, it is also arguably little short of insane to embark on an enterprise of questioning *every* moral value or practice on principle. Thus I am inclined to the view that the older moral philosophers like Plato, Aristotle and Kant were right to believe that there must be some ground of moral certainty or at least of objectivity even if, as I shall argue, some of them looked for it in unlikely places. This view seems to me to rest on a simple logical or conceptual point; just as there can be no counterfeit coins unless there are also real ones there can be no morally suspect or disreputable points of view unless there are also morally sound or reputable ones.[2] Moreover, we could not reasonably enter into intelligible disagreement about moral questions in the absence of some background of moral agreement shared by the opposed points of view.

It is common for philosophers of science to refer to a famous metaphor or analogy used by the Austrian logical positivist philosopher Otto Neurath to illustrate the nature of scientific progress.[3] With respect to his scientific theories, then, the scientist is roughly in the position of a sailor at sea in a leaky ship. Since it is not possible for him whilst he is afloat to dismantle his ship and rebuild it entirely, he must locate the leaks as best he can and patch the boat where they occur. The analogy is usually construed as a direct attack on epistemological foundationalism in science, as expressive of a perspective which regards it as futile for scientists to search for fundamental and incorrigible principles, laws and procedures upon which an absolutely certain and foolproof science might be constructed. Scientific theory and practice is a complex web or network of principles and procedures of varying degrees of soundness and reliability which it makes little sense to try to test or revise all at one go. Much the same point, I believe, can be made about our

2

moral perspectives and practices; these too comprise a complicated network of principles and procedures which – like the
sailor at sea in his leaky boat – we are stuck with and which
we must adjust where necessary in a piecemeal fashion because
we cannot overturn the lot all at once.

But what this image also suggests is that although it is only
sensible to admit that there is considerable uncertainty in
moral life, this cannot mean that there is *total* uncertainty; like
the seaborne sailor we must trust that some planks are water-
tight or will bear our weight – in this case the planks, as it
were, of moral thought and practice – in order to be able to
replace the rotten ones. In fact, however, the radical moral
scepticism which affects or infects popular modern thought
has usually taken two principal forms – the subjectivism which
says that since there are no objective moral truths I must make
up my own and the relativisim which maintains that since there
are no absolute or universally valid moral principles or truths
we might as well stick with the social and moral customs we
already have.[4] The moral subjectivist is a bit like the sailor who
tries to reconstruct his ship whilst still at sea and the moral
relativist stands in considerable danger of being like one who
turns a blind eye to the leaks and neglects to maintain his ship
at all.

The problem seems to be, oddly enough, that both these
kinds of sceptic – the subjectivist and the relativist – share a
common ideal of certainty, though it is a certainty for which it is
not really reasonable to seek; they both require a kind of fully
comprehensive moral insurance which will guarantee them
totally against unforseen disasters – new moral 'leaks' in
unexpected places. Like the older natural philosophers who
sought for an incorrigible system of ground rules or principles
upon which the whole edifice of scientific enquiry and practice
might be rationally constructed, the modern moral sceptics have
sought in vain for a foundational set of hard and fast principles
on the basis of which the whole of human moral life might be
constructed or from which all moral precepts might be derived.
Being unable to discover such hard and fast or incontrovertible
principles in any realm of human experience they have resorted
either to making them up – abandoning objectivity and under-
writing certainty with personal commitment – or abandoning
certainty they have clung onto what objectivity they could find

by committing themselves to the social conventions and moral codes nearest to hand.

In fact, however, these ways of proceeding have got things almost entirely the wrong way round, for we do not start with moral principles and proceed to moral practices, but – like the pilot of Neurath's craft – we find ourselves involved in a going concern, landed with certain moral practices and relationships, enmeshed in a complex web of ties of human community and association, in relation to which our moral codes represent an attempt to make some sort of sense. The moral principles that we have, then, are the product of a fallible human attempt to understand the web of moral association by reference to consideration of both a general and a particular kind about what sorts of conduct conduce to good and ill, wellbeing and harm, in human affairs; in short, the principles are underwritten by the practices, not the practices by the principles.

At this point two possible misconceptions about what has been said so far may need guarding against. First, it should be re-emphasised that the use of Neurath's metaphor to criticise foundationalism in moral thinking should not be construed as tantamount to a denial that there *can be* any moral certainties – that it is just not possible to form judgements of an objective character concerning what is morally right or wrong. To attack moral foundationalism is merely to reject the view that it is possible to discern any hard and fast incontrovertible *axioms* or *principles* from which our particular moral judgements might be deductively inferred or upon which our moral conduct might be rationally based. To affirm that the rough and ready moral principles that we have are underwritten by our actual moral practices, however, is precisely to acknowledge that there are genuine if general criteria of moral right and wrong, good and evil, to be discovered in the rough and tumble of human interpersonal relations and conduct.

Precisely they are to be discovered in those general human dispositions to good and ill, excellence and baseness, which are ordinarily called virtues and vices and with the nature of which this work is centrally concerned. It is the familiar enough human discourse of virtue and vice, in terms of which we ordinarily characterise human moral character and conduct, which is our best guide to the formulation of reliable moral precepts and principles. As we shall see, however, the moral virtues are very definitely not hard and fast principles which may be applied to any conceivable circumstances but general patterns or tendencies of conduct which require reasonable and cautious adjustment to particular and changing circumstances and which may even, in some situations, compete with each other for preference and priority. They are not so much the foundations of morality, then, if by this is meant a hard bedrock of principles upon which all moral conduct is based – rather they are the templates upon which the general contours of moral life are modelled; precisely, they are *criteria* rather than *axioms*.

The other possible source of misunderstanding concerning these observations about the pre-eminence of concepts of virtue for our thinking about the nature of moral life and ideas of right and wrong arises in relation to the notion of relativism. If, as appears to be widely believed, the notions of virtue and vice are socially defined and the practice of the moral virtues is a social phenomenon, must not any concepts of virtue and moral practice generally be relative to particular societies? In short, doesn't the attempt to explain moral life in terms of such heavily socially-implicated dispositions as the virtues, simply readmit the bogy of moral relativism by the back door? I think that the short answer here – we shall have much more to say in due course – is that it does not. It is clear enough that concepts of virtue and vice – however they may be differently interpreted in different societies – are nevertheless employed by all human agents to submit the range of available social, religious and political practices to question as unjust, self-serving, exploitative or whatever.

The crucial point is that although the moral virtues are often if not always socially-implicated dispositions, they are so in the very general and innocuous sense in which *all* human conduct is social, but not necessarily if at all in the very narrow or dubious sense of being ideologically or doctrinally biased. It is clear that the moral virtues operate at a much more fundamental level of human life, experience and interpersonal dealings than that with which particular religious or political creeds are concerned. To be sure, then, we live as human beings in a variety of different ways and according to diverse social customs but it is also true that fundamentally we all share a common physical or biological nature which inclines us to find pleasure, hurt, wellbeing, security and love in roughly the same places; so though it is easy enough to recognise two different interpretations or expressions of courage or charity in two different societies (or, for that matter, in the same society) it is hard to envisage a human community in which these qualities are not needed, recognised or held to be of any value at all.

Thus, though in one sense there are different versions of virtue – different ideas about how courage might be expressed, for example, by war or through pacifism – in another more profound sense it is certainly not true that we count *any* quality as courage except that which involves remaining resolute or not losing one's nerve in dangerous, difficult or painful circumstances and that must logically be the case for any human agent (as well as what renders rational debate about the nature and value of courage possible between members of different societies).

At any rate, in this work I have taken the view that some definite initiation into those virtues or qualities ordinarily acknowledged in the familiar human discourse of fundamental human association must lie at the heart of the moral education of *all* children and that parents and teachers who fail to acquaint their children with these fundamental dispositions of moral life are seriously reneging on the full educational implications of their roles as parents and teachers. It is clear enough, however, both from much recent literature about education and on the basis of observations of much contemporary social life that the various agencies of education *have* wavered about this – scared off perhaps by various bogies of indoctrination or illiberalism. Perhaps the most influential perspective on moral education of modern educational traditionalism is one that explicitly disparages and rejects what it calls the 'bag of virtues' approach and which is inclined rather, it seems, to try to get children thinking for themselves, more or less from scratch, about moral questions; other very influential brands of modern educational progressivism have in the name of some liberal notion of tolerance repudiated the idea of moral education altogether.[5]

It is my belief that these various views which cast suspicion on the idea of a basic moral education of the virtues are merely symptomatic of a failure of nerve on the part of moral educationalists which is itself the result of their subscription to certain dubious doctrines about moral life of a foundationalist nature. But be that as it may, it seems to be no more than a matter of common sense to recognise that most of the modern reservations about a basic moral education of the virtues under the influence of the bogy of indoctrination are just confused anyway; there is nothing but a dangerous muddle in the wake of the view that teaching, even instructing, a child in self-control is a matter of indoctrination or of a serious curtailment of his freedom.

The present work is intended to be one of moral education rather than moral philosophy – or, at any rate, it is intended as a contribution to the conceptual geography of problems about moral education from which the efforts of a more obviously practical kind of parents, teachers and other educationalists might derive some heart or inspiration. To that end, although I have not been able to avoid fairly protracted discussions of past and present moral philosophical theory, I have also engaged in equally extensive critical discussions of several important views of moral education and child development hailing from the social sciences.

I trust that it will be clear enough without much need for elaboration here why some discussion of various classical theories of morality and virtue is a prerequisite of any satisfactory treatment of moral education – it is roughly, of course, because we need to understand what kinds of items moral values, attitudes and dispositions are before we can see clearly what may be required to promote their growth. All the same, it should be said that I have here pursued the enquiry in my own highly idiosyncratic and selective way and students in search of an introductory text to the history of moral philosophy might be well advised to look elsewhere than to this volume; my survey of moral philosophies probably excludes more than it includes and so I doubt whether any very clear view of the history of the subject could be gained from this work.

But if the present work is undeniably unsatisfactory from this more refined theoretical end of things it is also very likely to be regarded as unsatisfactory from the more practical end as well. Many a professional educationalist approaching this book in the currently rather untheoretical climate of thinking about educational questions is bound to be struck by the observation that whilst purporting to be an essay concerned with the practical business of education, it nevertheless eschews any discussion of the practical apparatus of pedagogy and curriculum that might be considered necessary for implementing programmes of moral education.

Thus, this essay includes no attempt to develop a formal programme of study, contains no lesson plans, engages in no discussion of teaching methods, techniques, skills or strategies and the currently fashionable educational talk of 'management skills', 'delivering the curriculum' and so on is studiously avoided. Concerning these alleged omissions, however, I remain obstinately unrepentant. In fact, if the general drift of the present work is understood at all, it should also be grasped that nothing of this nature has here been omitted that does not trade in either the largely vacuous or the downright fatuous.

My basic view is that *all* the major mistakes about the moral educational role of the teacher with respect to the moral development of others to which people are nowadays inclined are based on *misconceptions* or *misunderstandings* of the nature of moral life from which have followed certain failures of nerve concerning the legitimacy of a fairly familiar and informal sort of enterprise. In short, teachers fail in the task of moral education not primarily on account of their lack of any pedagogical skill or technique or of a coherent curriculum theory, but rather because they have only an uncertain grasp of what moral life actually means.

There is a crucial sense, moreover, in which adequately grasping what moral life means is hardly consistent with failing to construct or reconstruct one's personal relations with others in a manner from which the only moral educational effects that we can reasonably hope for follow naturally enough. To be sure, merely being able to recognise what a morally decent life looks like is hardly of itself enough to turn us into the kind of people who are shining examples to others – for most of us much effort is still required to acquire the honesty, tolerance, self-control and so on which are at once both instrumental to and constitutive of such a life – but to understand adequately what a morally good life is, is to grasp that that life is worth aspiring to and also to acquire *some* insight into the right direction in which one should proceed.

But to recognise this is also to comprehend that a morally sound life is essentially a matter of *personal* effort and aspiration – not 'personal', of course, in the sense of 'subjective' or 'idiosyncratic' – but personal meaning that no one can do it for us. To this extent, however, all talk in relation to moral education of pedagogical skills, strategies and techniques, of management styles or delivering the curriculum becomes not just beside the point but runs *counter to* the point; a life characterised by those human excellences called the moral virtues is precisely not something which we accept because it has been required of or imposed on us, but something to which we aspire when we too have discerned the great value of those qualities of integrity, honesty, discipline, tolerance, care, courtesy and so on which shine forth in the lives and conduct of those who, with luck, have been charged with the task of instructing us.

What, of course, all this means is that moral education cannot be regarded as just another subject in the curriculum like physics or maths and that any pedagogy appropriate to its promotion is hardly susceptible of analysis in terms of techniques for the transmission or communication of academic theories or information. The supreme human value and significance of the moral virtues can be recognised only in their power to transform lives for the better in terms of individual character and social relations; we appreciate the worth of qualities of moral character by observing how they operate in the lives of others – admiring Miss Smith for her honesty and concern for others at the same time as we despise Mr Jones for his meanness and ill-temper.

But it follows also from this that the fundamental moral virtues cannot be learned in any context of socialisation or education apart from the example of those parents, teachers and friends who are able to exhibit to some degree how they work for the good in human life. Moreover, lacking the example of those who possess positive moral qualities, young people may well take as their models of behaviour those who possess only negative qualities – Mr Jones who is shifty, sarcastic and bullying.

So far, then, I have argued that proper moral education requires a full or adequate appreciation of the important contribution that certain basic moral dispositions have to make to any worthwhile form of human life, that the only sure indicator of such appreciation is that a person clearly aspires to possessing the qualities in question and that the example of such aspiration (none of us can hope to afford much more than this) is the *sine qua non* of effective moral instruction. In short a good moral educator can only be one who himself aspires to the achievement of some degree of moral excellence characterisable in terms of such attitudes and dispositions as honesty, courage, self-control, integrity, benevolence and so forth.

I am not unaware, moreover, of the extreme and far-reaching, not to say disquieting consequences, that this line of argument might be held to have for education, especially the professional preparation and training of teachers. It may well be said, for example, that it must if true have quite radical and far-reaching consequences for the business of teacher selection and appraisal. I am bound to concede that this is a distinct possibility, aware as I am of the quite serious potential that exists for the possible institutional abuse of this observation; it is also with some relief, however, that I am able to say that it is quite outside the scope of this book to examine this question here.

But whatever the consequences of my arguments so far for teacher appraisal, it is nevertheless clear enough that the drift of my discussion has profound and immediate consequences for teacher *education*. From this point of view I do regard it as a matter of grave concern that the relatively recent attacks of irresolution on the part of professional educationalists concerning the question of values education (following from the fear of indoctrination and the like) appear to have led to something approaching a conspiracy of silence among teacher educators on this topic. In an educational climate currently unconducive to the airing of any sort of difficult theoretical or conceptual problems about the purpose and conduct of education, it would appear that the college training of many student teachers has been focused well nigh exclusively on the procedural or mechanical aspects of teaching to the virtual neglect of any considerations concerning the ethical or moral dimensions of the teacher's role. To my mind, this circumstance is nothing less than a scandal and a disaster and I dread to see what such teacher educators will shortly be reaping from what they have already sown.[6]

For if it is true that the area of values education *is* generally problematic, it is equally clear that it just will not do *either* to bury one's head in the sand *or* to sit on the fence with respect to this question. Neither evasion nor neutrality over the question of values is a live option for educationalists simply because *all* education – not just moral education – is a value-laden matter. Unless one is an A.S. Neill content to leave children to their own devices – and the majority of professional educationalists employed in state educational institutions have little or no room for manoeuvre here since their general practice is at serious variance with Neill's at precisely this point – one is as a teacher constantly making choices about what is or is not good for children in educational terms and requiring them to abide by those choices.

It is also reasonably clear, moreover, that if student teachers are not required to address in a rational and honest way these thorny questions concerning the moral dimensions of the role of teaching – to try to see precisely where their moral responsibilities to children do or do not lie – they may be ripe for hijack or manipulation by various extreme forms of fanaticism about values of either an authoritarian–repressive or a permissive–libertarian kind. Where only an intellectual vacuum occupies the place of sensible reflection upon the moral character of human life and experience, the nature of values and the ethical aspects of the educationalist's role, the territory is fair target for invasion by the morally 'loony' right or the equally morally 'loony' left.

We do our student teachers in the colleges no great favours, then, by proceeding as though education and learning to teach are matters only of the mastery of certain pedagogical skills, knacks or strategies apt for the successful transmission of value-neutral knowledge or information. Worse still, we do the pupils in our schools an even more lamentable disservice by providing custodians of their development who view schools not as communities or cultures in which children can be nurtured to some kind of moral and spiritual growth, but as factories or assembly lines with respect to which the dominant value is productivity. Thus I believe that the contentious questions of value cannot and should not be shirked in teacher education and yet, so far as I can see, the opportunities for addressing such questions are widely on the decline in institutions concerned with teacher training and they may well in some places have disappeared altogether.

The present work, then, is not an educational essay concerned with the development of skills or techniques which lend themselves to direct practical application in the classroom – it is not a handbook of simple practical tips for teachers. Indeed, in

11

the area of educational endeavour with which we are here concerned I think that it is not to be expected that we can discover any simple practical tips that are not of a highly general and largely unhelpful nature. The moral–educational authority of the teacher consists not so much in his effective employment of practical strategies as in his efforts to understand the value of moral life, not at all in his arranging behavioural schedules of reinforcement but more in his demonstrating to children through his own conduct what decent and principled attitudes and behaviour towards others are like and how they enrich a human life.

The most urgent problems about moral education with which teachers, parents and other educationalists are faced, then, are precisely not pedagogical or technological but moral– philosophical and conceptual. Once we understand the nature of moral life and experience more clearly we can see that there are no pedagogical problems about moral education of a techno- logical kind – in the sense that there are, say, about how best to teach long division; thus the only practical moral educational problem – though it is one of supreme difficulty – is that of how to engage with and relate to our pupils in as wise, principled, decent and responsible a way as possible. We might express this by saying that whereas the major pedagogical problem about science education may concern how to get Faraday or Einstein into the heads of our pupils, the main pedagogical problem about moral education concerns how as teachers to get decency, integrity, virtue and justice into our own hearts.

This work, then, is concerned with understanding the impli- cations for education of a particular perspective on the nature of moral life – a perspective which is preferred over others for reasons which I have also tried to indicate in the book. In general, I have tried to start from scratch – to work from a position which assumes little or no prior knowledge on the part of anyone of moral and social theory or problems of moral education as such – and to proceed via critical appreciation of the work of some very great moral and social thinkers of past times towards a relatively original and distinctive perspective on the nature of moral life and virtue.

I say 'relatively original' because although the view I have tried to present in section three of this work is obviously heavily indebted in all crucial respects to the influence of such past figures of genius as Plato and Aristotle as well as to several more recent moral philosophers of far greater stature than the present author, the last four chapters of this work do nevertheless attempt to express points of view that are not to my knowledge *widely* aired, if at all, in the currently available literature of contemporary moral–educational philosophy.

It is worth re-emphasising here that although I have adopted the fairly standard procedure, at least in the first two sections, of discussing the work of great thinkers of the past, this essay should not be approached as an introductory text to historical problems of moral theory and moral education – or, at least, not one of a conventional or systematic kind. My choice of theorists and theories for discussion in this work is fairly personal and selective and I could not claim to have done adequate justice to every figure and every view of importance for the development of moral theory and moral education; anyone searching for a complete treatment of this matter must be struck, for example, by my *almost* complete neglect of any reference to the philosophy of utilitarianism.

Again, although many of the obvious great names of ethical theory such as Plato, Aristotle and Kant and many of the almost as well known prominent theorists of moral education like Durkheim, Piaget and Kohlberg are here, others may to some readers seem unaccountably missing. I must also plead guilty to some fairly uncrthodox and idiosyncratic treatments of some of the thinkers and their theories which I have discussed. I am well aware that I do not quite share the views of many of the great philosophers and social thinkers of the past which are widespread among present-day philosophers of education of the so-called liberal traditionalist persuasion. Thus, I have been almost perversely unsympathetic to some people and sympathetic to others in cases where it has seemed to me that the current orthodoxy of educational philosophy has leant too far in the other direction. What, however, has turned out to be the general form or plan of the book?

I have attempted to explore the problems which interest me in three main sections, each of which contains four chapters. In the first section I have set out to offer accounts of the ideas on moral life and virtue of some great philosophers of ancient to relatively recent times. It is worth noting here that although this work contains critical comment on all the philosophers I have tried to discuss, either directly or by implication, I have not indulged in the practice, fairly standard among recent educational philosophers, of first describing past views, then listing a number of possible criticisms of them. Instead, I have just been concerned to sketch – at least in the first three chapters – my own views of certain great past thinkers which highlight what I take to be of importance and originality about their contributions to our understanding of moral life; it is really necessary to read the rest of this work in order to discover and appreciate clearly what are my final judgements on the moral positions which I believe them to represent.

In the first chapter I have started – I do not really see how it would be reasonable to start anywhere else – at the very source of contemporary western moral philosophy, with the views of Socrates and Plato. From my earliest days as a student of philosophy I have been under the spell of Plato, I continue to return to his works for insight and I probably enjoyed writing this first chapter of the present work more than any other; irrespective of its doubtless defects, this chapter was written in a spirit of deep reverence for the author who first attracted me to philosophy and who has sustained my interest through the years. Moreover, although it is true that the particular line of enquiry concerning virtue and moral life which appears to have been initiated by Socrates and Plato is ultimately rejected in this work in favour of that developed by Aristotle, it is nevertheless also true that Platonic insights have informed the perspective of this work at various points and the Socratic influence is, for example, quite decisive for the argument of chapter 10.

It is my second chapter on Aristotle which is in general the most crucial for this work, of course, since I am ultimately concerned to defend something like an Aristotelian conception of moral life, moral education and the nature of virtue. All the same, however, I am inclined to regard this chapter as somewhat less successful than the first and as rather less well tied together. The basic and I suspect insuperable problem here, of course, is that there is just too much of importance in Aristotle's *Ethics* to deal with in the space of a short chapter. Thus, although it may seem extremely remiss to omit from a work on moral education any protracted discussion of, for example, Aristotle's important observations on the psychology of moral motivation, this is precisely what I have had to do.

The chapter concludes, then, with little more than a tantalising hint as to the importance of these sections of the *Ethics*; to have gone further would have taken me into the deep waters of some extremely abstract and complex metaphysical issues about freedom and so on and too far away from the rough path I have already had enough trouble clearing. Needless to say, the principal issues and topics which I have discussed in this chapter are re-examined and elaborated throughout the rest of this work – especially in the final section.

My third chapter on the ideas of Rousseau and Kant is concerned precisely to identify those views of the nature of moral life and experience to which the present work is largely antipathetic. All the same, my concern has still been to expound these highly influential doctrines which underpin modern liberalism as clearly and sympathetically as possible. Kant is, of course, a notoriously difficult philosopher to expound and that is one good reason for approaching his ideas through the influence on them of the more accessible doctrines of Rousseau. As in the case of the chapter on Aristotle the first problem I faced about giving an account of Rousseau and Kant was to avoid either leaving too much out or putting too much in.

The second problem was to avoid the various caricatures and distortions to which interpretations of both these thinkers are prone when authors are anxious to contrast their views reasonably sharply with those of other people. In the light of some very recent first rate work on the philosophy of Rousseau, I am not at all satisfied that I have managed to avoid a degree of distortion – particularly in relation to the alleged 'anti-social' elements of Rousseau's philosophy. Thus, for those who require a rather more accurate and sensitive account of Rousseau than I have been able to give in this work I cannot recommend too highly the fine recent study of him by Nicholas Dent.[7]

In the fourth and final chapter of the first section, I have attempted to draw up some initial battle lines by tracing the origins of various disputes of modern moral philosophy back to their sources in the conflicting perspectives of those past philosophers already discussed. In general, I have traced the modern orthodoxies of liberal thinking about moral education back to Kant and his Rousseauesque roots and the more recent discontent with modern liberal perspectives which we find expressed in neo-naturalism and allied doctrines to its fundamentally Aristotelian source.

As well as nailing my own colours to the mast at this point I have concluded this chapter with attempts at short accounts of two significant recent thinkers of a neo-Aristotelian turn of mind – Alasdair MacIntyre and John McDowell. The work of both these men is not greatly known beyond mainstream moral philosophy and has not yet been widely discussed by educational philosophers (MacIntyre somewhat, McDowell hardly at all). Given the immense difficulty of the thought of both these men, I also cannot feel sure that I have precisely or completely understood them, but it does seem right to have made the attempt.

In the second section, I have set out to discuss the ideas on moral life, education and development of a number of well-known theorists hailing from areas of social science rather than philosophy. It will hardly come as much of a surprise that I have taken a largely critical view of most of these ideas in the light of what I discern in the way of the frequent conceptual shortcomings of much of this (allegedly) empirically based work. All the same, I have still sought to be sympathetic where possible and to acknowledge the many occasions when at least people's hearts seem to have been in the right place.

With regard to my fifth chapter on the work of Durkheim, it still seems to me that despite the fatally flawed nature – from a philosophical point of view – of the French sociologist's work on moral education, his famous essay is nevertheless a civilised and serious work which contains many shrewd and insightful observations on moral life and deserves to be more widely read. It is certainly true that there is much to be learned about moral life from the peculiar character of Durkheim's conceptual errors.

In fact when we turn to the chapter on Freud and his influence on Homer Lane and (less directly) A.S. Neill, it may well be thought that I have been rather *too* sympathetic both to psychoanalysis and progressivism. My main aim in this chapter, however, has been to try to illuminate certain rather unorthodox views about moral education to be encountered in the theory and practice of some colourful modern representatives of progressive educational theory by tracing the influence on them of Freudian and psychoanalytic theory. I have also suggested that a certain degree of light on the origins of some 'problem' behaviour has been cast by such figures as Lane and Neill; the progressive interpretation and extended application of such psychoanalytic ideas as those of repression and sublimation has, I believe, afforded insight into the provenance of some morally problematic behaviour.

It does not seem to me that this observation is at all exceptionable especially as I conclude the chapter by insisting that neither Freud, Lane nor Neill should be understood as having discovered the *causes* of virtue and vice. Thus my sympathetic endorsement of the Lane–Neill observations about how some conditions of socialisation might serve to stunt moral development in certain respects should not be taken to imply sympathy towards any general metaphysical doctrines concerning the causal determination of human behaviour. I am also not at all inclined to the view that all bad behaviour is mad behaviour and that all wickedness should be seen as an illness to be cured. In fact I hold the common-sense view that most of us are for most of the time quite responsible (in the sense that, amongst other things, we could have chosen to do something other than what we actually did) for the wrong-doing we commit – but this does not invalidate the Lane–Neill point that some children might well have turned out rather better given a better upbringing.

Since the Piaget–Kohlberg view of moral development as largely a matter of the growth of moral reasoning constitutes, on the other hand, something like the orthodoxy of modern liberal thinking about moral education, and as its origins lie so clearly in the philosophy of the high enlightenment (particularly in the views of Kant), it is only to be expected that I have been highly critical in chapter 7 of what I take to be a potentially dangerous line of thought about the moral upbringing, training and education of children. I am reasonably satisfied, moreover, that the thought of this chapter or something like it is largely on the right lines about what is wrong with much of both modern psychology and modern educational thinking.

In the eighth and final chapter of the second section I am concerned to explore the significance of these various social theoretical perspectives on the nature and origins of moral concepts and dispositions with respect to that familiar dichotomy of educational-philosophical thought known as the traditional–progressive distinction. I argue that the distinction

17

in question is ultimately and properly to be understood in terms of a conflict between two different and opposed theories of the relationship between human nature and society which, though they cannot both be true, might nevertheless both be false. In fact, I am inclined to the view that these two different and crudely oversimplified pictures of human nature, social influence and the origins of virtue and vice urgently require replacement by a single new but more complex view of human nature, society and virtue which would allow us to form a clearer and more realistic picture of the proper direction of moral education.

It is precisely to an attempt to sketch the outlines of an account of moral virtue based on a more complex but also more realistic view of human nature and the individual and social dimensions of moral life that I turn in the third section of this work. The first three chapters of this section are concerned to explore the implications of the basic idea that a moral virtue is a distinctive kind of human disposition which is appropriately construed as a complex of reason, feeling and will.

To put the point another way, no explanation of the nature of moral virtue should be considered complete without some reference to the natural affective life of human agents, some account of the role that practical reason plays in the moral discipline of human sentiments and some reasonable story about the nature of moral motivation or of what inclines or disinclines human agents to the decent or principled conduct of their affairs. Thus the first three chapters of the third section cover the topics of feeling, motivation and reason in relation to virtue and each of them, it should be noted, is concerned to argue against what I take to be widespread misconceptions about these aspects of moral life.

In the ninth chapter I set out to argue against the common view (deriving originally perhaps from Platonic sources) that the moral virtues are concerned exclusively with the control or suppression of unruly instincts, inclinations and passions of a largely negative and destructive character. Undoubtedly this idea rests on a one-sidedly pessimistic view of untutored human nature which does not seem to be generally sustainable. In fact it seems clear enough that many moral virtues are founded upon natural human sentiments of a largely positive and constructive kind – sentiments which certainly require rational direction and discipline in order to count as virtues – but not necessarily, if at all, repression or subjection. In short, I argue that such altruistic virtues as charity, compassion and benevolence concern the disciplined *expression* of natural human sentiments rather than their firm *suppression*.

Likewise, I have tried to argue in the tenth chapter against another familiar and widespread view to the effect that moral motivation is to be understood largely as a matter of obligation or duty. Although I readily agree that on many of the occasions when we act in ways that may be considered to have moral significance we do so in recognition of particular duties and obligations, much if not most moral conduct is not appropriately regarded as obligatory behaviour. For my argument in this chapter I draw heavily for inspiration on an idea which seems to be common to all the great Greek philosophers of classical antiquity – Socrates, Plato and Aristotle – that genuine motivation with respect to the acquisition of the virtues should be regarded as a matter of personal *aspiration* (more than obligation).

The eleventh and penultimate chapter of this work is probably the most crucial and significant for my general thesis and it was certainly the most rewarding to work upon. In it I take the view that with the notable exception of Aristotle, moral philosophers of past times appear to have seriously misunderstood the nature and function of wisdom or deliberation with respect to moral life; specifically, they have construed moral reason and reflection as principally concerned with determining or establishing (from some Archimedean point of rational neutrality) the ultimate aims, goals and ends of moral life, whereas in reality the proper function of moral deliberation is to identify what constitutes moral conduct in particular circumstances of human indecision and uncertainty.

There is, then, a genuine sense in which the final goals of moral life are not matters to be decided by individual judgement or social consensus – a sense in which they are already *given* for human wisdom, reason or deliberation to work upon or in terms of. It is not for us to decide via some process of neutral rational reflection whether or not charity or courage are qualities of genuine moral value, only how to be rightly charitable or generous.

The twelfth and final chapter of this work is concerned to

explore, albeit too briefly, the implications for the teaching and learning of moral qualities and values of the foregoing observations about the nature of the virtues. In particular it is concerned to expose as basically confused all the forms of moral scepticism, subjectivism and relativism which have infected the views of educationalists about moral education and caused them, for fear of being regarded as indoctrinators, to lose their nerve with respect to the enterprise. Finally, it is my earnest hope that this work may have helped in its modest way to clear away some of the tangle of conceptual confusion in the way of a coherent conception of moral education and contributed something towards a clear view of what constitutes the rational conduct of not just a crucial but a perfectly legitimate educational enterprise.

Part I

IDEAS OF VIRTUE
IN
MORAL PHILOSOPHY

1

VIRTUE AS KNOWLEDGE: SOCRATES AND PLATO

Since the main question to which the present work is addressed concerns the nature of moral virtue and how those qualities of human character we call virtues might be taught in the course of human education, there can be no more appropriate place to begin than with a consideration of the views of Socrates and Plato on this matter. In the first place, of course, these two great philosophers of classical antiquity are the main source of western philosophical thinking in general and of thought about moral life and conduct in particular; but in the second place it is precisely with the question of how virtue might be taught that one of Plato's better known dialogues – the *Meno* – begins, a question to which Socrates seeks an answer in the course of that dialogue.[1]

To be sure, the response which Socrates returns to that question in the *Meno* is a notoriously problematic one from the point of view of moral education, since the conclusion that the nature of moral virtue is a matter of opinion more than genuine knowledge can hardly place teaching about moral matters beyond the realm of genuine controversy. In the dialogue called *Protagoras*, however, which is usually collected together with the *Meno*, Socrates is represented as defending the view that virtue is knowledge and thus teachable and this would appear to have been the final view of both Socrates and Plato in so far as a final view is to be found expressed in Plato's dialogues.

Here, of course, I can provide no more than a partial and simplified account of the views on moral life and education of these two great ancient philosophers. Of necessity, my account of Socrates and Plato will be simple and unsophisticated since as a lay reader rather than a professional scholar of Plato my reading of his works is at best innocent and at worst ignorant of the many subtle disputes concerning their proper interpretation that have continued down the centuries to modern times. Although my account of Plato and Socrates will be relatively simple, however, I trust that it will not be too controversial since I shall try to concentrate only on identifying some general Platonic arguments and insights into the nature of moral life and education concerning which there is considerable agreement.

My account of the Socratic–Platonic moral philosophy, however, will also be partial because besides avoiding unnecessary controversy, I also cannot enter here into the details, interesting as they are, of Plato's general social and educational philosophy. Unlike most educational philosophers before me, I shall show little apparent interest in Plato's programme of education for the philosopher-kings in the *Republic*, in his profound and insightful account of the nature of understanding in the *Meno* or in his observations on the nature of knowledge in the *Theaetetos* and other post-Republican dialogues. I shall concentrate mainly on Plato's moral psychology of virtue touching on as much of his general social, political and educational philosophy as it takes to understand his account of virtue. First, however, it is necessary to say something about Socrates.

What we know of Socrates as a historical figure from the dialogues of his greatest pupil Plato and from other sources[2] is that he was the first great martyr to truth of western philosophical enquiry. Inspired by the Delphic oracle, so his own autobiographical account in Plato's *Apology* went, to embark upon a quest to find a mind endowed with greater wisdom than his own, Socrates spent his life in energetic pursuit of an understanding of the nature and meaning of truth, virtue, knowledge and justice in the course of which he laid the foundations of much subsequent epistemological and moral enquiry and also attracted the disapproval of the Athenian authorities as an impious and dangerous subversive so that he was condemned to death by his own hand at around the age of seventy.

It is, of course, a notoriously difficult (and ultimately rather pointless) task to determine where in Plato's dialogues, Socratic philosophy as such leaves off and Platonic philosophy begins,[3] but it seems likely that well before Socrates ceases to appear as the central spokesman in the Platonic dialogues of the later period, Plato is using him as a dramatic character to explore and engage with epistemological and metaphysical questions that had been little more than hinted at by the actual historical Socrates. Having argued largely in the context of reflections upon social and political considerations that whatever is to be properly considered an expression of moral virtue must exhibit some kind of wisdom or knowledge, Socrates clearly stirred a hornet's nest of problems about the nature of knowledge, and that truth or reality which our knowledge is of, that were to continue to exercise the mature Plato of the *Republic* and beyond.

In the context of the present enquiry into the nature of moral virtue and education, however, clearly the right place to start is with the early Socratic dialogues in which it is likely that Plato is engaged in little more than a literary narrative or presentation of discussions about virtue and justice which were actually conducted by Socrates and attended by Plato. In these dialogues, we discover Socrates under the influence of his 'demon' engaged in philosophical argument with various younger contemporaries or with some of the most renowned professors or teachers of his day – the sophists.

By and large, the sophists have received an extremely bad press from Plato's dialogues, not unlike that which the scribes and Pharisees received from the authors of the Gospels. Indeed, the Platonic picture of the sophists and the Gospel image of the Pharisees have much in common; a certain worldly cynicism, a generally expedient and opportunist attitude to questions of political and social policy, a sanctimonious and hypocritical posture regarding questions of virtue, moral principle and conduct and a definite penchant for rhetoric and verbal trickery. Of course, just as there are 'good' Pharisees such as Nicodemus in the Gospels, so the Platonic portrait of the sophists is not one of unrelieved hostility and resentment – the great admiration of both Socrates and Plato for the Eleatic philosophers Parmenides and Zeno is conspicuous and the portraits of both Protagoras and Gorgias are gentle and affectionate even when their teachings are harshly criticised; but in general sophistical attitudes and perspectives on human nature and society are the main targets of criticism in Plato's dialogues.

What, then, was the nature of the Socratic objection to the teachings of the ancient Greek sophists? In general it was towards a certain shallow and cynical scepticism with respect to the nature of our knowledge of experience and the status of conventional or traditionally based values and principles. Sophists like Protagoras taught that since all claims to knowledge are rooted in human experience, and experience is basically a function of individual perception, there must be an inherently subjective quality about any human claims to knowledge. Since individuals frequently disagree with respect to the deliverances of perception and as there is no court beyond human perception to which appeal for an objective decision in any circumstance of disagreement might be made, human understanding of reality as given in experience cannot break out of the circle of the individual's perceptually based ideas. In that case whatever an individual perceives must be true for him and whatever he values or desires must be right for him. Thus Protagoras observed that 'man is the measure of all things',[4] by which he appears to have meant that there is nothing to the content of so-called knowledge over and above what may be construed in terms of human psychology or subjective experience.

These epistemological and metaphysical doubts about the nature of knowledge and what we can have knowledge of were translated at the level of moral, social and political life into a general scepticism about the status and validity of moral principles, social practices and political and religious institutions. Many sophists appear to have held that moral, social and political laws and principles are at best merely expressive of local customs and conventions and at worst rooted in tribal dogmas and superstitions with little or no rational basis; in short, they subscribed to beliefs which are also widely held in our own time and that is one reason why the arguments of Socrates and Plato against the sophistical view of these matters is of the highest relevance to contemporary discussions of these issues and should not be dismissed as of only historical interest.

How did the sophists propose that those who had grasped their doctrines (mainly the absolute truth that there is no absolute truth) should conduct their affairs in the light of them? In its most radical form the sophistical educational doctrine turns out to be remarkably like that taught some two thousand years later by the nineteenth-century German philosopher Friedrich Nietzsche. The beginning of wisdom in human affairs consists first and foremost in liberating oneself from the ties and constraints of conventional or traditional ideas and values in the interests of realising a transcendent set of goals and purposes in relation to which the generally accepted conventions are to be considered mere inhibitions or hindrances.[5]

In what, however, beyond conformity to accepted conventions can these goals and purposes consist? Essentially for the more radical sophists the answer to this question appears to have been construed in terms of the naked and unashamed pursuit of personal and political power. Traditional and conventional social and moral values were held to serve no genuine rational purpose beyond that of social control; they kept individuals in a state of slavish conformity and subservience to the interests of others and assisted the impediment of true individual self-fulfilment via the satisfaction of a person's deepest desires. Genuine self-realisation on the part of an individual, then, would be a matter of arranging circumstances to suit one's own advantage, largely through the manipulation of others, as much as possible. Power over the world and other people, should be the goal of the enlightened rational individual.

But how was this power to be exercised? The sophists were not at all the advocates of any kind of brutal or mindless control of others through physical coercion or violence for they knew of far better means of subtle persuasion which were more permanent and effective. This persuasive power was held by the sophists to reside mainly in the so-called art of rhetoric and it was the form of knowledge or skill of this name which the sophists professed to be able to teach others. In particular it was for instructing the sons of noble families in the art of rational persuasion that the sophists were mainly employed, for it was part of the general training of such young noblemen to learn how to exert influence over others by fair means or foul. In the primitive democracy of fourth-century Athens, power was to be won and wielded by means of flattering and seductive speeches in the assemblies through which the wills of others might be bent to the service of one's own. The ultimate aim was to secure for the individual all that he secretly desired in life in terms of personal honour, wealth and sensual pleasure; hence the rather curious mixture of Nietzscheanism and depravity that we often encounter in the Platonic dialogues among such young 'supermen' as Callicles and Thrasymachus who would have been graduates of this fashionable sophistical academy of self and power seeking.[6]

Socrates' response to all of this as it is represented in the early to middle period dialogues of Plato – particularly in the *Protagoras*, *Gorgias* and *Republic* – is quite uncompromising. In reply to Gorgias' claim that rhetoric is the art conducive to promoting the highest possible concerns of men, Socrates maintains that it is not any kind of art at all but merely a 'knack'. Genuine arts such as legislation, gymnastics or medicine are directed towards the achievement of some actual human good such as physical health or justice. Knacks like cookery and cosmetics, on the other hand, aim for the most part not at the achievement of some genuine good but at the mere disguise of what is substandard, defective or unwholesome; just as cookery often serves to make spoiled or unnutritious food more appetising through the addition of rich spices and sauces so the art of the beautician may be used to conceal the symptoms of physical deterioration or disease. Like cookery and cosmetics and unlike medicine and gymnastics, then, rhetoric aims only at pleasing people by flattering them and it proceeds largely indifferent to the moral corruption of those it flatters since the sole aim of the employer of rhetoric is to gain power over others through the manipulation and exploitation of them.[7]

At this point, then, Socrates has seriously called into question the idea on which the power of rhetoric depends, that promising or giving people what they desire or what they think they want is to be considered an unqualified good. Far from being an unqualified good Socrates maintains, it depends crucially on *what* an individual or society wants whether it should be given them. Tested by the suggestion (expressed, for example, in the story of the magical ring of Gyges) that given the opportunity to do anything one liked without fear of retribution any man would seek the satisfaction of his basic desires (no matter what beastliness this involved) as a good worth pursuing, Socrates replies that it cannot be considered good even for a man to *aspire* to the satisfaction of all his desires. Socrates, then, draws a sharp distinction between what men happen as a matter of fact to want or desire, which tends to be dictated by their natural instincts, passions and appetites and what men should desire or what it is in their interests to want which can only be established through mature rational reflection on the nature of human good as such.

Certainly, Socrates argued, what lies in men's interests can be quite other than what they desire as expressed in terms of instincts and appetites. A man with a poisoned wound may well want to avoid the agonising pain that would result from the wound being cleaned and cauterised but it lies in the interests of his very survival that the surgeon should turn a deaf ear to his cries to be left alone. By analogy, Socrates argues at this point for what is treated by his interlocutors as the quite extraordinary view that far from it being a piece of good fortune for a notorious tyrant or criminal to get away with his crimes, it is rather to be considered a great misfortune for the miscreant in question; for if a man dies because he refuses the painful operation that would save his life, he only loses his life and suffers bodily disintegration, whereas to go unpunished for our misdeeds according to Socrates is to risk the even more serious corruption of that spiritual part of ourselves which is called the soul.

In Plato's *Gorgias* this doctrine is greeted with no greater sympathy than it would generally receive in most ordinary contexts of moral debate today. But even if one does not subscribe to Plato's belief in the immortality of the soul (and it is not easy to do so in the particularly implausible form in which Socrates is made to express it in the *Phaedo* and elsewhere) it is not hard to make reasonably good sense of the idea that getting away with murder is generally bad for the moral character; that the more others turn a blind eye or fail to hold us accountable or responsible for our thoughtless, hurtful and selfish actions, the more thoughtless, hurtful and selfish we may become and, of course, we can hardly maintain that these qualities are expressive of a good or healthy character.

What was particularly difficult for Socrates' and Plato's contemporaries to swallow, however, and what would also be hard to take for many people today, is the idea that getting away with murder is actually a bad thing for the agent in question in anything like as serious a sense as it is a bad thing for those on the receiving end of his injustice or misdeeds. In short, it is relatively easy to show why the rest of us have an interest in turning a bad character into a good one – it is a simple matter of getting rid of an infernal nuisance; but the paradoxicality of Socrates' doctrine is contained in the idea that the way to spiritual or moral health and fulfilment lies not through getting everything that we want. It seems to be almost self-evident to many people that most of us live lives of decency, discipline and self-control only because we are poor and must work for a living or because if we get a little drunk then we land in gaol. But if suddenly we won the pools or if the police force was abolished then we could throw caution to the winds and realise true happiness in riotous and abandoned self-indulgence.

But as a matter of fact, the history of people who have been constrained by economic necessity to live lives of relative honesty and sobriety and who then suddenly win the pools goes some way towards supporting Plato's point. In those cases where honesty and sobriety have been viewed merely as shackles or constraints to be thrown off at the first opportunity the winners of big prizes have often gone on to wreck their lives in prodigal self-indulgence; the renunciation of moral virtue has ended not in true happiness but rather in very real tears. It is precisely the point of Socrates and Plato, then, that true human happiness, fulfilment and above all freedom is not to be had outside a moral context defined in terms of a life of self-control, sobriety and concern for others beside oneself – without precisely the virtues of wisdom, justice, temperance and courage.[8] One important reason for this is that it is characteristic of human desires as expressive of instincts, passions and appetites to be actually insatiable. The sybarite's primary appetites for alcohol, drugs and sex and the fixations of the miser or megalomaniac on the secondary reinforcements of money and power know no bounds and it is these things, above all, which enslave men, rather than the discipline of the moral virtues.

In fact it is only through the moral virtues or by their help that a man may become truly free to assume something like genuine control of his own life. The man whose whole life is enmeshed in an endless attempt to gratify his appetites in a round of drunken binges or sexual encounters may be aptly compared to a leaky vessel which cannot stay filled and stands in constant need of topping-up. Thus the unjust tyrant or oppressor who has absolute power of life and death over his subjects and who can require of them anything that he wants, he who is for the most part envied by other men, is for Socrates and Plato a figure to be pitied or ridiculed if he is not at all the master of his own fate or destiny but a mere slave of his passions. Many centuries later, Rousseau was to observe that 'those who regard themselves the masters of others are indeed greater slaves than they' and in so doing he expressed rather concisely the Socratic–Platonic view.[9]

For Socrates and Plato, then, the proper route to human freedom and happiness lies not via the pursuit of political power for the unbridled or unlicensed gratification of individual or personal appetites, but through the reasonable self-control and discipline of the moral virtues in the light of some principled conception of how it is right and proper for an individual to live or of what lies in his true interests. What is right for or in the true interests of the individual, however, is not a matter that may be determined by reference to his subjective desires and appetites; rather it requires the exercise of reason or the intellectual part of the soul to discover what this is. In the earlier dialogues of Plato we quickly encounter a basic perspective on the nature of virtue that might be aptly and conveniently called the 'Socratic' view. According to this view, moral virtue requires to be construed essentially as a function of the relationship between two relatively distinct aspects or dimensions of human nature which may be generally referred to as reason and passion. Roughly speaking, 'reason' comprehends what modern psychologists call the 'cognitive' side of human mental life – understanding, rational thought, deliberation, calculation, reflection, judgement and so forth; 'passion', on the other hand covers the 'affective' or feeling aspects of human experience – passions, emotions, moods, inclinations, instincts, appetites and so on.

It has been fashionable in recent analytical philosophy of mind to deny any such sharp distinction between the 'affective' and 'cognitive' aspects of human experience and to argue in particular that passions and emotions cannot properly be understood other than by reference to judgements, thoughts or cognitions; but whether or not this view is correct, it does not appear to have been quite that of Plato, for whom the 'passions' do seem to have been regarded as the 'unreasonable' aspects of experience (though there would appear to have been for him a motivational or passionate side to reason). To a considerable extent the two great philosophers we shall discuss in subsequent chapters – Aristotle and Kant – also seem to have constructed their moral psychology on a basic distinction between reason and passion that is closer to Plato than to some modern philosophers, but as we shall see, all three of these

31

great thinkers differ from each other in the ways that they see reason as related to passion in the practice of the virtues.

In the case of the 'Socratic' view of moral virtue of the early Platonic dialogues the relationship of reason to passion is fairly straightforward – it is one of simple conflict or opposition. By and large moral virtue is exhibited in those circumstances in which reason controls or overrules passion and vice or moral defect follows from the failure of passion, feeling or appetite to hearken to the voice of reason. The view of the passions that is generally and consistently sustained by Plato throughout all the dialogues, then, is an almost exclusively negative one; feelings, emotions, passions and appetites are regarded mainly as a source of temptation to wickedness and error and the principal function of human reason appears to be to help us avoid the various states of moral defect into which the passions would otherwise lead us.

The philosophy and moral psychology of Plato, then (whatever Socrates himself may have held), is generally considered to have inherited certain oriental or 'manichaean' tendencies towards a moral and metaphysical dualism of body and soul which probably later infected Christianity (via Plato) in the form of certain 'Gnostic' heresies. At any rate, in Plato's *Phaedo* we find the figure of the condemned Socrates looking forward to the death that will finally liberate his soul from the earthly imprisonment of the body by which it is tied to a lower or more mundane level of existence and concerns. Plato is very much the philosopher of that puritanical temperament which regards all involvement with carnal pleasures as something to be resisted and who associates the body and its appetites with tendencies towards spiritual degradation.

In general, then, it cannot lie in the true interests of an agent to be ruled by his instincts, feelings, appetites and passions for these will lead him almost certainly into wickedness and vice. The wise man will listen rather to the voice of his reason which directs him down the path of virtue in the direction of justice, self-restraint, courage and prudence. Since all men are endowed to some degree with powers of reason, deliberation and judgement what could it be that causes many men to pursue their passions and appetites into a life of vice rather than to lead a life of virtue? On the Socratic view it can only be a failure or refusal to make use of the divinely given powers of reason and judgement. Since no man who possessed a vision of the good life as given to him through reason could sensibly pursue a life that was worse – for example, the life of vice and self-indulgence involving the endless submission to insatiable appetites that must inevitably lead to personal ruin and dis-integration – it can only be the case that vice and moral error are the direct result of ignorance of the good; no man could err knowingly, so he must err unknowingly.

So the difference between virtue and vice is not just that reason subdues passion in the case of virtue but is on the contrary overcome by it in the case of vice; it is rather that the proper exercise of reason for a true knowledge of the good is naturally exhibited or expressed in the moral virtues whereas ignorance, wilful or otherwise of the good tends to express itself fairly directly in the form of vicious or morally defective conduct (given that for Socrates the passions and appetites which get their own way in the absence of reason are not really morally neutral forces but direct sources of temptation to wickedness). The position which is adopted most conspicuously in the *Protagoras*, although it is clearly foreshadowed in the treatment of particular virtues in some of the earlier minor Socratic dialogues, is that virtue is *knowledge*; the individual virtues are just expressions or aspects of wise or judicious reflection on the paramount question of the proper conduct of a just and decent human life. Thus in particular cases, the individual moral virtues are to be simply understood as particular rational responses to the various temptations, trials and tribulations characteristic of human life. Temperance or self-control, for example, ensures that a man's life is not wrecked or wasted through dissipation and prodigality and, though danger and difficulty inevitably beset the coward and the brave man alike, the courageous man is more likely to endure or persist in his enterprises to the point of success or honour than is the coward.

The 'Socratic' doctrine of the early Platonic dialogues that moral error is due to ignorance and that therefore no man can act wickedly in the knowledge of a better way to act is, however, clearly unsatisfactory. It seems to fly in the face of everyday evidence to the contrary. Even with respect to non-moral conduct (or, at least, issues of relatively slight moral signifi-cance) circumstances in which we know what is good for us but persist in doing what is not good for us are familiar enough:

a man knows all the compelling arguments against smoking but nevertheless cannot stop; a girl knows that over-eating is bad for her and she wants to lose weight but cannot stick to the prescribed diet. Thus, although conduct performed in the darkness of ignorance about what lies in our best interests is often describable as bad or even wicked, it represents by no means the only or most serious category of moral failure.

Moreover, from the moral point of view it is arguable that if no man ever errs knowingly then no man ever errs at all, in the morally important sense of being blameworthy or responsible for his actions. It has become familiar in modern times for social scientists to argue that crime and deviancy are to be understood as almost fully explicable in terms of adverse social circumstances to which crime and violence is the only intelligible or appropriate response. Juvenile delinquents really know no better than to assault and rob defenceless pensioners of paltry sums of money. If ideas of this sort are taken completely seriously then it may well be appropriate to constrain the individuals in question, to submit them to psychiatric treatment, to re-educate them out of the attitudes they have acquired in vicious environments or even to try to eradicate whatever might be understood to have caused the delinquent behaviour in those environments, but it is not really to the point to blame or hold agents responsible for actions concerning which they could not have known any better.

Far clearer cases of moral failure or defection than those which occur as a result of ignorance, however, are represented by those in which, as we have just seen, an agent knows well enough what he should do but does not do what he should (we have left undone those things which we ought to have done) and in which he knows what he shouldn't do but does it anyway (we have done those things which we ought not to have done). For the first kind of failure – that of failing to do what we should – the Greeks of Plato and Aristotle's time coined the word *akrasia* to mean something like weakness of will. To go ahead and do what we know we shouldn't, on the other hand, could be just another manifestation of *akrasia*, but it could also be understood as an expression of something rather more morally serious than simple weakness in the face of temptation – a certain preference for what is perverse or forbidden perhaps or a deliberate choice of evil over good. At any rate, the moral psychology of the early Socratic dialogues, expressed as it is through a simple analysis of moral life in terms of a conflict between reason and passion or the cognitive and the affective together with the idea that virtue is knowledge and vice is ignorance, is clearly inadequate to account for what is going on in these rather more complex cases of moral failure – *akrasia* and licentiousness.

A movement towards a rather more complex picture of the soul and the nature of virtue is made in the dialogues of Plato's middle period, notably in the *Republic*; here there is definite evidence of an awareness on Plato's part that the simple reason–passion dichotomy of the Socratic perspective is not adequate to do justice to the complexities of moral experience and moral failure. In the *Republic*, which is undoubtedly the first of the very great works of western social and political philosophy, Plato is concerned to argue again through the dramatic character of Socrates (though probably going well beyond the views of the historical Socrates) for a particular conception of the nature of justice in human affairs. Actually, a very large part of his aim is to characterise the nature of justice as it operates in the public context of society and politics, to describe the nature of the just state, but he sees this as intimately connected with the matter of understanding how justice is exhibited in the individual person.

In fact, for Plato, to understand the operations of justice in the individual is just to understand the nature of moral virtue, but he argues that we can gain a clearer perspective on this by seeing how justice works between men at the larger political level. Notoriously, in the course of trying to understand the government of the just state, Plato distinguished between three social classes each with a different function with respect to the task of maintaining a stable social and political order. The main distinction he observed was between the class of Guardians and that of the common run of ordinary people, but the Guardian class was further subdivided into the Guardian or ruling class proper and the Auxiliaries (or trainee Guardians) who help them to govern by ensuring that the policies of the rulers are effectively executed. Since the ruling classes are characterised by Plato in terms of their superior moral and political wisdom or intelligence over those they rule, the state may be considered healthy or just only in that case in which it continues in disciplined obedience to the decisions of the Guardians.

Plato's model of social and political justice in the *Republic* employs a tri-partite analysis of the membership of the state in terms of different political and economic functions, an analysis which he transfers to the individual person in order to understand the nature of moral virtue. So to begin with, just as a social order exhibits justice, according to Plato, when the vigorous but undisciplined body of human activity which sustains its economic life is wisely directed by intelligent government, so justice or virtue operates in the individual when reason or wisdom rules the passions and appetites. To this extent, of course, the 'Republican' model of virtue resembles the 'Socratic' model. But at the political level Plato has also identified a third group of individuals – the Auxiliaries – whose role is to carry out or enforce the legislation or policies formulated by the Guardians. What, in the individual person, could be said to correspond to the activities of the Auxiliary class in the ideal *Republic*? Plato in fact augments the Socratic distinction between reason and appetite with a third element *thumos* which is introduced in what is clearly intended to be an explanatory role with respect to certain kinds of moral failure or defect.

Most reliable commentators on ancient philosophy in general and Plato in particular caution against the translation of *thumos* by the modern English term 'will' and translators usually prefer to use such terms as 'spirit', 'energy' or 'initiative'. In so warning us against the translation of *thumos* as 'will', however, it seems to me that they acknowledge a fairly natural temptation so to translate it on the grounds that 'thumos' does have at least some if not all of the features we commonly associate with the term 'will'.[10] *Thumos* or high spirit, then, is introduced by Plato to express a quality of character or a source of motivation which may be available to be called upon in certain circumstances where an individual is vulnerable to weakness or temptation; if he is beset by fear in dangerous circumstances spirit will help him to be courageous or steadfast, if he is tested by intemperate passions or appetites, then spirit may be used to resist these appetites and Plato gives specific examples of these functions of spirit.

Plato even identifies a specific form of education – physical education – as concerned with the training of spirit or initiative;

to be sure, argues the character of Socrates, too much physical education may make a man coarse and uncivilised but an exclusively academic education in the absence of physical education will leave him spineless and effeminate. It would appear to be recognised clearly enough in the *Republic*, then, that wisdom, right reason or good judgement does not always operate as an effective bulwark against men's temptations to pleasure or fear of danger and that a certain strength of character expressed in the idea of *thumos* may be necessary to safeguard the individual from *akrasia* (or in the shape of the Auxiliaries, the state from revolution).

On the other hand, however, *thumos*, spirit or initiative seems to be quite unlike the modern concept of will in having anything like an autonomous life or identity of its own; it is characterised by Plato as something which stands quite definitely in the shadow or the service of right reason. The Christian idea of the will as something which operates as an independent source of motivation and choice and which is open to the influence of good or evil is quite different in these crucial respects from Plato's *thumos* and probably makes its first entrance into western thought with St Augustine.[11] Thus the wickedness that results from submission to fear or lust is still for Plato a largely involuntary matter, a failure of character rather than a perversion of character and therefore the main source of impetus towards virtue in the *Republic* is still right reason or good judgement.

At the political level, then, the just state is the one in which the majority of ordinary people who are bent on satisfying their personal desires are ruled by the wise and discriminating few with the *assistance* of the Auxiliaries who are the political embodiment of *thumos*; they are merely the executives of the decrees and decisions of the wise rulers. So although we can understand some cases of vice or moral defect in terms of failures of spirit or character rather than in terms of mere ignorance of the good, it is still obviously crucial to understanding moral virtue in Platonic terms to give some satisfactory account of moral wisdom or knowledge of the good. How is this to be done and what sort of knowledge is in question here?

Some of Plato's most important and difficult works – the *Meno*, the *Republic*, the *Parmenides*, the *Theaetetus* and so on – are precisely concerned with epistemological questions, questions about what knowledge and understanding are in general. Undoubtedly the Socratic view that virtue is to be understood in terms of a kind of knowledge led Plato into very deep theoretical waters from out of which he bequeathed to all subsequent philosophers a tangle of still unsettled problems. In the closing passages of this short account of Socrates' and Plato's views on the nature of moral virtue I cannot say much about these important questions but it is necessary to make certain observations.

First, both these ancient philosophers appear to have been well aware of precisely those problems of the possibility of speaking at all about moral knowledge which continue to embarrass many modern moral philosophers. The theoretical or empirical knowledge that a scientist claims to have of the world of nature can be tested by experiment or verified by observation; the mathematician's knowledge of his theorems and proofs can be checked against the validity or soundness of his deductive inferences; the artist's or technician's practical or procedural knowledge of his craft can be judged by reference to the effectiveness of his skills; but what is it that verifies or proves the soundness, rightness or validity of moral beliefs and judgements? To be sure, we encounter quite different responses to this question in different dialogues of Plato. In the *Meno*, for example, Plato appears precisely to entertain quite serious doubts about the very idea of moral knowledge; in matters of morals we are precisely concerned with judgements and prescriptions which cannot be demonstrated to be true. Moral judgements, then, can only express matters of opinion – true opinion perhaps – but we have no way of knowing for sure.

This is not, however, the final considered view of the epistemological status of moral judgements in Plato's works. Plato's final view appears to have been that a genuine kind of knowledge is exhibited in moral virtue, albeit knowledge of a very special and esoteric kind. Like many later 'rationalist' philosophers Plato deeply distrusted human experience as a potential source of genuine knowledge since he was keenly aware that our senses frequently mislead us concerning the true nature of things. He was also impressed by the observation that the greatest certainty and the least likelihood of being deceived is to be discovered in those forms of human enquiry which depend most exclusively on human reason and exhibit the highest degree of abstraction from the world of sensible appearances – mathematics and geometry, for example. For Plato, human reason represented the most reliable route to knowledge, empirical sensation and perception the least reliable.

Moreover, the intellect as the highest expression of the human soul could best come to a perfect understanding of the true nature of reality undistracted by or in a state of complete independence from any physical involvement with the world as given in empirical perception. For when we employ the various organs of sense to give us information about the world, we classify items of experience in terms of particular ideas and concepts – this object, a cricket ball, say, is red, round and hard. But in fact the ball is not absolutely round (because it has pits and bumps) or unequivocally red (because it's a bit faded) and so on, and no other object we may encounter in experience exhibits the perfect or unqualified roundness or redness that belongs to these and other ideas which we bring to the comprehension of experience. Obviously, then, our concepts of perfect or unqualified roundness and redness have not been derived or abstracted from any of the imperfect samples of them we have previously encountered in experience, so that they must relate to items in a supersensible world of reality to which we have access only by means of the exercise of human reason or intellect; it is a large part of the role of this intellect, moreover, to reason to the precise clarification or definition of these ideas and concepts of perfect reality.

This doctrine known as Plato's 'Theory of Forms' may appear to the lay-reader of philosophy only as far-fetched; but it is based on some very acute philosophical observations about the nature of concept-formation which are the source of genuine problems for epistemologists. From whence, for example, can we be said to get our concepts of number and mathematics? They can hardly be said to be derived or abstracted from empirical experience since where in experience do we find empirical instances of one million, minus two or the square root of minus two? There must be some sense in which such concepts are a product of human reason or intellect which are applied by human beings to the task of ordering or organising experience. It was Plato himself, of course, who raised some of the most serious difficulties for the Theory of Forms in his dialogue *Parmenides* and they are difficulties that he never appears to have been able to resolve satisfactorily.

The importance of the idea for the present discussion of Socrates' and Plato's account of the moral virtues, however, is that the sort of knowledge which the truly virtuous man may be said to possess is going to be, according to these two philosophers, of a very special and exalted kind. For if it is true that we cannot in experience find examples of perfect redness or roundness, it is even more unlikely that we shall be able to find examples of perfect justice, wisdom or temperance. A true knowledge of these qualities is only to be had via the rigorously disciplined practice of dialectic or rational enquiry; we cannot reasonably expect to be able directly to discern or abstract them from the imperfect realm of human experience where in reality anyway it is only injustice, license and ignorance that generally prevail.

In fact, then, whereas those who have discussed moral questions in more modern times have often pointed to the fact that moral judgements cannot be empirically verified in the same manner as scientific observations as to the disadvantage of the former – so much the worse for statements of morals since they can have no genuine warrant or justification – Plato turns the unlikeness of moral judgements and empirical observations in this respect to the rational advantage of the former. Moral judgements are considered to be closer to mathematical propositions than to observational or natural scientific ones in being at a further remove from the potentially deceptive or deluding world of empirical sensibility; but then mathematical statements would appear to have a more secure and certain rational basis for precisely that reason – they stand independent of or immune from the world of contingency and change.

For Plato, however, the moral philosopher's pursuit of a clear understanding of the concepts of wisdom, justice, virtue and so on represents the highest and most difficult of human concerns and the sort of rigorous training of the intellect that should follow from a serious study of the mathematical sciences cannot be but a preparation for the intellectual demands of the former task. As a consequence of this Plato would appear to have concluded in the *Republic* and subsequent works that the knowledge which is exhibited in the profession of true virtue is available only to a few privileged individuals of distinguished intellectual ability and then only after a lifetime of mental training and exercise, beginning with physical education and empirical studies and proceeding via mathematics to a serious study of the mode of intellectual enquiry called dialectic that will eventually yield a true comprehension of the absolute forms or abstract principles of justice and virtue.

Plato held, of course, that such individuals should be given this education or training with the ultimate aim that they might become the 'Guardians' of his ideal republic – those philosopher statesmen whose true vision of the nature of social and political justice would turn the idea of a perfectly just state into a political reality – the rule of the majority of indifferently decent but confused and undisciplined citizens by a wise and benevolent elite who possess true knowledge. Such government, of course, could only be *de haut bas*, a kind of direct dictatorship, albeit well-meaning, over the affairs of the undistinguished majority of men, because there could not be any possibility of the ignorant masses arriving at the slightest appreciation of the vision of justice vouchsafed to the enlightened few.

Hence Plato's famous allegory of the cave. The ignorant majority chained in the cave take themselves to be experiencing real people and objects by the light of the sun whereas in fact all they perceive are shadows cast by the flames of a fire in the otherwise cavernous darkness. The philosopher who has perceived the nature of perfect justice and virtue by the light of divine reason is like an individual who has escaped from the dark cave to experience the dazzling light of the sun which unveils reality in its true colours. Moreover, although he also recognises that it is his duty to return to the cave and help his erstwhile fellow prisoners as best he can, there can be little hope of his explaining successfully to them what he has seen, any more than a sighted man could hope to explain his experience of colour to the blind. This is more or less how moral knowledge is understood by Plato – as something highly theoretical, abstract and available only to the privileged few. Since for Aristotle this view of the nature and role of knowledge and reason in human moral life is almost wholly mistaken, it is high time we turned to his account.

2

VIRTUE AS CHARACTER: ARISTOTLE'S ETHICS

As we have just seen, despite certain misgivings about the matter, Plato's general view of the nature of moral virtue was that it is essentially expressive of a kind of knowledge or understanding. The life of virtue is to be understood as one lived in conformity to certain rational principles reflecting the true interests of an individual, as opposed to one in which individual conduct proceeds under the influence of a range of essentially destructive natural passions and appetites; virtue, then, is the rule of natural inclination or passion by right reason and vice not so much just the straightforward defeat of reason by passion, but rather a life of ignorance of the true good in which an individual knows no better than to act at the impulse of his irrational instincts and appetites. Plato also understood knowledge of the good to be of a particularly abstract and difficult intellectual character, however – of such a nature that only a privileged elite could hope to attain any real insight into it; only the Guardians after a long course of rigorous training and education might be vouchsafed a vision of the form of the good. These are just some of the views about the nature of human moral life and virtue that are essentially controverted by that other colossus of ancient philosophy and Plato's own most famous pupil – Aristotle.

Like those of Plato, Aristotle's views on moral philosophy and virtue require to be studied alongside or in the context of his social and political philosophy. In fact, of course, any moral philosopher worth his salt has sought to develop a conception of human society or of the sort of political order most conducive to human happiness and fulfilment which is consistent with or internally related to his ideas about human nature and individual virtue and Plato and Aristotle are perfect examples of this sensible tendency. Plato's view that virtue in the individual is exhibited only in that circumstance in which the blind and turbulent appetites and passions are strictly governed by right reason with the spirit's assistance exactly parallels his conception of social and political justice as a state in which a wise or enlightened minority rule the ignorant majority with the help of a disciplined auxiliary who will brook no nonsense.

This political view is, of course, profoundly anti-democratic (Plato made no secret of his deep antipathy to democracy) and some notable modern philosophers have located the origins of present day left and (more particularly) right wing totalitarianism in Plato's views. Aristotle's ethics, no less than Plato's, are inextricably linked to his politics and though he was as aware of the shortcomings of democracy as Socrates and Plato, his quite different understanding of human nature and moral virtue in the *Nicomachean Ethics* and elsewhere[1] is linked to a much more individualistic and liberal-democratic view in the *Politics* of what is conducive to human happiness and flourishing *vis-à-vis* social and political arrangements (although strictly *unqualified* democracy is actually labelled a 'perversion' in the *Politics*). Although in what follows, then, I shall need to concentrate mainly on Aristotle's account of moral virtue in the *Ethics*, it should be borne in mind and I shall try to indicate where possible, that that account is linked to a much more moderate and liberal view of the place of the individual in society than we find in Plato.

Again, as we saw when considering the views of Plato in relation to his use of the term *thumos*, a very real difficulty presents itself with respect to any discussion of ancient philosophy over the precise translation of terms. While it is quite true that very many of the everyday words we use have classical Greek or Latin roots, so much has usually happened to them down centuries of usage in changing social and historical circumstances that it is seldom safe to assume that they retain anything much like the same sense or meaning as the terms from which they were originally derived. In discussing the philosophy of Aristotle this problem of meaning shift becomes acute, although I shall try in the present context to avoid it except in relation to two crucial terms. In the first place, then, Aristotle maintains in the opening section of the *Nicomachean*

Ethics that all human endeavour aims at some good, and that the science or study of what is good for man is something like social or political science.[2]

The first question which arises naturally in response to this observation concerns what is the good for man, and Aristotle accepts the conventional view that it is *eudaimon*. Usually, however, *eudaimon* is translated as 'happiness' and this can give a misleading impression of what Aristotle appears to have thought the ultimate human good to consist in. We ask someone why they're singing in that breezy way and they reply 'because I'm happy today', and this suggests that happiness is some sort of inner state of mood or feeling – pleasure perhaps – of which the singing is an expression. Well, although Aristotle was certainly not hostile (as Plato often appears to have been) to the idea of pleasure as a human good, he is at pains to distinguish the *eudaimon* that is the proper object of human good from any kind of mere mood or feeling; in fact it would appear that we are meant to construe the happiness that is *eudaimon* as a quality of life or conduct rather than a state of feeling. It is often suggested, then, that *eudaimon* is better translated as 'well-being' or 'flourishing' than 'happiness'.[3]

But it may seem hardly helpful to be told in response to the question 'what is the ultimate good for human beings?', 'that which constitutes their well-being', for what we want to know is precisely what that is. The answer which Aristotle details at considerable length in the *Ethics* is that it is essentially a form of human life or activity to be characterised in terms of practice of the virtues or in which the virtues are prominently exhibited. But what are the virtues and how can we recognise them? For Aristotle we may come to know what the virtues are by the very same process by which we recognise them – essentially by observing how they operate in human affairs. Here, however, it is necessary to draw attention to a second important point of etymology in relation to understanding Aristotle – how we are to understand the Greek term *arete* which is normally rendered into our Latin-derived term 'virtue'.

First we need to appreciate that for the Greeks the term *arete* had a very much wider sense than that which we normally give to the English word 'virtue'. For us the term 'virtue' refers primarily to particular states or qualities of human character such as honesty or generosity or perhaps less surely to the idea of a rule or principle which people invest with some sort of moral value (for example 'she makes a virtue of cleanliness'); but for the Greeks the term *arete* was used to refer to excellence in things generally – not just human beings – with respect primarily to notions of their function and purpose. Since the function or purpose of an axe is to chop well, the *arete* of an axe (a *good* axe that is) would be its chopping power; since the job of a soldier (a *good* soldier, not necessarily a soldier who is a good *man*) is to fight or kill well, fighting or killing is the *arete* of a soldier. The *arete* of an agent or object, then, is just that characteristic of it that makes it a good (exemplary, representative, successful) object or agent of its kind – that property or quality of a thing which best fulfils its function or serves best to promote the end, good or purpose for which it was made or fashioned (or in the case of a human agent, trained).[4]

In the *Ethics*, of course, Aristotle is not interested in the *arete* of objects like axes or of human agents in their roles as farmers or soldiers concerning which proper functions are relatively easy to determine, he is interested rather in the *arete* of men as such. He is interested in determining the characteristics or properties in terms of which human beings might be said to fulfil their function or realise their end *qua* human beings. This attempt on Aristotle's part to comprehend the ultimate moral end or good for men as such in terms of a purposive notion like that of *arete* lends Aristotle's ethics a *teleological* orientation of a kind that has been unfashionable in moral philosophy at least in post-Enlightenment modern times (although it has just recently enjoyed something of a revival). The most conspicuous problem for Aristotle or anyone else inclined towards an ethics of this kind is to give some clear sense or content to the idea that we can determine what is the good for man – not man as farmer, soldier or sailor – but human nature as such.

In general, however, according to Aristotle, we are to determine the *arete* of man *qua* man in much the same way as we determine it in any other case; by their works shall we know them. We discover the difference between a good axe and a bad axe by trying them out and seeing which cuts the best; we tell a good from a bad farmer by the yield of his crops and the size of his herds; we tell a good man from a bad man by how well he prospers in his affairs and how much he benefits and is benefited or respected by his friends and neighbours. Unlike

Plato, then, who does not seem to think that much can ultimately be learned about the true nature of justice through observation of the actual affairs of men (or as some modern philosophers would say, we cannot learn how things *should* be from observing how in fact they *are*) Aristotle's approach to understanding human good or virtue is *naturalistic*; just as we learn what a good horse or a good slave is by observing and comparing actual horses and slaves in respect of the tasks we require of them, so learning about the virtue or goodness of men is similarly a matter of observation and comparison. Thus Aristotle insists that moral evaluation or reflection on matters of virtue cannot be an occupation for the young and inexperienced precisely because the road to wisdom about such things requires years of careful reflection upon a breadth of experience which the young do not possess.

Of course, Plato also thought that true understanding in relation to moral matters must await a stage of human maturity at which the mind was properly equipped for the task; but it is crucially important to see how different are Plato's reasons for saying this from Aristotle's. For Plato, the process of acquiring moral wisdom involves years of intense and highly abstruse intellectual reflection directed towards a clear apprehension of the form of the good and the search for the form of the good like the medieval knight's quest for the holy grail is open only to a privileged few. For Aristotle, on the other hand, the form of the good is merely a chimera, a creature of fancy which would be of no practical moral use even if we found it, and for him the search for moral wisdom or understanding cannot in any case have the character of precise scientific enquiry.

Aristotle, then, argues that it is merely the sign of a bad education to expect the same degree of exactness or precision in moral enquiry that one has a perfect right to expect in science or mathematics.[5] In science and mathematics we are, after all (or so Aristotle thought) in the realm of necessity, of things as they could not be otherwise, whereas moral action and conduct are inherently and irremediably contingent – enmeshed in a world of changing particularities rather than absolute certainties. It is vital to appreciate in relation to Aristotle's moral philosophy as distinct from Plato's that moral enquiry is to be construed as a form of *practical* enquiry, rather than as some kind of super-scientific or meta-theoretical search for an ideal realm of abstract, eternal and changeless principles.

Consequently greater experience is needed for the growth of moral wisdom not because long training is required to apprehend the precise, abstract and esoteric nature of the unchanging form of moral principles, but rather because of the greater appreciation that needs to be gradually acquired of the contingency, lack of precision and indistinct outline of them. Moreover, precisely because of the direct practical consequences which make virtue and the deep experience of human affairs which it presupposes of ultimate significance for all human lives, the sort of knowledge which is considered by Aristotle to be required for moral virtue must also be supposed to be available to all and not just to a privileged elect or elite; moral wisdom is not the concern solely of intellectuals since it is necessary for the perfection of *any* human life and it is not in any case an intellectual matter (in the sense of being exclusively for specialists or academicians).

For Aristotle, then, substantial experience is needed of human affairs for the making of successful moral evaluations or judgements; but in what contexts generally are we to observe and compare the operations of human agents in order to determine precisely in what virtue or excellence consists for men *qua* men. The particular science of good for man, Aristotle maintained, is politics – more generally perhaps that branch of enquiry we would call today social studies. The peculiar virtues of men *qua* men, then, are those which equip them for life in society, specifically for Aristotle those particular social-units familiar to the Greeks of his time – the ancient Greek city-states generally referred to by the term *polis*.

Broadly speaking, however, Aristotle is arguing for the quite reasonable view that what count as the kinds of qualities or virtues apt to promote the well-being or flourishing of human beings as such, are those that fit them for a life of harmonious and co-operative relations with their fellows in some sort of civil human community. One of the primary considerations about human nature for Aristotle, then, which goes to determine the character of the sort of virtues a man will need to live well is that man is essentially a social animal whose ultimate good even as an individual person can only be realised in the context of some sort of human society. Among the virtues that men require are those that fit them for successful social intercourse with others.

Just as important a consideration for determining what it is for human beings to live well or to realise their *telos* (end or goal) as human beings, however, is the Aristotelian observation that man is a rational as well as a social animal; indeed his rationality is presupposed to his particular form of human sociability. In general, to determine what constitutes the distinctive *arete* of a particular creature or artifact it is necessary to consider what are the characteristics or features of that creature or artifact which uniquely distinguish it from other things; thus it is the special characteristic of an axe to chop or a fish to swim. What characteristic, then, distinguishes men from other animals with whom they share so many natural functions – nutrition, sensation, perception, locomotion and so on? Most obviously the feature or characteristic which most clearly distinguishes men from other things of the natural or created orders is the power of reason or deliberation. Rational reflection and contemplation are for Aristotle, then, part and parcel of realising the *telos* or end of men; an important element (Aristotle concludes the *Ethics* by claiming more or less that it is the *most* important) in any satisfying, prosperous or fulfilling life for human beings must consist in the exercise of thought and reflection, not merely for practical or instrumental purposes, but also for its own sake.

Thus according to Aristotle the virtues that distinguish a worthwhile human life and which are themselves constitutive of such a life are of two main (though, as we shall see, importantly related) kinds; the *moral* virtues which adapt us to successful social relations with others and render us an asset rather than a liability in any civilised human community, and the *intellectual* virtues which permit and assist our successful engagement in a wide range of characteristically human rational enterprises of art, science and technology, all of which are attended by rewards in terms of both material gain and intrinsic satisfaction. All these moral and intellectual virtues, by the way, are understood by Aristotle to be qualities or manifestations of the human soul – as virtue, knowledge and rationality are expressions of soul for Plato. Once again, however, Aristotle's conception of the soul differs markedly and profoundly from Plato's and this issues directly in a quite different conception of virtue on Aristotle's part from that which we have found in Plato.

As we have seen, it was roughly Plato's view that the soul and the body of a person belong to two different worlds; the soul was to be understood essentially as an immortal, invisible and eternal entity that was in principle separable from the body and could expect to be freed from its association with it at the moment of death. In Plato's *Phaedo* Socrates is represented as looking forward to his death and the final liberation of his soul from its earthly prison. Again for Plato, as we have seen, physical or corporeal existence was to be regarded largely as a source of temptation to wickedness and vice, whereas something like a state of purely spiritual or intellectual existence represents the highest goal of human aspiration. In short, there is a strongly other-worldly and world-renouncing flavour to Plato's ideal of human moral perfection.

For Aristotle, on the contrary, little real sense is to be attached to this general Platonic view of the soul as something capable of existing separately from the body. Like the idea of virtue expressed through the notion of *arete*, that of soul (*psyche*) is construed by Aristotle teleologically, in terms of function and purpose. Thus in his work on descriptive psychology in the *De Anima* and elsewhere,[6] Aristotle takes the view that those activities of consciousness, perception, knowledge and understanding that we associate with the term 'soul' are to be construed as particular dispositions or powers of actual physical creatures rather than as the operations of some ghostly or spiritual entity only temporarily conjoined to a human body. In a striking analogy Aristotle observes that if the eye were an animal then sight would be its soul; likewise should we compare an axe to a person then the power to chop would correspond to its soul.

Thus thoughts, judgements, desires, intentions and so on are not to be regarded as immaterial spiritual objects but rather as particular forms of conduct or activity – or, at least, as dispositions or tendencies to conduct. Aristotle's view of the mind or soul is therefore, unlike Plato's, naturalistic and evolutionary, rather than supernaturalistic and manichean. This leads naturally to a quite different perspective on the world, the flesh and the passions in Aristotle's *Ethics*; no human inclinations or tendencies are to be considered bad in themselves, everything depends on the way in which they are expressed or exercised. This point is crucial in relation to understanding the precise nature of Aristotle's account of the moral virtues in particular.

For Aristotle, then, the moral virtues are among the excellences of the soul; but what is the precise character of these excellences and how do we acquire them? They cannot be merely passions according to Aristotle because we are not praised or blamed for feeling fear, anger or happiness and they would not appear to be faculties like sight and hearing because whereas we are innately endowed with these faculties we have to acquire the moral virtues. It is a point of emphasis in the *Ethics* that the virtues are neither natural in the sense of innate, nor unnatural in the sense of artificial or foreign to human nature, since as social animals we require the moral virtues and are fitted by nature to receive them.[7] Given the rational and social nature of man, then, there can be no serious doubt that he needs to acquire the virtues; the main question concerns how he does acquire them and to this question Aristotle again returns a quite different answer from Plato. Whereas for Plato, the road to learning which leads to the acquisition of virtue appears to be a kind of spiritual quest for enlightenment through the form of the good which lies open only to a privileged few, for Aristotle the acquisition of virtue is a matter of immediate practical concern to all men irrespective of their station and it requires much the same manner of learning that would appear to be necessary in the case of other forms of practical conduct.

First of all, Aristotle speaks of the acquisition of virtue in the very homely, familiar and quite unmysterious terms of the learning of a practical skill. Just as men learn to be skilled tradesmen, builders or carpenters, by practical initiation into the skills of building and carpentry; just as musicians, performers on the lyre or flute, become musicians by practising on the lyre and the flute; so, says Aristotle, men learn the moral virtues by the *practice* of courage and justice – they become courageous or just men by performing courageous or just acts. The moral virtues, like the arts, need to be both learned and taught – men need to be directed along the path of goodness or right conduct – but the learning in question, contrary to what Plato appears to have come to believe (though in the early dialogues Socrates also often appeared to pursue an analogy between moral knowledge and knowledge of skills), is primarily a form of practical rather than academic or theoretical learning. So having distinguished the moral virtues from mere states of passion or innate faculties, Aristotle takes the view that they are dispositions to conduct based in settled states of character which are acquired by a process of largely practical training.[8]

But the view that we become just or courageous by the performance of just or courageous acts has an obviously paradoxical ring to it. For how can we perform or practice just and courageous acts if we are not just and courageous already, and if we *are* just and courageous already why do we need to practice justice and courage? To a large extent this question can be illuminated by developing a little further Aristotle's analogy with learning in the arts. Clearly, the apprentice builder or novitiate pianist under the instruction of master craftsmen in these enterprises perform acts of building (laying one brick on top of another) and piano playing (executing scales and arpeggios) which are recognisable as such but which yet lack the precise quality of skill, art, mastery or craftsmanship that these acts would exhibit in the context of their teacher's work. What precisely they lack is the element of knowing properly what they are doing. The attention of the building apprentice or the learner at the piano is wholly taken up with executing that bit of skill or technique and with getting *it* right.

They will be aware, of course, that the particular closed skills they are performing are parts or details of the larger arts and crafts known as piano playing and building, but as yet they have a very long way to go before they acquire the level of knowledge, practical facility and experience of these enterprises which will eventually entitle them to be called builder or pianist; for that they will need to acquire the full range of craft skills, an understanding of how the skills are integrated into the craft, an ease of execution in relation to the basic skills which allows for the simultaneous exercise of intelligence, judgement and flexibility with respect to the shape of the whole enterprise and so on. It is in the light of all these considerations, moreover, that the most effective learning in such arts and crafts proceeds under the guidance of an experienced teacher who knows what he's about.

In a similar way Aristotle maintains with respect to moral virtue that those acts which we properly call just and courageous are acts such as would be done by a truly just or courageous man, not those only superficially similar acts that we might encourage a small child to perform in the course of his moral education in order that he may eventually grow up to be a just, courageous or unselfish person. As yet the small child might have only the foggiest idea why he is being encouraged

51

not to cry when he falls down and grazes his knee or why against his inclinations he is being encouraged to share his sweets with the hated little sister, but it is only by practising these aspects of virtue that he will acquire a grasp of the practicalities of moral life that may in time lead to his being a reflective and committed practitioner of it – in short, a just, courageous and temperate person. As it is not necessary in the case of a young person receiving piano lessons that he should either know (in the mastery sense) or even want to do what he is being required to do, so in the case of the requirement of a child that he should share his sweets.

It *is* a condition of the full possession of virtue or of being properly called a good man, however, that just or courageous men should both know what they are doing and choose virtuous conduct for its own sake. It is necessary not only that any action performed in a context requiring a moral response should be an appropriate one in the circumstances (in terms of the piano analogy the correct notes should be in the proper harmonic relationship) but also that the agent should also have a good reason for what he does and a genuine desire to do it; he must act from the right motive. It may, of course, be raised as an objection to all of this that just as compelling or even strongly encouraging a child to practise the piano may be the most effective form of aversion therapy with respect to music, so requiring him to share his sweets may actually be inimical rather than conducive to his moral development; but we may leave this point until the treatment of Freud and others in the next section.

At any rate, so far Aristotle has identified for us what he calls the 'genus' of moral virtue; it is a settled state of character acquired by practice which disposes us to certain forms of conduct describable as just, courageous, temperate and so on. The next important element in his definition of virtue, however, concerns what he calls its 'differentia' – the sort of state of character that it is. This brings us face to face with Aristotle's famous doctrine of the *mean*. As we have observed, the moral virtues are according to Aristotle what generally conduce to the promotion of human well-being, the good for man; in general he holds that justice, temperance, courage and so on are dispositions which conduce to the choice of conduct that preserves individual and social prosperity in both a moral and a material sense. But what sort of conduct is this and how is it to be precisely determined?

Plato and Socrates held that virtues and vices operated in simple opposition to each other; courage, for example, is that condition in which wisdom exhibited in a reasonably cool assessment of our genuine interests in dangerous circumstances enables us to act sensibly or honourably against the prompt-ings of our non-rational feelings of fear and panic, whereas cowardice, on the other hand, is simply that condition in which we allow fear to get the better of our good judgement. Aristotle, however, insists that whereas men are good in only one way, they are bad in many and he sees the opposition of virtue to vice as a rather more complicated matter than does Plato. He argues that the course of action which is the morally correct one to follow in any circumstances requiring the exercise of virtue may fall short of correctness in either of two main ways – by what he calls excess or defect.

To a large extent Plato had thought of virtue in general very much in terms of self-control – the control of fear by the courageous man, the control of the appetites by the temperate man – because he was very much inclined to regard the passions and appetites as negative and destructive forces in human moral life. Aristotle agrees that virtue is exhibited to a considerable degree in the rational control of the passions and appetites but he does not regard the passions and appetites as intrinsically bad. In themselves the natural inclinations of men are perfectly acceptable features and conditions of human existence; so much so that we could only regard a state of affairs in which men lacked the passions and appetites or denied them any expression whatsoever, as something abnormal or patho-logical. Fear for Aristotle is not something which is in itself bad or wicked – we do not or should not blame a person for experiencing reasonable fear in dangerous circumstances. We do rightly blame him, however, if he fails to exert reason-able self-control in such circumstances or if, by giving free reign to his panic, he places the lives of others in danger.

But by the same token, since it is very natural to feel fear in dangerous circumstances and there would be no need to exercise courage except in response to that natural fear, it can hardly be counted as courage when someone acts in genuinely dangerous circumstances as though he had no fear at all. Thus to meet danger in a state of blithe unconcern or without any kind of anxiety is for Aristotle almost as far from genuine courage as is cowardice, except that a response of reckless abandon to danger might be *mistaken* for courage in a way that cowardice is unlikely to be. And to be sure, to speak of 'Dutch' courage is to refer to a kind of bogus bravery in which the crutch of alcohol is substituted for genuine resolution; however ferociously they hurl themselves into battle, then, the courage of warriors high on hashish or amphetamines must be called into question. For Aristotle, then, courage is the rational and voluntary control of genuine fear or anxiety with the help of a disciplined character, not a state of obliviousness to that fear or anxiety to be achieved by working oneself into alternative states of emotion such as anger or euphoria, or by the use of drugs.

In Aristotelian terms corresponding to any given virtue – and Aristotle's discussion of moral life ranges over a far wider variety of virtues than we find in Plato including friendliness, generosity and so on – there are two defects of character rather than just one vice. It seems better, on the whole, to speak here of 'defects of character' because in relation to the virtue of courage, for example, it is clearly less appropriate to think of headstrong recklessness as opposed to cowardice as exactly a *vice*, but it is also quite clear that it represents a disposition which falls considerably short of the standards which Aristotle sets for the moral virtue of courage. It is characteristic of the virtues in general according to Aristotle, however, that they can be said to lie 'in a mean' between extremes of character in which certain defects or excesses are exhibited – excesses and defects, to be precise, of certain perfectly natural states of human passion, emotion and appetite.

In general, the doctrine of the mean expresses the idea that the conduct which conduces mostly effectively to the well-being of men in human society is that which exhibits reasonable moderation and avoids unreasonable extremes of action and passion. Whilst much ink has been spilt down the ages in either criticism or downright caricature of the doctrine of the mean it is possible to respect or commend the spirit of the doctrine at the very same time as one recognises its limitations or rejects it as a principle which is generalisable over all the qualities we call virtues. In relation to the general idea that the moral virtues are in some way concerned with self-control, for example, the doctrine may be understood to express a reasonable criticism of two diametrically opposed views of what is ultimately good for human beings.

In the first place, then, there is the philosophy of self-indulgent hedonism which advocates yielding to the passions and pleasures of the moment without any thought for the morrow; in the second place, there is the more severe puritan doctrine of world-renouncing asceticism which takes pride and pleasure in rigid discipline and self-mortification for its own or heaven's sake. Hedonism, of course, is probably for most men the more attractive of these alternative temptations; but we have also witnessed on the part of Plato the sort of powerful moral reaction to such hedonism that makes a virtue out of the renunciation of the world and the flesh. In the doctrine of the mean, Aristotle may be viewed as taking a stand against precisely this element in Plato's thought; to be sure, the passions and appetites require a reasonable degree of discipline and control, but they are also quite natural to men, and their proper expression, in the right place and at the right time, is not to be despised.

But even with respect to the virtue of temperance concerning which the doctrine of the mean might be expected to have the most force against the sort of extreme views of human life and purpose we have just mentioned, the doctrine already appears to be rather dubious. For whereas Aristotle has little trouble naming a familiar enough vice, profligacy or self-indulgence, which is opposed to temperance by an excess of pleasure; he has practically to invent one, that of insensibility, to express the state of character which represents a defect of inclination to sensual enjoyment. Although the condition by which men are tempted to the indulgence of their physical appetites is a common enough one, then, that in which human beings are prone to err by feeling no physical appetites at all is so rare that men have found no common name for it (Plato's asceticism is, of course, just an extreme form of the *control* of physical pleasure which in Aristotle's terms must still fall on the side of temperance rather than insensibility).

When we turn to such other moral virtues as honesty and justice, however, the doctrine of the mean appears even more implausible, since it is almost impossible to attach much sense to the idea that too much honesty or justice represent states of excess to be opposed like dishonesty and injustice to the virtues of sufficient honesty and justice – unless, of course, we insist on construing excess honesty and justice in rather special ways so that excess justice means something like favouritism and excess honesty is taken to imply an insensitive frankness. (Needless to say, however, these equations do not work since favouritism is just injustice and frankness however brutal is still honesty.)

Still, what is clearly worth preserving in the doctrine of the mean is the perfectly reasonable idea that the passions and appetites are not as some philosophers have suggested merely sources of temptation to be controlled by the virtues, but actually necessary conditions for the expression of them. By this I mean not only that courage would not be possible without fear but also that charity and compassion would not be possible in the absence of genuine human feelings of love and concern for other people. Thus it seems that the moral virtues may indeed be undermined or vitiated by failures or defects of emotion, passion or feeling (and we shall return to this point in the third section of this work) as well as by an excess of a feeling; they stand to be undermined by our lack of positive feelings as well as by our excess of negative ones.

In general, then, we may be inclined to accept entirely the first part of Aristotle's definition of virtue that it is expressed in states of character, and even to accept the spirit of the second part of his definition, interpreting the doctrine of the mean in terms of the idea that the virtues should exhibit the correct degree, moderate rather than extreme, of passion, feeling or appetite. More or less the complete definition given by Aristotle, however, is that:

> virtue is a state of character concerned with choice, lying in a mean, the mean relative to us, this being determined by a rational principle and by that principle by which the man of practical wisdom would determine it.[9]

Thus it could not be clearer that for Aristotle in so far as the moral virtues are concerned with the promotion of conduct which conduces to human happiness or well-being, they must involve some rational judgement and choice with respect to the determination of such courses of action and conduct. Although in the *Nicomachean Ethics*, then, Aristotle draws an initial distinction between the moral virtues – the virtues, as it were, of social interaction – and the intellectual virtues, it is a crucial and significant aspect of the moral virtues that they require the exercise of a kind of wisdom, rationality or judgement. It is not possible to enter into fine detail here about what Aristotle says of the intellectual virtues; he divides the operations of human intellect, rationality and understanding into five kinds, but for present purposes we need only acknowledge a broad distinction of a more fundamental kind which he draws between two quite different basic applications of reason.

He draws a crucial distinction, which has received a great deal of attention from modern philosophers and logicians in very recent times,[10] between the kind of reason or rationality that operates in scientific or theoretical forms of enquiry and that which is involved in enquiries or pursuits of a more practical (artistic, technical, moral) kind. Fundamentally for Aristotle the difference is between a kind of reasoning which begins from observations about how things stand in the world and proceeds to general judgements or conclusions about it of a scientific or theoretical nature, the judgements in question expressing necessary and eternal truths, and a kind of reasoning which is concerned with effective conduct rather than right belief and in which the procedure is generally from a state of desire expressed in some intention to change the world in a certain respect to some action which may effect that change.

Both art and morality, then, unlike the world of science which is concerned with the discovery (so Aristotle thought) of necessary and universal truths, are concerned rather with the world of contingency and change and both employ a superficially similar kind of means–end inference or reasoning which in the case of art is called *techne* (the disposition by which we make things by the aid of a true rule) and in the case of virtue, *phronesis* or practical wisdom. Art is a very inferior form of rational enterprise to morality, however, since because what we produce as craftsmen through artistic activity requires putting to use for the promotion of human good, it is anyway subordinate to moral virtue and practical wisdom.

But Aristotle's observation that moral virtue does involve or require a kind of knowledge, wisdom or reasoning which needs to be sharply distinguished from that which operates in the human contemplation of nature or in other theoretical enquiries is absolutely crucial for understanding his ethics and how his view of virtue differs markedly from that of Plato. For Aristotle, moral reasoning is not any kind of theoretical reflection upon a world of absolute and unchangeable forms of goodness and justice, because goodness and justice are not objects which exist in the domain of scientific or theoretical reflection but immensely practical concerns such that knowledge of them is only to be found expressed or exhibited in human action or conduct.

It is futile, then, to look for some abstract form of justice or the good which lies above and beyond particular instantiations of it in the hearts, actions and conduct of real individuals; justice and the good are to be discovered essentially in the extent to which those hearts and actions conform to the mean in particular circumstances and circumstances alter cases. Thus what may be a just action in one set of circumstances may be quite other than just in a different set; what may be a courageous or honourable action in the Assembly might be a cowardly action in battle and so on. If Aristotle is reasonably correct about all this, then Plato in the *Republic* would appear to have misunderstood the way in which knowledge operates through virtue by misunderstanding the nature of the knowledge that virtue involves.

To understand properly what sort of knowledge this is, however, we need to remind ourselves that moral virtue is concerned above all with *choice* – the choice of that course of action or conduct which best represents the true interests or good of an individual and his social circle in some actual set of circumstances. The choice in question is not, however, a matter of mere plumping or blind opting because, amongst other things, in order to establish the right thing to do in any circumstances we have to decide reasonably what the mean action would be in those circumstances. In general, Aristotle regards moral choice as itself the direct outcome or function of a kind of rational deliberation, and the particular mode of rationality which enables genuine choice with respect to moral action is precisely *phronesis* or practical wisdom. Thus, starting from some moral aim, plan or intention, we proceed to a consideration of the various possible means or procedures whereby that aim, plan or intention might be accomplished, we choose the best course of action to follow in the light of such deliberations and then we act on that choice. In short, moral wisdom of knowledge is a knowledge of how to make right moral choices.

It is most important to observe, however, that if our deliberations concerning matters of conduct are to be true expressions of moral wisdom, they must proceed subject to certain constraints. Aristotle distinguishes practical wisdom from a formally similar sort of means–end reasoning which he calls 'cleverness' and which is concerned only with getting what we want through the satisfaction of some given desire or appetite. So although, to be sure, genuine moral virtue requires the operations of *phronesis* or practical wisdom, it is also true that genuine *phronesis* is possible only in the context of moral virtue; only a man who has acquired through the sort of moral training we considered earlier a conception of the good or virtuous life can be effective at determining by means of practical wisdom what is the right thing to do in any circumstances requiring moral decision. Indeed, Aristotle maintains in one place that we deliberate practically only about the means and not the ends of action and in another that one important difference between virtuous and artistic conduct is that whereas the making of an intentional mistake is to be preferred in the arts to an unintentional mistake, in morals it is the other way about.[11]

What these observations indicate, I believe, is that for Aristotle, although mature reflection or reason is certainly required to recognise the meaning of virtue or the true ends of moral life, those ends are not themselves (as some later philosophers appear to have come to think) purely products of human reason in the sense that men decide or construct those ends either individually or socially. On the contrary, it is reasonable to argue that we can deliberate successfully in moral matters to conclusions about how we should act only in the light of certain considerations which are not open for us to decide about what constitutes right and wrong in human affairs; only given some conception of what constitutes human good or harm which is not negotiable or individually decidable, does the idea of reasoning to the choice of a course of moral conduct make much sense. So to have been properly educated in moral matters means precisely that certain choices are no longer available to us if we really wish to pursue the life of virtue.

All this might make it appear that Aristotle accepts the Platonic conclusion that no man can act wrongly except in ignorance, but this is by no means so. Aristotle has very interesting observations to make on the nature and variety of forms of human moral failure and he clearly recognises that there is a difference between the victim of *akrasia* who knows what he should do but fails to do it and the licentious man who prefers a life of vice, wickedness and self-indulgence to that of virtue because he really knows no better – he is the casualty of a faulty upbringing or moral education.[12] In fact, in the *Ethics* Aristotle makes a valiant attempt to account for the problem of weakness of will, though all of the solutions he rehearses seem to be less than satisfactory. All the same it is to his credit that the moral psychology of virtue he elaborated permitted the clear identification of such a wide range of kinds of moral defect, and all in all Aristotle provides us with an account of the structure of virtue and moral character that is quite without equal in moral philosophy. Next, however, we must turn to the account of moral life which has had perhaps the greatest influence on the ethical thinking of the present day.

3

VIRTUE AS SELF-DETERMINATION: ROUSSEAU AND KANT

The main aim of this chapter is to trace the emergence and development of a very important and historically influential view of the nature of virtue and moral life by which two well-known philosophers of the so-called Enlightenment – Kant and Rousseau – are linked. Immanuel Kant is, of course, one of the very great names – perhaps *the* great name – of modern western philosophy, and it is hard to think of a present day philosophical school or perspective which has not felt something of his impact. Rousseau on the other hand, is a relatively minor figure in the history of modern philosophy (despite the fact that he has been credited with having had a powerful influence on the development of some of the major radical ideologies of our day, especially Marxist or 'left wing' ones) whose name is encountered most frequently in the more 'peripheral' areas of political and educational philosophy.

All the same, there is small room for doubt that the fundamental ethical ideas of Rousseau and Kant are intimately connected, and connected moreover, via the debt of the latter to the former. In this chapter, then, we are concerned to explore, amongst other things, the influence of the relatively minor eighteenth-century social and political philosopher Rousseau on the man in whose shadow he and others must otherwise be seen to stand, that great German metaphysician and anti-metaphysician Kant who towers like a colossus at the gateway to modern philosophy. But Rousseau, who we shall consider first in this chapter, is also closely linked to some of the important views of moral life and moral education which we shall consider later in this work in at least two fairly direct ways.

First, through Kant, he is linked to certain modern liberal individualist views in moral philosophy such as prescriptivism and also to those post-Kantian perspectives on the psychology of moral development associated with the names of Piaget and Kohlberg – for all of which the idea of the promotion of individual rational autonomy represents the main aim of education. He stands, in short, at the beginning of a long and pervasive post-Enlightenment tradition of thought about moral life which the present author views as significantly mistaken. Second, however, Rousseau also stands at the start of an equally long tradition of progressivist thinking about the practice of education which reaches down to present times in the form of the Freudian-influenced work of Homer Lane, A.S. Neill and others, whose ideas about moral life, conduct and education and the influence of society on the individual strikingly resemble, despite their modern dress, those of Rousseau. What, then, are the ideas of Rousseau which have had such an extraordinary and enduring effect and influence?

In the cases of Socrates, Plato and Aristotle we saw that each of them in their different moral philosophies attempted to discover or to show how unschooled human nature might be made accountable to the demands of justice and civilised life through some particular conception of moral education or socialisation; their views involved conceptions of raw human nature, some vision of a just or decent form of human social life and certain prescriptive observations about how human nature might be educationally accommodated to the demands of moral and social life. In a similar fashion Rousseau's philosophy can be seen to exhibit three aspects – a view of basic pre-civilised human nature, a vision of the sort of human society or political arrangement which best conduces to the realisation of true human happiness and justice and an account of the sort of education that will be required to adapt people to such a constitution. At the level of individual morality or virtue for Rousseau the key notion is that of *self-determination*; at the social and political level it is *democracy*.

As is generally the case with philosophers, however, Rousseau's views require to be understood as a kind of response or reaction to those of other philosophers – in his case to the views of certain earlier political theorists, in particular those of the seventeenth-century English philosopher Thomas Hobbes

who had argued in his great work *Leviathan* on beh
view of human nature, society and justice.[1]
suggested, as we have seen, that man is by ɪ
potentially, both a rational and a social cre..
appeared to believe that there is something essentiaiɪy
natural or pathological about the solitary or asocial human
condition. Quite to the contrary, Hobbes argued that society is
fundamentally a condition which is alien to basic human nature
since it is of the nature of man to be a self-serving egoist who
knows no other motivation than that which concerns the fulfilment or satisfaction of his own immediate lusts and appetites.

Thus Hobbes portrayed a pre-social condition of human
existence which he called a 'state of nature', in which life is a
kind of continual war or struggle between each man and his
neighbour – each solely concerned for himself and his own
advantage. If there is anything at all to be said on behalf of the
state of nature as Hobbes depicts it, it is that in this condition a
certain kind of rugged independence or liberty is enjoyed by
each individual; each agent is totally free to act in the uninhibited pursuit of whatever he happens to want or desire. In
this state of affairs, the physically strong man in particular can
take from others who are weaker whatever he wants and can
overpower or kill them if they resist. But such is the level of
insecurity under these conditions that even the physically
strong man is vulnerable to the hostility of others; he has to
sleep, he may fall ill, a single weaker foe might ensnare him
through superior cunning or the many enemies he makes
through his depredations might band together to overpower
him jointly. So whilst human life in the pre-social state of nature
envisaged by Hobbes is characterised by a certain degree of
freedom it is also a deplorably insecure condition; in Hobbes'
own words 'the life of man [is] solitary, poor, nasty, brutish and
short'.[2]

According to Hobbes man is redeemed from this generally
uncongenial condition only by entering into a form of contract
with other men whereby they all agree to renounce their natural
liberties to prey on their neighbours and place themselves under
certain obligations to respect the lives and property of other
people. Like other social and political theorists of the time,
Hobbes referred to the agreement into which men enter in order
to become social beings as a 'Social Contract'. On this view,

.hen, society and morality are institutions constructed on a system of external obligations which men acknowledge towards others out of an enlightened self-interest which teaches them the benefits that they may expect from the respect in which those same obligations are held by others.

In short, Hobbes subscribes to a contractual view of the nature and origins of both civil society and morality which grounds social and moral rules in considerations of reciprocal advantage. Obviously, of course, the obligations and constraints which the social contract imposes on men are seriously restrictive of the individual freedom they enjoy in a state of nature, but such restrictions may be regarded as adequately compensated for in terms of the relative security which permits the achievement of greater individual satisfaction and fulfilment through the realisation of the longer term plans and goals that men are able to pursue when these are not so prone to violent interruption by others.

Nevertheless, the system of obligations which underpins Hobbes' social contract is not the result of any kind of 'gentleman's agreement' and it is not reasonable to expect that any such agreement would be willingly honoured by untutored human nature. Thus the co-operation of men in the social contract can be efficiently secured only by something like coercion; the rules and laws which are designed to constrain unruly human nature require to be honoured in the breach by effective penalties and sanctions so that any who try to exploit the protection afforded them against others by the social contract whilst still continuing to violate the rights of others may be punished as criminals and outlaws.

But since men are in general touched with the criminal tendencies of the natural human state, it is clear that some coercive external authority or power will in every case be necessary to ensure that the clauses of the social contract are treated with due reverence. Hobbes was inclined to grant absolute powers of sovereignty to any given civil and political administration and he emphatically cautions against any undue relaxation of control by any given government, however appointed, with respect to the social order over which it has to preside. For Hobbes the worst tyranny was to be preferred to social anarchy, for whereas tyranny implies only sporadic or localised expressions of injustice or oppression, anarchy means the total collapse of a society into that pre-social state of nature characterised by the war of all against all.

Basically, then, the reconciliation of human nature as Hobbes sees it to the conditions and values of civilised society presents a problem which is expressed in the dilemma that men can have the kind of civil society that requires submission to government and laws or they can have the freedom of the state of nature but they cannot reasonably have both of these things. It is idle to talk of genuine liberty or freedom in the context of civilised human society because such a state effectively means the coercion of individuals in certain basic ways – the forced submission of them to rules and laws which are designed precisely to restrict their freedom to behave as they please. If human beings want real freedom they must return to the state of nature together with the nightmare of insecurity which it implies; otherwise they may continue to enjoy the safety and security of civil society and give up bleating about freedom.

Now Rousseau questions not merely the conclusion of this argument but also the premises which lead to it – though he does so in a rather piecemeal way at different stages and in different parts of his work.[3] In the early stages of his work Rousseau questions the Hobbesian view of human nature and the origins of social life at the level of sociological or anthropological analysis in a certain spirit of nostalgia for pre-civilised life whereby his name has come to be associated with a kind of 'back to nature' philosophy. At any rate, Rousseau does not appear to have believed at this or any subsequent stage of his work that aggressive self-interest is the distinguishing feature or characteristic of pre-civilised man. In fact, though there are limits to the comparison, Rousseau like Aristotle does not appear to have been generally sympathetic to the idea of a pre-social human state and he seems to have held that it is part of man's nature to require a state of mutually dependent and co-operative relations with other human beings.

Against Hobbes, then, it can be argued that the pre-civilised state of human existence is still to be characterised in terms of social co-operation and that even in the state of nature the asocial or anti-social human being is a kind of monster. And in fact it seems to be characteristic of primitive nomadic hunter-gatherer cultures to confront the problems of survival as closely-knit co-operative social units. In such primitive social units, often no more than extended families, there is no very strong sense of either individual personal identity or private interest. The tribesman returning from a successful hunt will readily share his kill with the rest of the group including those and the relatives of those who have been less successful; all enterprises are approached communally and the products and benefits of those enterprises are held in common. Contrary to the view of Hobbes, then, it can be argued that individual selfishness and aggression is almost unknown at stages of human evolution preceding that of civil society (or at least this can be argued on the basis of certain carefully chosen examples – the Caribbean Arawaks rather than the Caribs for example).

But, of course, selfishness is by no means unknown at subsequent stages of human development. Rousseau's major work on political and social philosophy – *The Social Contract* – opens with the famous words: 'Man was born free but he is everywhere in chains.'[4] The most conspicuous feature of the so-called enlightened civilized world of the eighteenth century for Rousseau was the widespread injustice and selfish exploitation of men by other men which it was possible to observe throughout society. Rousseau was acutely aware, then, of the lengths to which 'civilised men' would go to gain as much privilege, wealth and power as possible for themselves at the expense of others, largely indifferent to the deprivation, poverty and suffering of those they cheerfully exploit. So how could this state of affairs have evolved from that in which primitive man readily assisted his fellows and selflessly shielded their families against suffering and want? Whereas for Hobbes the origins of civil society are marked by the social contract and the imposition of restrictions and constraints and some sense of justice on man's natural selfishness and egotism, for Rousseau, at least in the early stages of his thought, the entry into civil society is marked rather by the emergence of the self-centred and possessive individual.

The watershed of human social evolution for Rousseau is marked by the shift in the economic circumstances of human life which occurs when the essentially nomadic hunter-gatherer cultures develop a settled way of life through the discovery of agriculture and commerce. Along with the larger social units which now have become possible through the growth of towns and cities there emerges a very much more complicated and sophisticated form of life based on an inevitable division of labour. Whereas the primitive nomad built his own temporary shelter, made his own clothes and utensils, raised his own few crops and fought together with other tribesmen his own wars, these functions now become in the more advanced societies the skilled occupations of particular specialists – builders, tailors, farmers, soldiers and so on. People now divide into classes, defined, as Marx is later to say, in terms of their particular relation to the means of production or, at least, to some sort of public service; as farmers, weavers, tinkers and tailors they exchange their skills for other services or just sell them for money.

In turn, however, such commercial transactions enable the personal accumulation of great private wealth and property through the economic exploitation of those whose bargaining powers are limited by those whose skills or services are in short supply and great demand. Thus the division of labour is responsible for the emergence of unfair competition which leads first to the unjust accumulation of private property as a result of widespread exploitation of one class by another and from thence to an exaggerated sense of personal worth on the part of those who exploit successfully and gain economic ascendancy. According to Rousseau the very idea of personal possession or individual ownership is one of the most dubious inheritances of the transition to so-called civilised life. In his *Discourse on Inequality*, Rousseau observed:

> The first man who, after fencing off a piece of land, took it upon himself to say 'This belongs to me' and found people simple-minded enough to believe him, was the true founder of civil society.[5]

(It is a recurring theme of those modern Westerns in which the Red Indian has had a rather better press than formerly, that the tribesmen of the great plains and elsewhere could not grasp the white man's concept of land ownership.)

Thus for Rousseau many of the widespread injustices and inhumanities readily discernible in the conduct of so-called civilised human beings were to be explained precisely in terms of the rise of civilisation itself. In his early work at least, then, Rousseau is inclined to reverse Hobbes' judgement about the relationship between untutored human state and civilised social life; whereas Hobbes regarded the natural human state as one of aggressive self-interest to be improved only through the imposition of the rules and regulations of civilised life, Rousseau was more inclined to regard human nature as basically well-meaning and benevolent but liable to perversion or corruption in the course of its transition to the civil state. (And this difference is crucial, as we shall later show, to understanding properly the familiar distinction of educational theory between traditionalism and progressivism).

But if human nature is liable to be corrupted in the course of its entry into a civilised way of life how, according to Rousseau, is this circumstance to be remedied, if at all? Clearly it does not seem at all realistic to try to reverse the process of social evolution by which men have made the transition from primitive hunter-gatherer cultures with their uncertain conditions of existence to the more secure and comfortable circumstances of modern urban life; certainly the mature Rousseau finds the idea of such a return to the condition of the primitive 'noble' savage neither possible nor congenial. On the other hand, however, there can be little real hope of justice or freedom for human beings in so-called civilised society given the prevalence of those generally self-interested and exploitative attitudes among men that Rousseau was able to observe around him.

Despite his reputation in some quarters as a philosophical forerunner of modern totalitarianism, Rousseau would not have seen the solution to these moral ills of civilisation in terms of some kind of state-imposed redistribution of wealth which could issue in only further injustices. The proper solution to the problem for Rousseau, then, lies not in a return to the pre-civil state of the noble savage but in a certain kind of human moral evolution. If true justice is ever to be realised in human affairs then men must become good or virtuous in a sense quite other than that in which they have been regarded as virtuous hitherto – the sense in which to be virtuous is to be both rational and responsible. In general for Rousseau the noble savage is by nature good, but he does not exhibit genuine moral virtue because his goodness is not the expression or outcome of a deliberate choice between good and evil; the goodness of the untutored savage is like that of a small child who behaves well because she wishes to please – we may praise such goodness but we should not regard it as expressive of genuine moral responsibility. Once more in contrast to Hobbes, then, Rousseau does not attribute freedom in any real sense to natural pre-civilised man, since however unconstrained his conduct may be it does not represent genuine moral choice.

On the other hand, the wickedness and injustice of most men in civil society can hardly be regarded as expressive of a definite choice in favour of evil either since very many post-natural men are blinded by a kind of false sentiment or passion of self-esteem which Rousseau calls *amour propre*. To be sure, civilised men have a degree or level of self-consciousness which the noble savage has not, but it is also a false consciousness filled with vanity and self-importance which blinds men to any larger or higher interests beyond self-gratification and aggrandisement. In fact Rousseau's analysis of the problem of the self-centred possessive individual is not at all unlike that of Socrates and Plato – he is a slave to the extent that he regards himself as the master of or superior to others.[6] The more that he is driven or motivated by delusions of superiority over other men, then, the less an individual is able to take a detached and objective view of the appropriate direction of his own life and, if he is a member of a ruling elite or aristocracy, of the best interests of those he governs. So for Rousseau, vice and injustice turn out to be much as they are for Socrates and Plato, a matter of a kind of ignorance or false consciousness in the grip of which men mistakenly believe they are pursuing their own best interests when they seek the immediate satisfaction of their own personal desires, inclinations and passions.

But what does lie in men's best interests and how can they discover what it is? Rousseau is ready with a direct answer to this question in his major work *The Social Contract* in which he observes: 'There is undoubtedly a universal justice which springs from reason alone. . . .'[7] Not unlike Socrates and Plato, Rousseau holds that the best interests of men both individually and socially are expressed in a concept of universal justice which it is possible to discover by the proper exercise of human reason; by means of rational deliberation we may free ourselves from the condition of false consciousness whereby our vision of the true good for man is clouded by vanity, pride and self-love. Unlike Socrates and Plato, however, Rousseau does not regard virtue as the suppression of passion by reason, since the natural co-operation and altruism of the noble savage represent natural sentiments and inclinations which are entirely in harmony with moral virtue – though, of course, these sentiments are not genuine moral virtues for Rousseau since they are not freely chosen. It is not sufficient in order to possess true virtue, then, merely that the individual should come to have knowledge of what is good and undergo conversion from his condition of passion-clouded ignorance, he must also come to choose what is good by the free exercise of his will.

Thus, as Rousseau observes in his *Discourse on Political Economy* – 'every man is virtuous when his particular will is in all things conformable to the general will' – where, by the 'general will', he means essentially the law of universal justice discernible by the free use of unclouded reason.[8] For Rousseau, virtuous conduct is that which is chosen by an individual whose will is informed by impartial and objective reason. Thus there can be no genuine justice on a general social and political scale until men have acquired powers of individual self-determination through the control of their subjective states of personal desire and passion in accordance with the deliverances of disinterested rational deliberation. The answer to problems of large-scale social injustice and exploitation can only lie, according to Rousseau, in something like the widespread re-education of individuals in genuine moral virtue which reflects an impartial concern for all in the light of considerations of general justice and benevolence.

It can now be seen that the educational philosophy of Rousseau's *Emile* is not merely a sideshow to his political and social theories but part and parcel of them, for it is precisely in his *Emile* that Rousseau is concerned to sketch the conditions for the development of individual rational self-determination or autonomy through which the emergence of those moral qualities expressive of a true concern for the promotion of justice in human social affairs is most surely guaranteed. Two principal educational strategies are to be adopted in turn. First, since the conditions of false consciousness and *amour propre* which distort men's perceptions of themselves and others are socially acquired through various kinds of indoctrination or conditioning – to be brought up as the child of aristocratic parents, for example, is to inherit not only wealth and property but also certain attitudes of contempt for the lower orders and, likewise, early material poverty might lead to the formation of certain negative attitudes of envy and resentment – it is important that children should be shielded from such potential sources of moral corruption from an early age. This is what Rousseau means by a 'negative' education.

But second, Rousseau is also concerned to plot the course of that proper rational moral development (and *Emile* contains a theory of child development which predates that of Piaget and his followers by a couple of centuries) which will eventually issue in the formation of capacities on the part of a young person to reason clearly and objectively – quite without personal bias or prejudice – on questions of general social and moral significance. Thus Rousseau's idea of virtue seems to be essentially that of unbiased rational self-determination and in his *Emile* he is concerned to trace the development of the totally un-prejudiced, reasonable and free agent.

It is important to grasp the immediate bearing that all of this has on the Hobbesian problem of political philosophy which says that men cannot be both governed and free. Basically Rousseau's view is that Hobbes' dilemma rests on a mistake about the nature of genuine freedom; true human freedom consists not in a mere lack of constraint and that is why neither the predatory savages of Hobbes state of nature nor the noble savages of his own pre-civilised state can be considered properly free. Genuine freedom in human affairs is exhibited only in that self-determined conduct which occurs when, through the exercise of impartial and disinterested reason, men have liberated themselves from bondage to the passions and pre-judices which inform the false consciousness of *amour propre*. Thus true freedom precisely requires the submission of the individual will to certain objective and universally binding *laws* of reason; human agents are free only when their conduct conforms to the rules of universal justice expressed in the moral law. But this being the case, according to Rousseau, it is necessary for a man to be *ruled* in order for him to be free; more precisely, since rational self-determination is the key to moral virtue, a man can be free only on the condition that he rules himself.

But, of course, since no single individual can be confident that justice on a larger social scale will follow from his own particular impartial and disinterested judgements, what general social and political arrangements may be made to ensure the promotion of fair play in society at large? Rousseau's solution to this problem, which we cannot explore in detail here, consists essentially in the defence of a democratic system of government in which the greatest possible degree of political power and sovereignty remains ultimately in the hands of the people; thus, by such a system, all men of good will – presumably educated for democracy in the right Rousseauesque way – will have the opportunity to make their rightful contribution to the rational determination of a just public policy and their own social destiny.

In fact, it is reasonably easy to see how, in the terms of Rousseau's philosophy, moral virtue – construed at the individual level as rational self-determination – and freedom and justice – understood at the social level as enshrined in some form of democratic process – are crucially presupposed to each other. For just as any genuine kind of democracy can hardly exist in the absence of the individual freedom of thought and conscience which is a precondition for Rousseau of individual moral virtue (for without this there could only be the ignorant mob rule feared by Socrates and Plato), so also personal or individual autonomy will hardly be possible in circumstances in which at least the spirit of democracy is not respected. On the one hand it is only in circumstances in which free thought or the free exchange of opinions is at least permitted and at most actively encouraged that we can hope to find the relatively rational and unbiased individuals who represent Rousseau's ideal of moral virtue; but on the other hand it is also clear enough that if the democratic process is to contribute effectively to the general well-being of all members of a given society then it is a requirement that the population should be generally motivated and informed by the reasonable, fair-minded and not wholly self-interested attitudes that Rousseau associated with the autonomous individual.

In short, individual autonomy and social democracy would appear to be presupposed by each other. In that case, however, it would seem that Plato was sailing dangerously close to paradox in the *Republic* when he envisaged a politically closed society in which most people would be required to do only as they were told by a ruling elite whose intellectual development depends precisely on the sort of free exchange of ideas which would in general be discouraged in that society. Looked at from this perspective it is difficult to see how any practical implementation of Plato's ideal might not result in certain intolerable tensions.

Be that as it may, the extent to which Rousseau's ideas concerning moral virtue and the nature of justice are reflected in the much more complex and systematic moral philosophy of Immanuel Kant is hard to exaggerate. For Rousseau, as we have seen, virtue is essentially a matter of rational self-determination resulting from the submission of the individual will to the general will which is understood to express 'a universal justice which springs from reason alone'. Kant's ideas of virtue, duty and the moral law are constructed on very much the same pattern of ethical analysis as Rousseau's, but they are also crucially conjoined to a system of metaphysical (though in some important respects anti-metaphysical) and epistemological thought which represents arguably *the* most difficult and abstruse body of work in the whole of modern western philosophy.

Although the essentials of Kant's ideas on moral philosophy are not ultimately much harder to grasp than those of Rousseau which we have just examined, in his case they are part and parcel and follow as a direct consequence of his views on the nature of reality and the limits of our knowledge of it, as these are set out in his forbidding *Critique of Pure Reason*. Thus at this point it is really necessary to attempt the well nigh impossible task of saying something both brief and useful about Kant's ideas on theoretical (scientific) reason in order to shed some light on his work on practical (moral) reason.

Just as Rousseau's moral and social philosophy requires to be understood as a kind of response to the views of such earlier contract theorists as Hobbes, so Kant's theoretical and practical philosophy needs to be seen as a reaction to the growing influence in his day of empiricist philosophy, especially the empiricism of such British philosophers as Locke, Berkeley and Hume (an Englishman, an Irishman and a Scotsman). It is Hume, however, who seems to have made the most direct and profound impression on Kant. Like other empiricists, Hume held that the only reliable source of human knowledge lay in experience as it is revealed to us by our ordinary human powers or faculties of sensation and perception; Locke, for example, had argued that prior to experience and the awakening of perception the human mind is to be compared only to a blank state (*tabula rasa*) or a piece of paper on which nothing has yet been written – there can be no knowledge or understanding of the world in advance of sensory perception. But as sure as he seems to be that the deliverances of sense perception can be the only reliable source of human knowledge – since like other empiricists he denies innate ideas – Hume is sceptical about almost everything else; his empiricism is radical in a way that no previous empiricism had been.[9]

Effectively, Hume maintained that no determinate sense can be assigned to any term in a given human language to which no item of sensory perceptual experience – in Hume's own terminology an 'impression' – corresponds. In the light of this view he acknowledged only two classes of meaningful utterance – sentences or statements, that is – which can properly be said to express some kind of truth or give some sort of genuine information. The first he calls 'matters of fact'; sentences such as 'the boy stood on the burning deck' have at least the potential for giving us knowledge or information about how things stand in the world, because they contain terms to which appropriately related items of sensory experience will correspond if the sentence is true. The second class of meaningful sentences, however, Hume calls 'relations of ideas'; such sentences as 'a square is an equilateral rectangle' do not give us any information about the world in the way of matters of fact, because they are true by definition rather than confirmed by experience. Hume's relations of ideas are what some philosophers would call 'trivially true' or even 'self-evident', but they have nevertheless a significant role to play in language and thought by way of the explication of unfamiliar terms and the licensing of certain kinds of inferences.

The crucial point which lies behind this rather barren sounding distinction of Hume's is that if a sentence purports to express what cannot be shown to be either a matter of fact or a relation of ideas, it is to be regarded as essentially *meaningless*. Thus, for Hume, most of what previous philosophers had tried to say concerning the nature of God, freedom, immortality, the good and so on, must count as meaningless. So-called 'metaphysical' statements such as 'God is eternal and changeless' and 'the will is free' could not be said to express any determinate sense, according to Hume, basically because they are unverifiable; there is nothing to be discerned in experience – no sensory impression – which answers to the ideas of God and the will.

To be sure, with respect to talk about the freedom of the will, we may as human agents claim to be able to identify some sort of experience of causing things to happen in the world through our actions. Isn't my feeling of causing or being responsible for the letters forming at the end of my pen, an impression of the will in operation? The problem is, replies Hume, that to account for the will in this way as some kind of inner cause of outer events is to explain the obscure in terms of what is even more obscure, since we cannot attach much clear sense to the idea of a *cause* either. What item of experience, what sensory impression, after all, corresponds to the familiar idea of a cause? When all is said and done what do we actually perceive when we claim to observe one event in the world causing another? Nothing, says Hume, except a regular conjunction or association of events.

Thus when the white snooker ball strikes the red and appears to transfer its motion to it we observe nothing more than the movement of one ball followed immediately by that of the other; strictly speaking we observe nothing further which warrants our saying that the one movement *causes* the other (and we do not say this when the arrival of one train in the station is followed immediately by the departure of another). From whence comes, then, the idea of a cause? Hume's answer is that the idea simply expresses or reflects a kind of psychological or behavioural trait whereby human beings are habituated to the contingencies of experience; human nature responds to what regularity it is able to discern in experience with certain attitudes of expectancy. Brute experience conditions the human expectation that, for example, the sun will rise tomorrow. We are in serious error, however, if we mistake the habits of expectation thus acquired for genuine laws of nature predicated on the idea of cause and effect because we have no sure knowledge that the contingencies of experience respect any such laws; the sun might not, for example, rise as expected tomorrow and for no particular reason derived from or related to considerations about causal necessity.

Anyway, it is this fundamental scepticism about our knowledge of reality that Kant is concerned to respond to in his awesome *Critique of Pure Reason*.[10] Well nigh lost to view beneath

75

a barrage of abstruse technical terms and convoluted philosophical arguments are two main points; one essentially
sympathetic to Hume and the other empiricists and the other
quite unsympathetic to him. Kant seems to agree with the
general empiricist position that the limits of human knowledge
– what human beings can achieve demonstrable understanding
of – coincide with the boundaries of human empirical experience; but Kant also wants to say that empiricists of a Humean
temper have a badly distorted idea of the nature of experience.
For Hume seems to have construed our available knowledge of
experience as something like a matter of passive acquaintance
with a flux of discrete sensory impressions – sounds, colours,
textures and so on – from which quite without legitimate
warrant we *infer* ideas of causality and objectivity.
(Hume had even considered the formal concept of an object to
be something that nothing corresponds to in our actual experience – we do not perceive objects but only colours, shapes,
textures and so on).

According to Kant, however, this is simply an incoherent
view of experience, for under the conditions which Hume
describes we could make absolutely no sense of anything at all
and no knowledge of the world whatsoever would be possible.
Kant argues that notions of objectivity and causality, far from
being added to human experience as a kind of afterthought are
actually *presupposed* to anything that might reasonably count as
intelligible human experience. Our knowledge of reality is not to
be construed as the consequence of a kind of haphazard
conditioning of human responses by an essentially protean
experience, it is the accommodation of an inherently intelligible
and objective world to certain human powers of rational and
intellectual organisation.

For empirical experience to be at all intelligible, then, it must
be capable of exhibiting precisely those features of objectivity
and causal regularity in terms of which it is normally understood by human reason; but if it does exhibit these features then
those very same rational categories of objectivity and causality
by which human reason construes experience may be reasonably expected to answer to something actually existing in a
reality beyond our mere experience of it – a world of objects and
events ordered in terms of cause and effect. Thus for Kant
objectivity and causality are not unlicensed inferences from

experience, they are among the basic logical preconditions of the possibility of any sort of intelligible experience at all.

One effect of Kant's prodigious work on theoretical under-standing is to vindicate up to a point the views of earlier rationalist philosophers concerning the relationship between human reason and human knowledge; not, to be sure, the view that pure reason provides the exclusive source of knowledge, but certainly the reasonable insight that human rationality has an important role to play in relation to the structure of under-standing and the discovery of truth. But Kant is also to a very large extent on the side of Hume and the empiricists in arguing that the limits of empirical experience are the limits of demon-strable knowledge in human terms. What Kant calls the 'phenomenal' world – the world of empirically discriminable objects enmeshed in relationships of cause and effect – is the only world of which we can claim genuine knowledge as human observers and agents. But this would appear to leave Kant in much the same position as Hume regarding judgements per-taining to God, freedom, immortality and so forth. Statements concerning the nature of God cannot be empirically verified, assertions about freedom seem to be idle in a world in which all physical events are apparently determined by causal laws, and observations concerning life after death are again clearly unsusceptible of proof this side of the grave.

Of particular interest in the present context, however, Kant is left with a large and conspicuous problem about the nature and logical status of moral judgements – a problem which he set out to solve in his *Groundwork of the Metaphysic of Morals* and his second great critique, *The Critique of Practical Reason*.[11] Once again it is quite clear that Kant's moral philosophical thought was very much stimulated by that of empiricist influenced contemporary moral theorists and in this connection Hume's own views on the nature of morality assume importance once more.

Entirely consistent with his general epistemological views concerning the origins of our knowledge and understanding in sensory experience, and with his effective denial that human theoretical reason plays any active organising role with respect to that experience, Hume is also deeply sceptical about the alleged causal role of human reason in relation to agency; in short, he denies that reason as he understands it has any power whatsoever to move men to action, observing that 'reason is and ought only to be the slave of the passions'.[12] Consequently, for Hume, anything that we are inclined to construe as moral conduct can issue only from those desires that men generally have in society for the fellowship, well-being and approval of others around them; morality is thus a matter of sentiment more than reason. In the terms of Hume's thoroughgoing and uncompromising empiricist analysis, then, the impetus behind human moral life and conduct is located in the idea of a 'moral sense' which is held to be expressed or exhibited in certain 'calm passions' or inclinations to kindness or benevolence.

All of this, of course, is totally unacceptable to Kant who anyway takes quite a different view of the role of reason in human affairs; for him, unless we suppose some degree of agency or some active organising principle to be inherent in human reason, it is well nigh impossible to see how there might be any such thing as intelligible or coherent human experience at all. For Kant, no reasonable concept of morality may be constructed upon or derived from the deliverances of any empirically given 'moral sense' mainly because the world of empirically given experience, both 'inner' (mental) and 'outer' (physical), is a world of phenomenal events governed by inexorable laws of cause and effect. But neither causes nor effects, natural or human, can be intelligibly praised or blamed; we do not praise the lightning when it misses the man and strikes the tree instead, and likewise we cannot reasonably praise a man for giving generously to a flag-seller because he happened to get out of the right side of the bed that morning (yesterday he got out the wrong side and ignored her completely).

We may properly regard the kind actions which follow from warm or hearty feelings as conducive to human good, then, and we might reasonably wish that such sentiments were more widely and generously distributed among men, but we cannot, according to Kant, regard such actions as especially expressive of moral motives. Thus moods or feelings of kindness or benevolence towards others are far too vague and inconstant to form the basis of morality and in any case, even when humanly positive actions do follow from a settled disposition towards kindness, it is merely a man's good fortune that he has such a disposition – it is hardly something for which he should be commended or held responsible.

In fact, Kant's view is that we have within us an idea of moral law and correct moral conduct which, whilst it is expressed in the recognition that it is right to be just or benevolent, is nevertheless not just based on a mere just or benevolent sentiment. Indeed, this idea of justice and benevolence tells us quite clearly that we *should* or *ought* to behave fairly or kindly even, or perhaps most of all, when we are temperamentally disposed to be unkind or unfair. For Kant, true morality can consist only in a *dutiful* obedience to that concept of the moral law or of right and wrong which is independent of any kind of empirical knowledge we might have, inner or outer, of the phenomenal world; moreover, we cannot have derived our knowledge of the moral law or our sense of moral duty from any experience of the phenomenal world as it is given to us by inner or outer sensory perception. But in that case, from whence comes this idea of the moral law or this understanding of right and wrong if not from that empirical experience which the empiricists had insisted is the only legitimate source of human knowledge?

As we have seen, Kant had already argued in his work on theoretical reason that the sensory impressions or 'intuitions' which constitute the raw data or bare deliverances of empirical perception are in themselves 'blind' or meaningless so that in order to become meaningful they require to be intelligibly arranged or ordered by some active source or principle of judgement and interpretation which stands, in some sense, outside the experiences it organises; he referred to this significance-conferring agency as the transcendental or 'noumenal' self. This self cannot be known either in or through experience because it is not itself a part of experience; all the same, it must be logically presupposed to any idea of experience construed as an intelligible and ordered perspective on the world. In his work on reason generally Kant leans heavily on this idea of a transcendental self which contributes actively to the organisation of experience via the imposition on it of the basic categories of theoretical understanding, but in the context of his philosophy of practical reason he construes the noumenal self as essentially a legislator or law-giver with respect to human moral life.

Kant's objection to the moral sense view is that agents cannot properly be held responsible – praised or blamed – for actions which follow as the causal effects of certain natural sentiments and dispositions; we can attribute moral value or responsibility only to conduct which is the expression or product of a genuine choice in favour of this course of action rather than that. But in that case genuine freedom must be presupposed to action in accordance with the moral law. This freedom cannot be attributed to any natural human sentiments or dispositions but it can be attributed, according to Kant, to the noumenal self which lies beyond any empirical knowledge we may have of our inner phenomenal nature.

Of course, precisely because it lies beyond the realm of what is empirically ascertainable, neither this self nor any freedom of which it might be supposed to be the source can be proved or demonstrated to exist in theoretical terms (for to explain freedom in theoretical terms would be to put it under certain causal laws, but then it would not *be* freedom) but freedom as what Kant calls an 'idea of reason' must be seriously presupposed to any coherent concept of moral action. What, then, are the main features of the moral law which the non-empirical self promulgates by virtue of this freedom? In general Kant argues that judgements which express the moral law must be both *pure* and *a priori*. By describing expressions of the moral law as pure, Kant means that they should be quite innocent of substantive empirical content; the moral law is not to be regarded as any kind of abstraction or generalisation from sensible experience. Even in a world wherein all men are disposed to act wickedly and in which they had never acted well, it would still be the case under the moral law that they *ought* to act rightly; but obviously no idea of their actual moral obligations could be formed from observations of their existing conduct.

In this connection Kant draws an important logical distinction between different kinds of 'ought' statements or imperatives in order to mark off those in which the moral law is exhibited from those in which it is not. The latter sort of imperative he refers to as 'hypothetical' and they are of two main kinds; first, rules of skill, and second, counsels of prudence. Rules of skill are concerned with taking necessary means to the achievement of certain technical ends (for example, installing radiators to provide central heating) and counsels of prudence are concerned with the adoption of practical means to the achievement of personal well-being or happiness (for example, installing central heating to make the house more comfortable to live in). According to Kant, the main logical feature showed by both these types of imperative is that they are of the 'If A then B' form; that is, the antecedent clause of the statement (A) expresses some desire or need of the agent, the consequent (B) states some course of action that it is open for the agent to take and the satisfaction of the need or desire is conditional on the performance of the action.

For Kant, however, moral imperatives are not of this hypothetical 'If A then B' form. He refers to expressions of the moral law as 'categorical imperatives' because they are not to be regarded as contingent upon particular human desires, needs or wishes of any kind whatsoever. Indeed, the moral law is required not on behalf of any such wants and desires which we might happen to have as human agents living in a world of change and decay, but precisely despite such wants and desires many of which often run counter to the demands of morality.

On the other hand, however, it is important to emphasise here that Kant is not inclined to dismiss natural human desires and dispositions as of little moral significance because he regards them in the manner of Plato as generally bad or harmful; on the contrary, like Hume, he appears to regard many human sentiments and inclinations to kindness, charity, fairmindedness and so on as perfectly conducive to human well-being. Kant's point is rather that as mere natural feelings, passions and inclinations such states cannot be considered to be expressions of the moral law and so in terms of net moral value they are simply beside the point. In this respect, however, Kant also differs from Aristotle for whom explicit reference to feelings and passions must enter into any account of the nature of moral virtue; indeed, for Aristotle, some states of character are to be regarded as deviating from the path of virtue precisely because they are defective with respect to the realm of what Kant would call inclination.

The other important logical characteristic which Kant identifies in relation to the moral law is expressed in the idea that moral imperatives exercise absolute or universal and not merely particular or contingent authority. Thus he held that the categorical imperative – unlike the hypothetical – commands absolutely and it commands all men (or all rational beings) at all times and in all places, irrespective of local customs and circumstances.

Kant, then, regards the categorical imperative as akin to a necessary proposition – one that a rational agent cannot reasonably deny without becoming implicated in something like self-contradiction. Precisely, the general form of the moral law for Kant is expressed in the rule: 'Act only on that maxim through which you can at the same time will that it should become a universal law.'[13]

Undoubtedly this formal principle of the will owes a good deal to Rousseau's idea of the general will as universal justice. In *The Social Contract* and elsewhere Rousseau had argued that the sort of decisions about public policy which should be aimed at by the properly self-determined citizens of a true democracy would not simply be those which expressed the wants or desires or the majority over the minority – such decisions would express only what Rousseau calls the *will of all* – rather they should be decisions which follow from a disinterested and impartial attempt on the part of all participants in the democratic process to form a clear view of the *common* good or interest. Rousseau, then, requires the rational agent to step outside of himself as a centre of empirically conditioned egocentric desires and interests in order that he might acquire some vision of what is just and good regardless of partisan perspectives; he is arguing for a conception of the rational will as a disinterested source of moral and political action.

Clearly this is very close to what Kant is after in the *Groundwork* and the second *Critique*, but he also wishes to go even further than Rousseau, for whom the decisions expressing the general will are, after all, still localised to the interests of a given social group. Kant, however, wants his moral law to apply not only to the citizens of a particular democratic community, but to all members of what he calls 'the kingdom of ends' – the entire community of past, present and future rational agents.[14] Moreover, it is precisely because Kant views the moral law in this way and regards each rational agent, at least in principle, as an autonomous executor of the moral law, that he places the absolutely unconditioned value on individual human beings which is expressed in the following principle: 'So act that you treat humanity in your own person and in the person of everyone else always at the same time as an end and not merely as a means.'[15] To regard humanity in general and not just the members of your own social group or circle as a community of potential moral legislators, then, is in all circumstances to preclude the exploitation or manipulation of others for our own selfish ends and to place the highest possible value on the moral principle of respect for persons.

Thus, for Kant, if moral imperatives are to be absolutely binding they must be shown to exhibit something like the necessity and universality characteristic of logical and mathematical statements; they must be such as to give any rational agent a compelling reason for acting in accordance with them and to make any breach of such principles appear rationally self-defeating or unthinkable. This is quite a tall order, of course, but Kant does take himself to have discovered, in the already mentioned idea of universalisation, the rational procedure whereby such imperatives can be generated.

Although the soundness of Kant's general strategy of universalisation has been much criticised and many of his illustrations have been disputed, perhaps his strongest candidate for an absolutely universal moral prescription whose denial would involve an agent in something approaching a contradiction is the general requirement that human beings should always keep their promises. Thus, so Kant asks us to believe, since a rational agent cannot consistently wish that promises should not in all circumstances be kept or that they should in any circumstances be treated casually – for so to wish is to undermine the moral institution of promise keeping upon which any agent relies for his own promises to be kept – it is not rational for any agent to wish for anything other than that promises should universally be kept. In short, then, with respect to a large number of requirements of conventional morality, Kant believes that any attempt to deny them is in some crucial way opposed to reason; such denials would inevitably lead an agent into a hopelessly self-contradictory position *vis-à-vis* rational exercise of the moral will.

And Kant's final view is, of course, that the only thing in the world that can be generally and unreservedly called good is the *good will*; that will which is identified in terms of an impartial and disinterested reason which always puts *duty* to the moral law before personal desire and inclination. The truly good man, then, is he who acts in obedience to a moral law which is neither God-given nor made by man himself, but which is nevertheless discernible by human reason through the universalisation of certain imperatives of moral conduct. Reason enjoins the agent to the performance of that conduct sanctioned by the moral law though, of course, the agent is otherwise quite free (in the sense of unconstrained) whether to obey the law or follow his personal inclinations.

As in the case of Rousseau, then, the key notion in Kant for understanding virtue and moral life is that of self-determination or rational autonomy; the idea of a moral agent is that of an autonomous moral legislator who acts in disinterested obedience to the voice of reason rather than personal inclination and in that way realises his true freedom. Next, in the context of a short survey of some more recent developments in moral philosophy, we must try to take stock by considering some of the merits and defects of the various avenues of enquiry to which we have so far been introduced.

4

MODERN MORAL PHILOSOPHY: TWO CONCEPTS OF MORALITY

After three substantial chapters on the moral theories of great philosophers of the past I shall conclude the first section of this work with just one chapter on the moral philosophy of recent times. This is not at all because I believe that nothing of any importance has occurred in moral philosophy since the time of Kant – clearly very much has; it is rather because I am not all concerned in this work to offer an historical overview of developments in moral philosophy, but only to identify some coherent perspective on the nature of moral virtue and its educational implications.

From this viewpoint I believe that the main philosophical options are evident in the work of the great philosophers we have already considered; certainly, none of the moral philosophies of the modern period may be understood properly without a reasonable grasp of the ideas of Plato, Aristotle and Kant. So though it is necessary to give some consideration to some of the more recent developments of moral philosophical thought, this more recent work should not for a moment be construed as having displaced or rendered obsolete that of the great philosophical giants of yesteryear, but only as having contributed, albeit significantly, to the clarification of certain perspectives first explored by such figures as Plato, Aristotle and Kant.

In fact, because excellent surveys of modern moral philosophy are readily available elsewhere, I shall entertain but one limited purpose in this chapter; I shall merely try to make the point that all recent developments in moral philosophy *are* continuous with the three classical perspectives on the nature of virtue and morality which we have already considered and that the major debate of modern times has occurred mainly between the philosophical heirs of Kant and Aristotle. This is not at all, of course, to dismiss Socrates and Plato as of little or no significance to modern moral philosophical thought – on the contrary their powerful insights have in many and various ways continued to exert a profound influence on all manner of serious reflection about the nature of moral life. Platonic elements are to be readily enough found in the thinking of all important modern contributors to moral philosophy and when all is said and done we could hardly have had either Aristotle or Kant without Plato.

But for all that serious moral philosophers of all persuasions would give up the works of Plato only as a very last resort, it does not seem to be straightforwardly possible to forge Plato's numerous and varied insights into a single systematic approach to understanding moral life or a unified perspective on the nature of moral virtue, and in this respect some of his crucial ideas seem to be attended by serious conceptual difficulties. The only 'school' of moral philosophy of recent times which strikes me as having been focused on themes of a markedly Platonic character is that which flourished early in the present century under the name of 'intuitionism', and in fact intuitionism proved very vulnerable to precisely the kind of criticisms brought by Aristotle and others against the philosophy of Plato. It is difficult to see in the case of both Plato and the intuitionists, for example, what role their not dissimilar 'ideas' of the good might have in the way of practical application to actual human affairs and it is also rather unclear by what process of rational deliberation or reflection these ideas are supposed to be arrived at.

It seems that for all their enormous power to inspire, then, the two great founding fathers of moral philosophy, Socrates and Plato, have not left us with any unambiguous strategy or route to follow in our pursuit of a developed account or theory of the mechanics of moral life and moral reasoning. The cave allegory in Plato's *Republic* is perhaps the most profound of all insights into the nature of wisdom and understanding in general and moral wisdom in particular, but it does not provide much of a clear idea of the way in which such wisdom might be acquired; it is arguable, moreover, that what Plato has to say about this elsewhere in the dialogues is rather less than promising. Still, we have by no means done with Plato in this work and in due course we shall return to reaffirm the significance of certain Platonic insights.

It seems to me, however, that if we are to go to ethics or moral philosophy with a view to understanding how moral education is possible in practice, then there are only two really promising options, one which basically takes its cue from Kant and the other which stands fairly squarely in the tradition of Aristotle; the really significant debates in recent moral philosophy with important bearings on the nature and conduct of moral education have occurred between philosophers and educationalists standing roughly in traditions which it is not misleading to call Kantian and Aristotelian. For the present it may also be useful to oversimplify somewhat by characterising the main difference between these two traditions in terms of a basic conflict between the advocates of an ethics of *obligation* and those who subscribe to an ethics of *virtue*.

As we have already seen, Aristotle attempts to construct a theory of moral life on the idea of virtue interpreted in terms of certain natural *dispositions* towards human well-being as opposed to harm; Kant, on the other hand, effectively denies that the natural dispositions of men have much significance for human moral life and he emphasises instead the importance of duty and obligation as these are standardly expressed in certain *rules* of conduct discerned by pure practical reason in accordance with the dictates of a universal moral law. It would be a distortion, of course, in relation to either Kant or Aristotle or any other important moral theorist, to suggest that morality is for them exclusively *either* a matter of rules *or* of dispositions; as we have seen, there is in Aristotle, for example, a reasonably well-developed account of moral rationality which contains an important place for the observance of rules and in Kant there is at least one moral disposition of supreme importance – the *good will*.

It is much more a matter of emphasis; whereas for Aristotle moral rules expressed in practical deliberation make sense only as a means to the promotion of moral virtues which are at heart dispositions, for Kant human dispositions only make any kind of moral sense when expressed in terms of duties and obligations of a rule-governed nature – the will is good only to the extent that it is informed by the moral law. Much the same considerations also apply to other moral theorists of any importance. In order to respect the actual course of recent historical developments in this chapter I shall begin by considering a modern excursion into an ethics of obligation and then proceed to air some of the general objections to such an approach by recent advocates of the ethics of virtue. I shall not, of course, attempt to conceal my own sympathies in the process.

Speaking roughly again, post-Kantian attempts to develop some kind of ethics of obligation have assumed two main forms. The first inclines to account for the idea of duty or obligation in terms of some ideal of individual rational moral autonomy – to show how the recognition of duties and obligations is important for the individual from the point of view of acting rationally, consistently and with some degree of personal integrity in his relationships with others. The second attempts to explain concepts of duty and obligation more in terms of their social and political utility (though many of such attempts have been avowedly non-utilitarian) – to derive ideas of moral duty and obligation from the consideration that the social-contractual nature of our relationships with others is such as to require us from a moral point of view to return to them precisely those social benefits (freedom, equality, justice, protection under the law and so on) which we are in receipt of ourselves.

As I have not the space to consider both the individual autonomy and social-contractual forms of the ethics of obligation I shall discuss only one version of the first. Among my reasons for this are that the more influential of modern social-contractual theories are primarily social and political and only secondarily moral theories and that in the chapter on Durkheim in the next section of this work I shall be concentrating on some of the special intractable difficulties about the common idea that moral laws and obligations have their basic origins in social conventions or contracts. An added reason for concentrating critically on the individual autonomy version of the ethics of obligation in the form of the doctrine known as *prescriptivism*, however, is that it also enables us to see more plainly some of the defects of subjectivism as an approach to understanding the nature of moral judgement and experience.

To a considerable extent, the emergence of prescriptivism as an account of the nature of moral judgement and principle duplicates the story of Kant's reaction to the moral philosophy of the empiricist 'moral sense' school as exemplified by Hume.

Prescriptivism was itself a response to *emotivism* – that peculiar subjectivist moral side-show to the influential philosophical movement of the early part of this century known as 'logical positivism' – and to the view of meaning inherent in positivist philosophy known as *verificationism*. In fact, the logical positivists stood very firmly in the classical tradition of British empiricism as represented by David Hume and arguably the movement was little more than a modern dress version of the views of Hume – specifically a Humean sceptical empiricism to which modern philosophical techniques of logical analysis developed by such philosophers as Frege, Russell and Carnap had been added for good measure.

Just like Hume, then, the positivists made the principal test of the meaningfulness of any given expression or statement of natural language whether or not it could be held to correspond to some element or fragment of empirical experience or, failing that, whether it could supply some useful or illuminating elucidation.[1] In short, meaningful statements of natural language were held to be of two kinds; those reporting contingent facts susceptible of verification by appeal to experience, for example, 'water expands when frozen'; and those which are useful for the explication of terms, for example, 'presditigitation is sleight-of-hand'. Again like Hume, however, the logical positivists were reluctant to attribute determinate sense to other categories of statement; hence such religious and moral judgements as 'God gave his only begotten son' and 'thou shalt not commit adultery' being not obviously either reports on empirical experience or kinds of definition, could not easily be credited with genuine significance.

But also like Hume, the positivists wanted to be able to make some sense of the *point* of moral utterance; to be able to say at least something about what people were attempting to do in using forms of words employing such expressions as 'right', 'duty', 'wicked', 'evil' and so on. Hume had himself, of course, explained conduct generally conducive to human individual and social well-being as expressive of certain calm passions or sentiments; he held that it was a natural part of the human constitution to be disposed to acts of kindness and benevolence through feelings of fellowship or other attachment towards others. To call an action 'good', then, was basically to say that it was motivated or caused by a benevolent feeling and to call some other action 'bad' was to construe it as expressive rather of some negative feeling or emotion. At all events, the idea of moral action was definitely associated by Hume with the realm of human emotion more than reason.

Likewise the logical positivists (especially A. J. Ayer and C. L. Stevenson, though most positivists endorsed some version of the emotivist story) also associated moral judgement with an emotional response, but whereas for Hume moral judgements such as 'he behaved kindly' were held to *report* the objective presence or causal operation of feelings and emotions, in the case of the emotivists moral judgements were believed to *express* the subjective feelings of those uttering them. Thus, for someone to say 'that was a decent thing to do' or 'he behaved like a cad' would be to express his preference for or his aversion to a certain kind of action or conduct. For the positivists the term 'good' was to be construed in a so-called moral context as a term of approval; it referred to no objective quality of any action to which it might be applied but merely served to express a given agent's subjective response or attitude to that action. Thus 'x is good' was held to be tantamount to 'I approve of x' and 'x is bad' to 'I don't like x'.

Since the story of emotivism has been told and retold in greater detail elsewhere, we may be reasonably brief with it here. It should suffice to say that even if it were not the consequence of a general theory of meaning which is now widely held to be mistaken, it would still be objectionable as a view of moral judgement; moreover, in addition to suffering from much the same defects that were exposed in the philosophy of moral sense by Kant, it exhibits its own peculiar flaws. In the first place it is just plainly erroneous to equate 'x is good' with 'I like x', since both 'x is good (for me) but I don't like x' (for example, cabbage is good for me but I don't like it) and 'I enjoy x though I know it's bad for me' (for example, I enjoy smoking but I know it's bad for me) are obviously neither self-contradictory nor unintelligible utterances (as they would certainly be if emotivism were true). As Kant argued, to judge that something is (morally) good is to express rather more than just one's subjective preference or personal taste, and even for Hume there are objective criteria for the goodness of actions and conduct – precisely whether they are conducive to human well-being or caused by benevolent sentiments and so forth.

In the second place, moral judgements are obviously in some

genuine sense contentious or debatable; arguments may occur over moral issues of a kind that would not arise if moral disagreement amounted to no more than a difference of personal tastes. Thus if someone disagrees with me concerning whether raspberries are more delicious than strawberries, I should not normally require of him a reason for his own preference, but I am interested in the reasons for his support of a particular moral or social policy (the death penalty or the abortion bill) which I find repugnant. In fact, all the great moral philosophers whose views we have so far examined in this work considered reason or rational deliberation to be crucially implicated in moral life and all of them would I think have taken a very dim view of emotivist ethics (and, of course, did – Socrates offered the first clear resistance to a position much like modern emotivism).

Thus most of the moral philosophical reactions to emotivism of recent times would appear to agree that one of the outstanding problems inherent in understanding the nature of moral life and experience concerns the functioning of human reason in relation to moral judgement. Indeed, what especially characterises the diverse modern moral views in a way that serves to distinguish them quite markedly from their classical predecessors is a very large concern with the nature and extent of moral disagreement (between different communities as well as between individuals) and with the question of whether such disagreement is ultimately susceptible of satisfactory rational resolution. To be sure, Plato, Aristotle and Kant were also preoccupied with the problem of understanding the nature of moral wisdom and rationality and with the question of how moral judgements might ultimately be justified, but none of these philosophers seems to to have doubted very strongly that perfectly good sense is to be made of the notions of moral knowledge and moral truth.

In the wake of such subjectivist moral perspectives of the modern period as emotivism, questions concerning the relativity or otherwise of moral views and attitudes have moved to the forefront of philosophical work in ethics, and modern moral theorists have been forced to confront squarely the issue of whether morality is ultimately enshrined in an absolute code of principles of universal validity (as both Plato and Kant appear to have thought in their rather different ways) or is better understood as exhibited in a wide variety of different and often conflicting codes of conduct in different individual and social circumstances.

Although we have indeed noticed that certain forms of moral and social relativism were common enough even in the days of Socrates and Plato, the question of the relativity or plurality (or otherwise) of moral codes really becomes a burning issue in the post-emotivist moral philosophy of the present century. Perhaps this is because the wholesale human migration, improved communications and widespread foreign travel of modern times no longer leave much room for circumstances whereby a particular individual or society can remain comfortably isolated from or oblivious to the different values, habits and customs of others. But whatever the reason, today's moral philosophers are more or less obliged to provide at least some explanation or interpretation of the apparent differences between human cultures with respect to moral values.

As one direct response to emotivism the doctrine known as prescriptivism was very largely concerned to provide an account of the nature of moral rationality in a climate of modern opinion impressed by the apparent possibility of a multiplicity of conflicting moral codes and values. Originally formulated by the Oxford philosopher R. M. Hare,[2] prescriptivism is also one of the best possible examples to be found of post-Enlightenment liberal thinking about the nature of morality in the mainstream tradition of the ethics of obligation. Like emotivism, prescriptivism is also best understood as just a particular application to problems of ethics of a more general philosophical theory of meaning – in this case, that branch of Oxford ordinary language analysis called 'speech act theory' which flourished just after the Second World War.

Speech act theorists were profoundly impressed by the idea given its most influential philosophical airing in Wittgenstein's powerful *Philosophical Investigations* that language has numerous functions and uses other than simple *description* and that therefore the meanings of the particular terms of any given natural language might best be understood as directly derivative of these functions.[3] In short, we should not be misled (as Wittgenstein appears to have believed many previous philosophers were) by the semantic assumption that words are always in the business of describing the world. Even in those cases in which it might appear from a grammatical point of view that we are presented with a noun qualified by an adjective – such an appearance can be both grammatically and philosophically deceptive. For just as we would simply be in error to take the 'No Smoking' sign to be describing the absence of smokers (so that by lighting up we might make the notice false), we have merely committed a minor social solecism if someone greets us with 'Good morning' in foul weather and we reply 'Well, it isn't really'.

The simple point, then, is that just as the 'No Smoking' sign is there to *forbid* us from smoking rather than to *inform* us of the absence of smokers, so 'Good morning' is meant not as a description of the morning but rather as a greeting or a wish that one might have a good day. In an attempt to develop this semantic insight, speech act theorists set about constructing accounts of the meaning of certain philosophically contentious terms based on observations about the different sorts of tasks or activities that people might be said to be performing in the course of using them. True to the spirit of this view, for example, the logician P. F. Strawson maintained that to say of something that it is *true* is not to attribute some strange property to a particular sentence – a property, say, of 'fact-statingness' – instead it is to perform the 'act' of endorsing or confirming the sentence in question.[4]

In the first place, prescriptivism alleges that the term 'good' is susceptible of different linguistic uses and that consequently it can be said to have different meanings in different contexts of use. To be sure, often it does indeed operate in a descriptive way; if a labourer building a wall asks to be handed a *good* brick, we know that he requires a regular, well-made and unchipped one. But, say prescriptivists, it is not this simple descriptive sense of good which mainly applies in moral contexts in which to refer to a particular action or to a particular man on account of his actions as good is to do something above and beyond describing. In moral contexts, then, the term good is used not to *describe* agents and their actions but *assess* or *evaluate* them in a certain way and it is this that helps to explain the large element of disagreement and controversy in relation to moral uses of the term.

It is now possible to see, for example, why in the case of an unmarried mother's indecision about whether or not to have her child aborted, one person might regard abortion as a good decision and another might regard it as precisely a bad or a monstrous one. If the term good was only susceptible of an exclusively descriptive use we should have to say – since these two judgements about abortion clearly conflict – that only one of them (at most) is correct. But prescriptivists want to say that since good is being used here in a *prescriptive* rather than a descriptive sense, *each* of these judgements may be supported by reasons which justify them or at least entitle those who utter them to their own potentially valid point of view. In short, the view of the precriptivist is that in contexts of moral discourse the significant use of the term good is not to describe but to *commend*.

This perspective obviously goes some way towards vindicating the emotivist view that to call something right or good is to express one's approval of that thing. The striking contrast between the emotivists and the prescriptivists here lies in the fact that whereas for the former moral utterances are little more than expressions of non-rational sentiment, the latter maintain that they are rational judgements which require to be supported by reasons – they are not just expressions of personal taste or preference. At least to this extent, the prescriptivist response to emotivism does indeed appear to be a case of history repeating something like Kant's response to the empiricist moralists of his time. This appearance of philosophical *déjà vu* is reinforced somewhat as the prescriptivists proceed to explicate the precise nature of the rational backing which is held to be appropriate to moral judgements or evaluations. To call some action good is not to describe it but to commend it; but which actions are to be commended in moral terms?

Like Kant (one of their major influences) the prescriptivists recognise that morality is an essentially practical human concern and that reason as it operates through morality is concerned with the grounding or justification of imperatives; the job of practical reason with respect to moral life is to inform us about what we ought to do in circumstances requiring moral action and decision. So which actions ought we to commend or call good? Precisely those we ought to perform. But which actions ought we to perform? Precisely those we are inclined to commend. Now, however, we seem to have landed ourselves in a hopeless *impasse*. But in fact the prescriptivists' way out of this *impasse* is roughly that taken by Kant – an appeal to the universalisation of prescriptions. We commend or call good precisely those actions which we can reasonably will to be done by everyone in similar circumstances; both 'ought' and 'good', then, are basically to be construed in terms of something very like the Kantian universalisation of imperatives or prescriptions.

In short, the idea of rational self-legislation again surfaces as the proposed solution to certain problems concerning the sort of character human action ought to have in order to be considered moral. In order to qualify as genuine moral action, human conduct must be voluntary, rational and autonomous; it should not merely be the expression or causal product of irrational or non-rational moods, inclinations or feelings over which we have little or no control and for the occurrence of which we could hardly be praised or faulted.

But though moral conduct is to be regarded as an essentially rational business, the prescriptivists endorse both the fact–value and is–ought distinctions (or some unholy wedlock of these) and they insist that our reasons for action are not derived in any direct way from empirical experience; as we have been emphasising, moral judgements are not for them descriptions of the world but rather disguised injunctions to act in the world to change it in some way. Thus the true or authentic origins of moral judgements or prescriptions lie in the individual himself – in moral matters the individual is his own independent rational law-giver.

Here, however, there is a crucial respect in which the prescriptivists would appear to deviate quite significantly from their Kantian roots. For whereas Kant appears to have thought that by the right exercise of human reason in moral matters we could discern or establish a moral law with a genuine claim to absolute or universal authority over any rational being irrespective of his local or personal circumstances, for prescriptivists the individual universalisation of prescriptions is not bound to produce the same moral imperatives for all men. It is not necessarily to be expected, then, that all individuals will agree to universalise the same prescriptions (though some prescriptivists strongly suggest that this might reasonably be expected as a general tendency with respect to certain common enough human prohibitions on murder, theft, adultery and so on).

Indeed, most prescriptivists regard this as one of the main advantages of their theory, since it helps to explain what they take to be the irrefutable evidence of moral pluralism and disagreement within and between particular societies. Thus, although it *may* be the case that those from other cultures who disagree with us concerning the rightness or otherwise of certain forms of conduct are so inclined only because they have been uncritically indoctrinated into various irrational religious faiths or political dogmas, it might yet be that they have arrived logically at different rational conclusions from ours as a result of universalising different or alternative prescriptions.

Despite the fact that the philosophical heyday of prescriptivism is now a quarter of a century into the past, it is not unreasonable to suggest that it has been a moral perspective of no little significance and considerable influence both within academic contexts and beyond them. Moreover, it is plausible to claim that its influence is still strong in educational philosophy which like some other areas of 'applied' philosophy has tended to lag somewhat behind the mainstream of academic philosophical work and, beyond educational philosophical circles as such, various rather confused versions of the prescriptivist viewpoint are readily enough encountered from time to time in 'official' educational policy documents from state departments of education. (Clearly related to these observations, I suspect that something like a prescriptivist perspective is well-entrenched in the philosophically unsophisticated thought and practice of very many otherwise reasonably educated people in contemporary western society).

Yet again, prescriptivism is certainly consistent with and has probably had a fair amount of impact on certain psychological theories of moral development associated with such by now familiar names as Piaget and Kohlberg (to be considered in due course); at any rate, the cognitive–psychological views of moral development in question are quite explicitly Kantian in most of the crucial respects in which prescriptivism is itself Kantian. Thus it is on something like the view that the main aim of moral education consists in the promotion of certain capacities for autonomous rational decision making that large numbers of educational philosophers *and* psychologists have in recent years been largely agreed. (And it may be sensible to regard such large scale agreement between philosophers and empirical psychologists as not just a rare occurrence, but also one of which to be profoundly suspicious).

In light of all these considerations, it is not too great an exaggeration to suggest that variously specified versions of something like prescriptivism would appear to have constituted the principal orthodoxy of thinking about moral education in much of the western world from the mid-sixties to the present. And if, as many mainstream moral philosophers have been arguing for some time now, prescriptivism and related individualistic ethical doctrines are deeply flawed as accounts of moral life and action, this is so much the worse for the moral education that many children will currently and recently have been receiving.

Criticisms of prescriptivism have arisen from various sources often as hostile to each other as to doctrines of individual rational moral autonomy. In the present context, however, I am mainly interested in objections to prescriptivism as an ethics of law and obligation, an attempt to provide an account of moral life and action in terms of the idea that it is possible to devise or discern strict moral rules and principles by the free exercise of a human reason which is largely indifferent or neutral with respect to the claims or interests of any natural dispositions, desires or inclinations as these are given in human experience. I am interested, then, in criticisms of prescriptivism which have come from the general direction of the ethics of virtue and I shall further limit my observations in what follows to a consideration of three not entirely compatible or mutually sympathetic sources of this criticism.

The earliest and most immediate hostile response to prescriptivism came from a group of philosophers whose general position (ignoring differences of fine detail) I shall call 'naturalism' (though the more common term seems to have been 'neo-naturalism'[5]). Like both emotivism and the philosophy of Kant, prescriptivism is profoundly *anti-naturalist* in character in precisely the sense that it refuses to regard any statement about what is valuable or what ought to be done in moral terms as derivable from considerations about how things happen to stand in human individual and social affairs. Kant, for example, insists that moral imperatives are categorical and that they command absolutely, irrespective of personal or local circumstances; quite unlike hypothetical imperatives they are not at all contingent on natural human desires and interests.

Modern naturalists, however, like their great intellectual predecessor of classical antiquity Aristotle, believe that views about what is morally good or valuable and hence statements about what men ought morally to do must bear some logical or internal relation to considerations concerning the needs and desires of men as agents who are naturally interested in their ultimate welfare and happiness. To believe otherwise, they maintain, can lead one only to precisely the sort of incoherences that in fact one encounters in prescriptivism.

To begin with, let us reconsider the prescriptivist view about what 'good' means in moral contexts; that such-and-such an action is good, they hold, means that that is the sort of action I am ready to commend. Goodness, in other words, is explained in terms of commendation much in the same way that truth was explained in terms of confirmation by other speech-act theorists. But the doctrine about goodness suffers from precisely the same defects as that about truth. For if we try to explain the expression 'x is true' in terms of 'I confirm x', how then are we to explain the idea of confirmation? Surely only in terms of the belief that x is true. Likewise it seems possible to understand the prescriptivist's notion of 'commending x' only in terms of believing (as distinct from deciding to call) x good.

In short, just as it is more naturally explanatory to account for confirmation in terms of truth rather than vice versa, so it is with commendation and goodness; in fact apart from the idea of believing something to be good, the notion of commendation can make hardly any sense at all – consequently goodness, moral or otherwise, must be explicable by reference to criteria other than or beyond our mere preparedness to commend individuals or actions. But in that case it is reasonable to suppose that these criteria are objectively specifiable; we consider a given object or action to be good because, for example, we discern in it certain properties or qualities which are more conducive than others to certain needs and interests that we naturally have as human agents. In the moral and social sphere, then, we regard hospitality as good conduct because it generally conduces to human welfare by oiling the wheels of social co-operation; on the other hand, we regard aggression and hostility as bad because these have precisely the opposite effect.

What amounts basically to the same point can be put in other ways. Prescriptivists consider their theory to be superior to emotivism because it shows rational moral argument and debate to be a genuine possibility. But where two individuals disagree sharply concerning the goodness of a particular object, person or item of conduct, how is their rational argument about the matter to proceed and on what possible basis might it be resolved? Since prescriptivists recognise no 'factual' or objective criteria upon which judgements of moral worth might be based, any arguments of this nature must eventually run into flat disagreement between individuals who are stubbornly disposed to universalise different prescriptions based ultimately on criterionless decisions about what is morally valuable. Thus the possibility of rational moral argument and debate which prescriptivists claim to be a positive advantage of their theory over others is rather more apparent than real; it amounts finally to much the same direct conflict of subjective preferences that we earlier noticed as characteristic of emotivism.

Seen from a variety of perspectives, then, a fundamental problem is that the very idea that reason or rationality has a genuine part to play in human moral life seems not to have much of a purchase if too strict a gap or distinction is observed between concepts of moral obligation and considerations pertaining to the actual circumstances of human life as these stand to be expressed in certain natural human dispositions, interests and purposes. Thus, the critical literature on prescriptivism of recent times has also contained many criticisms of a more technical nature directed against the prescriptivist denial of the possibility of logically deriving moral 'ought' statements from 'factual' premises and also against the prescriptivist account of moral inference as such; these need not, however, detain us here.[6]

It is clear enough, at any rate, that the new naturalists who have raised just these sorts of objections hark back to quite a different philosophical tradition of moral thought from that which is discernible in the case of prescriptivism, the tradition in question being precisely that begun by Aristotle and sustained throughout the Middle Ages by certain of his philosophical followers and heirs, the most distinguished of which was St Thomas Aquinas. In particular, naturalism revives a profoundly *teleological* (purposive) conception of human moral life in opposition to the *deontological* (duty-based) conception of Kant and his various descendants.

Of course, the most familiar of all modern moral theories which is commonly regarded as a teleological ethics is that developed in the nineteenth century by Jeremy Bentham and John Stuart Mill[7] under the name *utilitarianism* – the view that all actions with a claim to moral value or significance are to be judged good or bad according to the amounts of pleasure (Bentham) or happiness (Mill) they produce. Utilitarianism, then, is a kind of *consequentialist* ethics – it attempts to assess the moral worth of human actions in terms of the felicity of their outcomes or consequences. In defending their own teleological conception of ethics, however, modern naturalists have usually been as resolutely opposed to consequentialism in general and utilitarianism in particular as they have been towards the ethics of duty in general and prescriptivism in particular.

The main point for emphasis here is that the new naturalists are advocates not just of a teleological ethics but also of an ethics of *virtue* – precisely in the great tradition of Aristotle and Aquinas; thus they regard moral life as essentially exhibited in the disciplined cultivation of certain human dispositions or states of character which are to be seen as related *internally* to the achievement of a certain quality of decent individual and social life. Like utilitarians and other consequentialists they regard moral action as in a crucial sense productive of or related to the achievement of human well-being or happiness (*eudaimon*) but unlike them they do not believe that this happiness is susceptible of independent specification from the conduct which brings it about; moral action is not viewed by naturalists as related only *externally* or *causally* to beneficial outcomes – it is not merely a means instrumental to the achievement of happiness but constitutive of human happiness and well-being itself.

Suppose, for example, that a series of cowardly or dishonest actions, which as it happens do not harm anyone else, leads to a life of material ease and sensual pleasure for a particular individual and that an heroic stand by another, from which as it happens no one benefits, leads to his torture and death. For those in the mainstream tradition of naturalism, the moral quality of a man's life – whether or not he has lived decently, courageously and with some degree of personal integrity – itself contributes to determining what should count as a man's ultimate well-being or happiness; this is not something to be specified or quantified in terms of amounts of ease and prosperity independently of the character or quality of a man's actions.

Thus there is little good or benefit to be discerned in pleasure or prosperity bought at the price of cowardice, dishonesty and dishonour (what profit a man to gain the whole world and lose his soul) but there is much human good to be discovered in the courage whereby a man endures unjust persecution. Like Kantians and other deontologists, naturalists insist that moral conduct requires to be evaluated in terms of the quality of will or motivation by which it is informed rather than just by reference to felicitous outcomes or consequences (which they also rightly point out cannot be safely predicted anyway); but unlike them they hold that the good will or moral motives and intentions generally cannot be properly characterised apart from some reference to the natural purposes and interests which men have for pursuing moral life in some actual range of human circumstances.

Despite the fact that naturalism and certain other ethical positions drawing inspiration from it have gained considerable ground and influence in mainstream moral philosophy of recent years, however, they have had relatively little impact on recent educational philosophy except in a few peripheral cases. In this respect the educational philosopher Mary Warnock is notable for having offered a rather rough-and-ready if not too precisely detailed defence of a naturalist position amid some telling criticisms of post-prescriptivist moral education in several recent works.[8]

Not all virtue theorists are naturalists, however, and in the remaining space of this chapter I want to give brief consideration to the recent work of two quite individual philosophers of crucial importance in relation to the modern development of an ethics of virtue in opposition to deontological perspectives. The first of these is John McDowell, whose formidably difficult papers on ethics have appeared from the late seventies onwards scattered throughout a variety of professional philosophical journals and anthologies.[9] McDowell's point of departure is essentially from a criticism of what he calls 'non-cognitivism' – basically his own term for prescriptivism and related points of view. So far as I understand him, McDowell's main complaint against basically any position in ethics which tries to derive a system of strict moral obligations from the universalisation procedures inherent in some notion of pure or disinterested practical reason is that essentially it puts the cart before the horse; in fact, he appears to regard such an ideal system of rational obligations as something of a chimera – it is just idle to believe that it is there for moral enquiry to discover.

The truth of the matter is not that our moral lives are to be construed in terms of more or less unsatisfactory conformity to some platonically ideal code of moral laws accessible to human reason via some process of disinterested and abstract intellectual theorising, but rather that moral reasons, laws and principles are rough and ready rules of thumb which are constantly being devised and revised in the interests of helping us to negotiate in something like a principled way the maze of problems of human association and personal relationship which characterise what we call human life. As Aristotle insisted, then (and McDowell takes himself to be faithfully Aristotelian in all of this) morality is a practical affair, and reasoning in morality is concerned with contingencies rather than necessities, with particularities more than what is absolutely or universally true. In this respect McDowell appears to believe that his 'non-cognitivists' are held captive by a very mistaken picture not only of moral reasoning in particular but also of human rationality in general, since *all* our reasoning, according to him, is contingent in this sense.

It is for basically this reason that McDowell is also critical of naturalism – or, at any rate, of some naturalists. The principal point at which the naturalist critics disagree with their non-cognitive opponents, according to McDowell, is over the question of whether moral beliefs give a person a sufficient reason or motive for acting in the world. Since the prescriptivists hold that a moral judgement is not formed in accordance with objective considerations pertaining to how things actually stand in human affairs, but rather expresses an agent's personal commitment or obligation to act in a particular way, they hold that moral judgements are effective motives for action. However, since naturalists in general believe that moral terms and judgements do apply descriptively to certain objective features and properties of agents and their actions in the world, they do not attribute any special prescriptive force to moral beliefs and so they do not hold that moral reasons give an agent a sufficient reason for action; thus an agent may regard martyrdom as an objectively admirable form of conduct without thereby being provided with a reason to undergo martyrdom (in similar circumstances) himself.

According to McDowell the trouble is that both the naturalists and the non-cognitivists here conspire together in the same fundamental error about human moral life – the error of regarding the moral values which propel people into action as somehow lying beyond or outside the sphere of reason and understanding; both ethical positions are *non-cognitive* about values. Thus the heart of the difficulty here for McDowell relates to precisely that false conception of rationality in general and moral reason in particular to which we have previously alluded – the conception of reason as somehow located at a neutral archimedean point lying beyond any particular or actual human goals, purposes or interests. It is not the case that interests and values are added by human beings, in the manner of some sort of afterthought, to an objective reality which is discerned by disinterested reason, but rather that the only objective reality that we can ever know just *is* a world shaped by human values and interests which is only more or less adequately described by human reason.

Thus McDowell's point seems to be that in order to engage in practical deliberation with a view to forming a moral judgement one has *already* to possess a motive for acting morally, for practical reason can operate effectively only where reason recognises a world of objective facts *and* values – or, from the standpoint of a conception of reality which is, as it were, impregnated with value. A sincere effort on the part of any human agent to understand his world clearly and with some sensitivity is sufficient to provide him with reasons for acting well rather than badly in it (for doing things which benefit people and avoiding doing whatever causes them pain or harm) and he does not require any extra non-cognitive motivational element in his character to kick-start him into moral action. For McDowell, then, moral beliefs are cognitive but they also thereby provide reasons for action; the naturalist view of the relationship between reason and motivation is thus just as unreasonable and distorted in his view as that of the non-cognitivist.

Ideas of a related nature have also exercised Alastair McIntyre[10] in a very important and prolific body of work produced over the last decade; one widely influential book *After Virtue* was published at the beginning of the eighties, and another, *Whose Justice, Which Rationality?* at the end, (at which time he also delivered the prestigious Gifford lectures at the University of Edinburgh). In the more recent work McIntyre has remarked that his earlier *After Virtue* was widely misconstrued as a defence of an ethics of virtue over an ethics of rules, but though he is clearly right to insist that *both* rules and dispositions are required to complete the general picture of human moral life, there can be little or no doubt that McIntyre falls into the philosophical category of those who endorse an ethics of virtue rather than an ethics of obligation as this distinction is understood in this chapter.

In fact he starts off, as have quite a number of others, by taking to heart certain fundamental theses in what might be considered the very manifesto of modern naturalism – Elizabeth Anscombe's difficult but battle-rallying essay 'Modern moral philosophy' which appeared in the mid-1950s.[11] Among the quite astonishing points that Anscombe made in that article are two which quite clearly inform McIntyre's own thinking; first, the idea that the most urgent task facing philosophers interested in ethical questions is the elucidation or clarification of certain psychological concepts of intention, desire, action and so on (so that, as she suggests, philosophers ought to abandon moral philosophy until they have done more philosophy of mind) and second, that moral philosophers ought in any case to abandon (as far as it is psychologically possible) the idea that there are special *moral* concepts of duty, obligation and right, because these are really just survivals into modern times of ideas that had a genuine sense only in the context of a divine law conception of ethics to which the modern world no longer widely subscribes.

McIntyre's work takes both these ideas very seriously indeed and he argues in some detail and at some length that moral philosophy from the Enlightenment onwards has been set largely on the wrong course due mainly to the mistake of believing that a coherent and intelligible system of moral principles of absolute value and universal application might be discerned or construed via the exercise of purely disinterested powers of human reason. In particular he rejects the appeal to canons of rationality which lie wholly outside of all existing human traditions of reflection about the nature of moral life and its goals and purposes as these are expressed in specific conceptions of human good or well-being. Thus McIntyre is entirely in accord with some of the basic tenets of naturalism – that, for example, most modern moral philosophers have been preoccupied with an entirely inappropriate set of questions about the epistemological basis of duty and obligation and that the really significant questions of moral life and value require rather to be understood in terms of a basically teleological conception of human good. In its own way, McIntyre's work drives yet another nail into the coffin of prescriptivism as one of the principal heirs to a moral tradition central to which is a notion of moral reason or rationality which is itself quite disinherited.

But like McDowell, McIntyre also appears to depart quite significantly from naturalism since, for him, moral perspectives are inevitably and unavoidably social in origin and they arise in response to the particular contingencies and circumstances of specific contexts of human individual and social life. Neither moral virtue nor rationality and justice themselves can be properly understood apart from particular moral and social traditions and so there cannot logically be any abstract concept of pure, absolute or universal moral rationality which cuts across or is well placed to adjudicate neutrally between such different traditions. Thus McIntyre may be construed as unsympathetic to at least one idea which seems to lie at the root of modern naturalism – that there is some concept of human virtue or good that might be identified, at least in principle, as applicable to something conceivable as *human nature as such*, irrespective of social circumstances; if we respect what would appear to be the interpretations of Aristotle of both McIntyre and McDowell regarding this point, then it would seem that there cannot be any human nature which is independent of social circumstances and influences.

On this issue, McIntyre's arguments may seem reminiscent of certain criticisms directed at both naturalism and prescriptivism in the 1960s by a group of British moral philosophers generally influenced by the teachings of Wittgenstein's pupil Rush Rhees. The philosophers in question such as Phillips and Mounce,[12] however, argued that because of the social–contextual nature of morality, prescriptivists must be at least right (albeit for the wrong reasons) about the impossibility of resolving certain moral disputes, whereas naturalists must be quite wrong to think that any resolution of such moral disagreements is reachable even in principle; in this manner they preached what sounded to many ears like a vicious social relativism about moral values. By contrast McIntyre denies vehemently that he is endorsing or propounding any kind of relativism of this fundamentalist kind; he does not appear to accept the inference that the social origins of moral values leads to radical incommensurabilty – the position that the adherents of different moral perspectives must ultimately have to agree to differ on certain moral questions.

Indeed, McIntyre seems most unwilling to abandon at least some notion of moral truth as the ultimate aim of moral enquiry even though he also appears entirely persuaded that, as in other fields of human enquiry and endeavour, this truth will never be completely within our grasp. But in this respect moral enquiry *is* precisely in no different a position from any other; just as in the case of scientific enquiry we are destined as the occupants of limited human perspectives always to see only through a glass darkly, we must nevertheless continue to believe in the possibility of seeing *more clearly*. In fact, McIntyre is quite keen to insist on the objective reality of moral progress and innovation which, he maintains, occurs precisely as the result of collisions and conflicts between different moral traditions when the adherents of such conflicting traditions engage in serious attempts to understand each other. Such attempts at mutual understanding may lead (and McIntyre gives numerous examples) to a genuine re-evaluation of the ideas fundamental to each perspective and perhaps to the emergence (as with intelligent scientific enquiry) of a single new view which both transcends the limitations and reconciles the valuable insights of the parent perspectives in terms of a larger and more comprehensive vision – a richer general view, perhaps, of what constitutes ultimate human flourishing.

Such is something of the current state of play regarding the modern philosophical debate between those who are inclined to try to understand moral life in terms of some sort of ethics of obligation and those who are persuaded that it is more promising to try to understand morality from the general standpoint of an ethics of virtue. It will be apparent, of course, that the arguments in this chapter have been plainly biased towards the ethics of virtue, and I have largely been concerned to show how and why I believe the case for such an ethics to be the stronger. From this viewpoint, by the way, I do not here need to decide between the different versions of the case against deontology which I have noticed; the positions of naturalism, McDowell and McIntyre all have much to be said in their favour and the influence of insights from all three of these important perspectives is clearly discernible (without, I hope, too much obvious incongruence) in the arguments of subsequent sections of this work.[13] Before we encounter these arguments, however, we must first examine, in the next section, a number of important views on the nature of moral life and education hailing from the direction of the human and social sciences.

Part II

SOCIAL SCIENCE AND MORAL DEVELOPMENT

5

MORAL EDUCATION AS SOCIALISATION: EMILE DURKHEIM

To date we have been considering some of the ideas about moral life and the development of virtue of certain great philosophers of the past and we have tried to identify some of the moral theories which have had a formative influence on present day ethical thought. So far, then, we have largely been concerned with forms of conceptual analysis – with enquires and disputes about the *meaning* of various ethical terms. Clearly, however, moral conduct is just one kind of behaviour and it is not possible to ignore the fact that various modes of scientific discipline have developed during the modern period which are exclusively concerned with understanding either animal behaviour in general or specific kinds of human behaviour in particular – biology, ethology, psychology, anthropology, sociology, social psychology, politics and economics, to name just a few.

Moreover, although some of these modes of empirical enquiry, like biology, have sought to remain largely naturalistic or topic-neutral with respect to considerations of human value – rather in the manner of such 'hard' natural sciences as physics and chemistry – most of the others have acknowledged and attempted directly to address the problems raised by the normative character of much human conduct. Thus it would not be unreasonable to suppose that some of the modern social and behavioural sciences might have something illuminating to contribute to the understanding of those problems of morality and moral education in which we are presently interested.

In fact, it will soon become clear that I am inclined to a somewhat pessimistic conclusion about the contribution of empirical theories to any genuine understanding of moral life and moral development; in short, I do not think that they have

111

much of real value to offer because I believe that it is a deep mistake to suppose that conclusions about moral life and purpose may be arrived at as a result of anything like standard scientific generalisations or on the basis of anything that should reasonably be construed as scientific enquiry. Nevertheless, since there is always much to be learned from critical reflection on important intellectual mistakes I shall devote this section largely to a consideration of certain well-known social scientific theories of moral education and moral development for the purposes of instruction; in any case, as I shall indicate, I do not believe that all of the theories I shall consider have been *entirely* mistaken.

At any rate, the empirical work cannot be ignored since, for example, one obvious question of present interest on which it has seemed to people to be natural to seek help from empirical studies concerns the individual acquisition of moral attitudes and dispositions – the problem of how moral life gets (or fails to get) as it were, 'inside' the individual – and in due course I shall consider the views of Freud, Piaget, Kohlberg and others on this question. (It is currently fashionable, I suppose, to be relatively sympathetic to Piaget and Kohlberg but hostile to Freud, but I shall be friendly to Freud and some of his educational followers and somewhat unenthusiastic about Piaget and Kohlberg.)

But, of course, questions about how morality gets 'inside' the individual are obviously in some sense secondary to questions about the nature of that which is to be got inside; very many social scientists have viewed moral education or socialisation generally as essentially a matter of the 'internalisation' (a social scientific term of art) of norms and values in a manner which clearly implies that such values and norms are objective or 'outside' the individual – that they are not to be construed merely as personal or subjective human responses. We have so far argued that virtues are essentially dispositions, but dispositions which are moulded by or defined in terms of certain kinds of principles, conventions and rules which introduce a certain sort of extra-personal discipline into the life of an individual. From whence, then, come these rules and conventions and what 'real' or 'objective' existence do they have?

Clearly many of the normative features of human moral life are of a *social* nature – they are concerned with the complexities of human association. Duties and obligations are owed primarily to other people (there is, as we shall see, something rather fishy about the Kantian notion of duties to oneself), roles and responsibilities are defined by reference to public and largely other-regarding functions, and customs and conventions help to constitute the civilised social context in which decent human intercourse can take place. If there is any science to which we might make a justified appeal to cast some light on the nature of moral rules and contracts, then, it would seem to be the discipline of sociology which regards it as its business to investigate the nature of social and interpersonal rules in general. (And in most of this chapter we shall be giving close critical attention to the work of one great sociologist who had much of importance to say on the nature of social rules in general and moral rules and education in particular.)

Clearly social and moral rules *are* crucial to understanding human association (though the main thesis of the present work is that they are not *exclusively* so) and so the question of their provenance is a pressing one; moreover, in the course of our examination of some classic moral philosophies we have already identified a number of different responses to this question. Hobbes, for example, certainly well represents one time-honoured response to the problem of social cohesion – a response which seems to have endured in the more recent work of philosophers and social theorists of the modern period. Hobbes held, as we have seen, that social norms, contracts and conventions are quite literally human artifacts – they are invented by men as instruments to serve the general purpose of self-interest. Individual human beings have certain innate impulses, instincts and desires of a basically asocial and competitive kind which are susceptible of reasonable satisfaction only through the submission of the individual to certain legal constraints and his entry into those contracts and agreements by which he might secure the co-operation or at least the non-interference of others in his enterprises.

Hobbes, then, adopts what might be called an 'externalist' perspective on moral and social rules and regulations. Social and moral constraints certainly bind individual human beings together in some form of civil human community, but their authority and influence over men is entirely external; they are regarded as at best a necessary nuisance by individuals otherwise disposed to the uninhibited pursuit of their natural desires and inclinations. Men endure the unwelcome imposition on them of social and moral constraints only because they do not wish to return to the condition of unbridled internecine strife that is Hobbes' state of nature. This generally 'externalist' view of moral and social rules and regulations would appear to be a feature of many post-Enlightment social and political philosophies of a liberal individualist temper. In particular, it seems to be characteristic of the nineteenth-century utilitarian tradition which has had a powerful influence on modern social and political thought; it is especially characteristic of this tradition to view the imposition on the individual of various legal constraints, particularly through the mechanism of state bureaucracy, with considerable suspicion and distaste. For many modern social and political theorists, then, individual freedom would appear to be construed in terms of the minimum of legal constraints.

As we have seen, however, both the Hobbesian analysis of the problem of social cohesion and his account of the nature and place of moral and social rules in human life and experience seem most unsatisfactory. If individual human beings are as naturally asocial and unco-operative as Hobbes makes out, then it is well nigh impossible to see how human society could ever get started at all; it seems more intelligible to suppose that some human co-operation is presupposed even to the pursuit of rational self-interest. Indeed, it is scarcely intelligible to speak either of self or self-interest under the conditions which are for Hobbes characteristic of a state of nature. It is surely just mistaken to regard the human self or personality as a mere bundle of natural or raw instincts and desires which becomes overlaid by various laws and conventions in the course of the individual's entry into civil society, for we do not regard anything as a self or personality which is not itself informed or constituted by such rules and conventions. We do not, for example, regard non-human animals and small pre-social human children as real persons, though they have instincts and desires in abundance, either because they are in principle unable or because they are not yet able to take responsibility for their own conduct via the recognition of duties, contracts and obligations.

It would seem to be a serious error, then, to regard the soul or personality as something which exists essentially prior to or independent of some initiation into moral rules, conventions, obligations and so on. Aristotle expressed this point by characterising man as an essentially social or political animal whose nature can be properly understood only by reference to his relationship to the *polis* – his membership, in short, of something like a civil human community. Very much later Karl Marx was to make a very similar point by observing that: 'it is not the consciousness of men that determines their being, but, on the contrary, their social being that determines their consciousness.'[1] According to Marx, then, we have the mentality we have as human beings, including the desires, inclinations and aspirations we have, due to particular social influences and patterns of cultural conditioning; it can make little or no sense to speak of men's natural desires and inclinations in advance of such influences.

Within social theory Marx has sometimes been classified as a 'conflict' theorist because like Hobbes he was inclined to emphasise the aggressive, self-serving and potentially divisive aspects of human nature; he regards competition as expressed in the form of class-conflict as the key mechanism of human social evolution (at least historically) – economic changes and concomitant improvements in human material circumstances occur largely because men strive for power and advantage over other men through control of the very circumstances of their economic existence. His fundamentally un-Hobbesian view of the relationship between human society and the individual, however, by which he regards the rules and conventions inherent in social perspectives as actually constitutive of individual personal identity expresses an 'internalist' perspective on the normative features of human experience which is actually more characteristic of what social scientists have called 'consensus' theorists.

The response of consensus theorists to the Hobbesian problem about how basically asocial individuals might be bound together in something like a civil human society and made to submit to conventional constraints and laws is just really that there is no such problem if we regard people as essentially social; we need precisely to grasp the point that social norms and values are constitutive of anything we should intelligibly want to regard as a human self or personality. Even the pursuit of self-interest for consensus theorists presupposes a background of social contract and agreement – there must be some form of human association in order even for selfishness to be possible. (When a wild animal snatches food from another it is not being selfish – nor is it being altruistic when it gives its life for its young).

At all events, one very important figure in the development of consensus theory was the nineteenth-century French sociologist Emile Durkheim, to whose views we shall devote the remainder of this chapter – first, because Durkheim offers a first-rate example of a serious attempt within mainstream sociology to account generally for the origins, nature and place of social rules and conventions in human life, and second, because he is the author of a well-known work on moral education in which he attempted to demonstrate how such rules may make their entry into individual human psychology.[2] In all of his significant contributions to the development of empirical sociology – in his *Rules of Sociological Method* and *Suicide* as well as in those other works of his we shall be considering shortly – Durkheim is a good example of an 'internalist' about social and moral rules. He was very highly critical of the social utilitarians and evolutionists of his day such as Jeremy Bentham and Herbert Spencer who construed human community precisely in terms of a collection of largely competitive individual interests and social rules as devices for securing the maximum possible satisfaction of those interests in terms of the greatest collective happiness.[3]

Moreover, Benthamite utilitarians held that human happiness was reducible to or susceptible of measurement in terms of quantities of crude hedonic pleasure and that genuine human fulfilment consisted ultimately in the achievement of such pleasure. Like such great moral philosophers as Plato, Aristotle and Kant, however, Durkheim is convinced that true human satisfaction and well-being is not to be discovered in this notion of raw or primitive pleasure even if it could, *per impossibile,* be quantified; he holds rather that human flourishing is truly possible only in those circumstances in which individual human life and psychology is properly constituted and appropriately informed by norms and values conducive to harmonious, orderly and co-operative social relations.

In fact, Durkheim takes the view that the most grievous human ills are those which follow in the wake of any kind of serious erosion of traditional or conventional values. It is when men begin to lose faith or confidence in the values that sustained their fathers and grandfathers that society in general and individuals in particular really start to fall apart. For Durkheim, then, suicide – the last counsel of despair – is ultimately explicable in terms of *anomie*, a state of radical loss of purpose brought on as a result of the old order losing all power and authority over the minds and hearts of men. A religious agnostic himself, Durkheim felt strongly that this radical loss of purpose was precisely what was happening to the western Europe of his time with a widespread decline in general public subscription to the old traditional Christian beliefs and values and the corresponding rise of popular secularism.

Durkheim also seems to have thought that this was itself the inevitable consequence of the natural process of social evolution from more primitive to more sophisticated human communities and cultures. Rather like Rousseau, he held that a crucial and traumatic social event occurs when men make the transition from economically relatively simple cultures to more complex settled communities which require or give rise to the division of labour. Durkheim characterises the earlier and simpler cultures in terms of what he calls 'mechanical solidarity' – a state of social and cultural homogeneity in which there is little personal individuality and all members of a community subscribe to basically the same set of values.

More complex civil communities constructed upon the division of labour, however, are characterised by what Durkheim calls 'organic solidarity' – a greater degree of personal individuality and a plurality of interests and values which require very much more sophisticated and delicate negotiation and harmonisation from a social point of view. This is essentially because whereas the division of labour can issue in the development of a richer and more interesting form of human life and social cohesion, it can also result in that combination of the erosion of traditional norms and values and a conflict of interests which tends towards *anomie*. In fact, with respect to his own time, Durkheim precisely believed that the emergence of secular interests had led both to the demise of the socially unifying influence of traditional Christian values – no longer considered by many, especially in the light of the growth of scientific knowledge, to be relevant to the modern world – and also to a radical conflict of individual interests to which nothing higher might be appealed in the way of their resolution.

Consequently, the aim that Durkheim set himself was to demonstrate that there are secular rational values in terms of which men's lives might be reasonably ordered and which might re-establish in those lives a genuine authority capable of transcending personal and individual desires and interests. Basically, in place of traditional concepts of God or the divine, Durkheim tries to put society itself – social norms and rules are themselves to become the chief objects of individual moral respect and reverence. Let us now consider how this works out in detail in the context of Durkheim's account of moral life and conduct in his work *Moral Education*. In what follows, I shall explore what seem to me to be the main problems with his account in relation to what Durkheim identifies as the three main elements of morality – discipline, social attachment and autonomy – in the order in which he deals with them in his book.

Durkheim begins by identifying the idea of discipline as a crucial element of morality defined essentially in terms of regularity and authority:

> To conduct oneself morally is a matter of abiding by a norm, determining what conduct should obtain in a given instance, even before one is required to act. The domain of morality is the domain of duty; duty is prescribed behaviour.[4]

For Durkheim, then, morality consists in conformity of conduct to a rule which expresses some sort of imperative force. It is also characteristic of the rules we regard as moral, however, that they set certain definite limits to the free expression of our personal desires, feelings and appetites. Durkheim agrees with most of the great moral philosophers (for example, Plato, Aristotle and Kant) that moral discipline involves some degree of self-control; our individual or personal inclinations require to be subordinated to considerations of some higher interest. What is this higher interest for Durkheim?

In fact he employs arguments for discipline which remind one strongly of both Plato and Aristotle. Durkheim sounds strikingly like Plato (and also Rousseau) when he argues that discipline is an important condition of genuine moral freedom.

Since to live a life of the uninhibited pursuit of instincts and appetites for pleasure is to be a slave of the passions rather than master of one's own destiny, self-restraint should not be viewed as an unwelcome limitation on human aspiration but as necessary to its proper fulfilment; self-mastery through moral discipline is an essentially *enabling* condition. Thus like Plato, Durkheim argues that the freedom necessary for virtue and the achievement of other important human goals is only possible if certain aspects of human nature are tamed or controlled. But he also argues very much in the manner of Aristotle that the virtues are by no means contrary to nature since we are fitted by nature to receive them; in other words, the self-control required by the virtues should not be held to involve any unnatural or artificial constraint.

As Durkheim sets out these arguments in *Moral Education* they do not look at all inconsistent, but as they occur in the contexts of the work of Plato and Aristotle they *are* tied to potentially conflicting views about the relation of discipline to human nature. In the *Nicomachean Ethics* Aristotle insists that the passions and appetites controlled by the virtuous man are not in themselves *bad* – they are morally neutral. In fact, Aristotle clearly thought that certain states of human defect or vice were to be characterised in terms of an *insufficient* degree of feeling, sentiment or passion. And here there is much implied criticism of the much more ascetic or manichaean attitude to the passionate and appetitive aspects of human nature adopted by Socrates and Plato who both seem to have viewed the suppression of appetite as a good in itself. On the face of it, Durkheim would appear to take Aristotle's side on this question since he states explicitly that 'asceticism is not good in and of itself'.[5] On closer inspection, however Durkheim's Aristotelianism is not as thoroughgoing as it first appears.

For it is not, of course, just any sort of discipline that has moral value for Durkheim, only discipline that has a disinterested or altruistic purpose. Thus he goes so far as to maintain that we do not engage in moral appraisals of conduct that conduces to the interest of its author; anything an agent does on his own behalf rather than in the interests of others cannot be said to have genuine moral value. Now although this denial of the moral relevance of any conduct performed on behalf of the self (probably founded on a conflation of the notions of selfishness and self-interest) does not perhaps extend as far as Platonic manichaeanism or any idea of 'asceticism for its own sake', it is certainly at odds with the general thought of Aristotle.

Moreover, although Durkheim's characteristic use here of the locution 'we do not say that . . .' in relation to his views on self-regarding conduct may make it appear that he is engaged in something like conceptual analysis of an 'ordinary language' kind, I think that what we have here amounts to little more than a rather dubious stipulative definition. It just does not seem to be the case that we do not attach moral significance to self-regarding conduct. We do distinguish, for example, between a man who courageously undergoes a painful operation for the sake of his own health and another who shirks it in a cowardly fashion and we admire a man who resists strong temptations to conduct that would harm him despite the fact it would neither harm nor benefit others, and in doing so we clearly engage in moral appraisals.

Furthermore, of course, we do not automatically regard as of moral value all conduct that is motivated by considerations of altruistic concern for the well-being or happiness of others. It is clear, for example, that the indulgence of spoiling parents towards their children may involve considerable self-denial and express genuine altruistic concern but nevertheless promote nothing but moral harm on the part of those to whom it is directed. Again, as Aristotle observed, a man may err morally in the direction of too *much* altruistic concern, by being (say) too generous. Perhaps the over-generous man really does benefit those towards whom his largesse is directed, but if his prodigality leaves him in dire economic straits we shall rightly condemn his folly in terms it seems appropriate to call moral. It has been suggested, of course, that Aristotle's moral philosophy appears altogether too self-centred but even if that is true it supports no case for rejecting the reasonable view that there are self-regarding virtues and that moral value may be expressed in terms of the benefits of self-control for the individual who practises it as well as others.

It is clear enough why Durkheim wants to argue as he does about the contribution of self-discipline to the moral growth of the individual; the reasons are set out in *Moral Education* in his discussion of the second element of morality, that of 'attachment to social groups'. In such works as *Suicide* and *The Division of Labour in Society*, Durkheim recognises that understanding the moral life of a community contributes crucially to any reasonable explanation of the basis of social cohesion and consensus; he concludes that it is an altruistic morality rather than one of self-interest (however enlightened) that holds society together and so it is easy to see how he conceives the main goal of moral education in terms of the promotion of those characteristics that conduce most readily to social cohesion – qualities of altruistic attachment.

In order to investigate the nature of the moral practices that have this end, then, Durkheim proposes to regard them as social *facts*, and true to his first rule of sociological method 'to consider social facts as *things*', he proceeds in the Appendix to *Division of Labour* to describe the sort of thing that a moral fact is. Here it is important to notice that Durkheim clearly wishes to eschew the customary *a priori* approach to understanding moral life characteristic of the great moral philosophers; Kant and the utilitarians are among those who attract considerable censure from him for being insufficiently scientific.

According to Durkheim, the trouble with moral philosophers is that they invariably set out with some kind of axe to grind; they start out with some pet definition of morality and proceed in the direction of procrustean accommodation of the facts of moral life to that definition, rather than via proper empirical observation of the actual facts of human moral experience on which a proper science of morality might be built. In *Moral Education* Durkheim aims towards establishing a genuine 'scientific morality' which is both free from religious and metaphysical commitments and firmly based on the facts of social–moral life. Without doubt, it is this conception of nature of moral life that gives rise to all the serious problems in Durkheim's account.

Now whilst many modern moral philosophers would doubt the very intelligibility of talk of 'moral facts' I am not one of them; I do think, however, that serious mischief is done by construing moral facts as *social* facts and only deep confusion lies at the heart of any idea of a 'science of morality'. Let us see, however, how moral practices are understood in Durkheim's work. As we have said, essentially they are to be regarded as social rules expressing other-regarding obligations which promote the harmonious and co-operative conduct of communal life and to which conformity is enjoined under pain of certain associated sanctions involving social disapproval and so on. It is first of all an occasion for some (but not much) surprise, to discover that hard upon his severe strictures on the *a prioristic* stipulations of the moral philosophers in *Division of Labour*, Durkheim has turned up with what can only be reasonably regarded as one of his own. To the perfectly reasonable objection that at least some of the altruistic conduct that we ordinarily consider to be moral is *not* conduct that anyone is under some obligation or pain of sanction to perform, Durkheim offers the astonishing response that such behaviour is better regarded as having *aesthetic* rather than moral significance.[6]

For the moment, however, we need to notice one very important concomitant of the view that moral practices are a species of social rule – one that is accepted by Durkheim without any hesitation; this is that moral rules may be considered to be as diverse in kind as social rules and customs and to vary as they do between different human cultures: 'the fact that morality varies from society to society certainly shows that it is a social product.'[7] Clearly for Durkheim there is no such thing as a code of absolute or universally valid moral laws or principles which are applicable to human conduct in any place and at any time; he repeatedly makes the point that what is suitable in terms of moral conduct for one society at a particular stage of development may be quite unsuitable for that or another society at some other stage of social evolution. If we truly wish to understand what morality is, then, we must attend to the social facts and conditions that constitute and underpin the reality that is human moral life and the facts will inevitably vary from society to society. It is no easy matter to assess or evaluate the precise nature of Durkheim's views on this rather vexed topic since his discussion of it does not readily impress one as a model of consistency; still, I shall make a try.

For a start, what could be meant by saying that morality varies from society to society? Clearly Durkheim cannot just mean that different human groups have different *conceptions* of what is morally right and wrong; it would not follow from this that what *is* actually morally right varies from society to society. In fact what he seems to mean is that since different social circumstances constrain those living under them to adopt and accept different patterns of behaviour and obligation, there just *are* different and distinct moralities which are valid in their own right precisely to the degree that they are suited to the different social conditions which give rise to them. Does it follow as a consequence of this, then, that for Durkheim any one socially constructed morality is as right or correct as any other and that therefore there is no possibility of moral comparison between them?

Since in general Durkheim is engaged in the enterprise of constructing a new rational–scientific morality on the grounds that it is in some respect *superior* to traditional religiously grounded ones, it is by no means clear that this is what he does believe; evidently he regards any social climate under which his secular morality would *not* operate as somehow less congenial than one in which it would. In short, the view that moral principles are just a function or product of social practices sits not at all well with Durkheim's apparent conviction that a society which conforms to his code of secular morality is in some sense a *better* society than one which does not.

But in what could the superiority of Durkheim's rational secular morality over other moralities consist? In the terms of his general social theory it could only be that it tends to the promotion of something like greater social cohesion or stability. But what is the value of greater social cohesion? The answer that springs most readily to mind would be expressed in terms of the greater level of happiness in society, its more efficient functioning or enhanced potential for survival. Again, however, Durkheim explicitly and expressly *rejects* this sort of explanation of the function and purpose of morality. In the Appendix to *Division of Labour* he quite rightly takes utilitarianism to task precisely on account of its crude attempt to reduce notions of moral value to considerations of utility.

As matter of fact, some of the most historically stable and enduring of human societies have probably been the most utilitarian, but they have very seldom been the most civilised in terms of moral sensibility. Durkheim himself correctly observes that rational and civilised societies readily bestow moral status and rights on the infirm, the insane, the unproductive and even the criminal elements of society which would not be extended by societies influenced largely by utilitarian considerations. On the other hand, however, those civilised societies which subscribe to something like democratic moral principles are probably characterised by rather less stability and cohesion than those which operate via the repressive coercion and violent denial of basic human rights and liberties. So the precise value of Durkheim's rational secular morality which is expressed at least partly in terms of its enlightened, tolerant and even indulgent attitude to the less socially desirable or cost-effective of social units can hardly be measured in terms of its contribution to social utility.

It seems doubtful that this talk of the social relativity of moral values will really do; how, then, has Durkheim got into this bind? We have observed that he rejects the claims of traditional religiously affiliated moralities on the ground that they substitute blind faith for reason; the new secular morality is to be rational and scientific. But if the purpose of this new morality is no longer, as Durkheim insists, to express the divine will, in what *does* its authority and purpose consist? We have already seen that Durkheim dismisses the view that it is directed towards individual benefit or wellbeing since 'we cannot call moral' anything that an agent may do on his own behalf. But by the same token, he argues, whatever a man does in the interests of other *individuals* cannot have any greater claim to moral significance.

In general, then, whatever invests morality with its authority must be something that transcends the person and his individual concerns. This transcendence was located in the will of God by traditional moralities but Durkheim locates it in the idea of *Society*. Society, one is required to see, is not just a collection of individuals with individual interests, it is some kind of super-personal self-existent entity which represents a higher interest, a whole which is greater than its parts. It is Society viewed in this light that is to be regarded as the ultimate source of moral authority and as the final object or goal of all genuine moral endeavour.

But none of this is remotely plausible. We have already suggested that there is no good reason for denying the moral significance of at least some conduct that serves only the interests of the agent who performs it, but nothing short of the most fanatical prejudice should tempt us to dismiss the moral value of anything that a man does with the interests of other individuals at heart on the grounds that the interest of something called 'Society' has priority. Suppose a man tempted to adultery or murder resists the temptation. Is his forbearance to be regarded as all the more morally commendable on the grounds that he feels obliged to respect the moral laws of society, than if he is 'merely' moved by considerations of how his wife or potential victim would suffer?

I think that really not much in the way of argument is required to show that Durkheim's idea of 'Society' as the source of moral authority and the goal of moral endeavour is little more than a piece of philosophical fiction. Although it would still be to court possible misunderstanding, it would nevertheless be *more* accurate, I think, to identify the individual person as the proper object or goal of the moral response since it is of course individuals who stand to be harmed or benefited by moral or immoral acts. To say this is not at all to deny that morality is a *social* matter in the sense that its main sphere of concern is the realm of inter-personal relations; it is just to deny that the ultimate goal or concern of morality could be 'Society' in Durkheim's sense.

In any case, Durkheim's attempt to ground moral authority in the idea of Society just does *not* solve the problem he wants to solve. If he is indeed right to recognise a difficulty about the source or origin of moral principles, then it is still of no avail to locate it in the rules or customs of Society rather than the will of God, since essentially the precise problems about the traditional religious morality he is anxious to avoid resurface in much the same form. Philosophical theologians have long acknowledged a problem (probably first raised in Plato's *Euthyphro*) about whether what is morally good is so because God wills it or God wills it because it is good, and some have argued that it is conceptions of deity that require moral evelution rather than vice versa. (We may be certain that such and such a claim to divine revelation is true, for example, only if what it commands us to do can be independently judged to be morally right rather than wrong.[8]) Clearly, Durkheim is faced with a precisely analogous problem about whether the good is so because Society wills it or Society wills it because it is good. The first position must be regarded as intolerable because it requires us to suspend judgement on the moral character and status of the many undoubtedly barbarous and repulsive social practices of many ancient and modern societies; the second, since it implies a genuine distinction between social practices and moral criteria and the possibility therefore that the former may be accountable to the latter, obviously undermines any social relativist position concerning the origins of morality.

Arising as it does from the general context of his social thought, Durkheim's treatment of his third element of morality – autonomy – must be considered rather eccentric, especially compared to other modern treatments of the topic. He recognises correctly enough that his first two elements of discipline and social attachment may not be considered jointly sufficient to explain the nature of genuine moral conduct since both these dispositions may be fostered in an individual in the absence of any sort of voluntary rational commitment on his part to the value of moral life.

He agrees with the general opinion of moral philosophers, then, that in the absence of some degree of free rational engagement in moral conduct, there can be no real moral responsibility. Equally clearly, Durkheim's conception of rational moral autonomy is a long way from that view of it which has developed in modern times largely under the influence of Kant. The most immediately striking respect in which some more recent constructions on the idea of autonomy differ from Durkheim's concerns the way in which the individual rational agent has come to be viewed as the ultimate source of rational moral values and decisions.

Like Durkheim, many modern theorists take very (perhaps *too*) seriously the idea of a plurality of moral codes and values but unlike him this has led them to view morality as more of an *individual* or personal matter than a collective concern. Most recent work by moral autonomy theorists has been directed towards identifying the rational procedures whereby the individual generates and formulates his own personal moral perspective. Usually, as we have already indicated, these have been understood in terms of something like the agent's acceptance or endorsement of certain moral prescriptions which he wills to have a general or universal application. On this view the main emphasis is placed on the development of capacities for free, independent and critical thinking about moral questions; as individuals we can and should be encouraged to conduct our own lives responsibly according to our own decisions concerning what is right or wrong in moral matters.

It is easy to see how Durkheim would have been repelled by this extremely individualistic conception of the nature and origins of morality. Although it would be foolish to deny that morality requires to be understood at least partly in terms of individual responses of a voluntary rational nature, the modern advocates of rational autonomy would appear to take this notion too far. If the good is not good because God or 'Society' wills it, it is all the less likely to be so merely because the individual wills it. As we shall in due course further emphasise it is surely implausible to suppose that it is just up to the individual to decide whether murder, adultery and promisebreaking are right or wrong, or that there are not basic moral principles concerning which our own personal decisions and preferences, whether or not they are formally consistent, are neither here nor there. Of course, rational thought may assist us to see that something is morally wrong – but only if it *is* morally wrong; it cannot be that something becomes right or wrong just because (as the Prince of Denmark puts it) thinking makes it so.[9]

I should be generally sympathetic, then, to the predictable reaction of Durkheim to the excesses of modern individualistic autonomy theory; unfortunately, however, his own view cannot be considered to be in much better shape. It is also worth noting here that although Durkheim clearly regards autonomy as an important element of morality he devotes conspicuously less space to discussing how it should be developed in practical educational terms than he does to the question of the practical promotion of the other elements. In any event, it is difficult to believe in Durkheim's notion of autonomy as a genuine concept of reason or rationality since it appears to consist mainly in getting an individual to acknowledge the justifications given by his society for the moral rules and conduct it prescribes.

From this point of view, it is a little disturbing to discover, in an otherwise balanced and enlightened discussion of punishment in which Durkheim offers some insightful criticism of crude retributive and deterrence theorists, the argument that punishment ought to be viewed as symbolic or expressive of the disapproval of the group. Far from being encouraged to adopt a detached or critical moral perspective on what is regarded as acceptable or unacceptable in his society, then, the child is apparently to be manoeuvered by dint of praise and blame into conformity with the conventional conduct of the group and into acceptance of *its* reasons for that conduct; on the face of it, this amounts to little more than the ethics of gang loyalty. All that Durkheim's concept of autonomy appears to add up to is the promotion of the individual's *psychological* conformity to current socially approved principles; it is less a concept of rationality than of what the psychoanalysts would call *rationalisation*.

Clearly, then, with respect to the details of Durkheim's account of the nature of moral life and education what he has to say about his third element of morality – autonomy – is much less satisfactory than anything he has to say about the first two. Regarding self-discipline and altruism Durkheim has much of value to contribute and the way in which he is generally inclined to characterise these aspects of moral life – as states of character or dispositions apt for right conduct – is not at all uncongenial to the general drift of the present work. What is basically at fault with Durkheim's account of moral autonomy or the role of practical deliberation in moral life is that it requires to be accommodated to his more general thesis of the nature and status of moral rules as kinds or species of social rule.

But if moral rules are essentially social rules, then moral education can be little more than a matter of adapting the individual to the social customs, conventions and other practices of his particular community; if what is right or wrong is to be defined for him by reference to what is judged in general to be so by his own social group, there can be no place for the genuine exercise of individual moral reason and judgement beyond what is minimally required to recognise or acknowledge what that group ordains. In short, Durkheim offers a view of moral education which is essentially an account of how individuals can and should be *socialised* into the traditions and customs of the tribe and to the extent that his account provides no clear (critical) role for moral deliberation beyond what is needed for such socialisation, it is not clear that what has been given may reasonably be regarded as a concept of moral *education*.[10]

My own view of Durkheim's *Moral Education* is that it is an impressive work with many admirable features; but it is nevertheless a work which is *importantly* wrong. Durkheim provides us with the clearest possible statement of a view which is very widely held today, though usually in a much more vague and confused way. Very many people of a reasonable level of general education today can be persuaded without much trouble to endorse the general position that moral rules and codes are hardly more than matters of social custom and convention (a perspective often entertained simultaneously with the view, which is of course inconsistent with it, that it is up to the individual to decide for himself). It is quite widely held that like the rules in the Highway Code, those laws which we blame or praise people morally for breaking or observing have been man-made simply to make life in society more orderly and relations between people more smooth-running; they exist for the sake of social convenience and have no other purpose. In particular, they have no absolute or universal status and what may be found to be socially convenient by one society or community may be regarded as inconvenient by another.

As is the case with most views widely regarded as plausible, of course, there is *some* truth to be found here. It can hardly be denied, for example, that moral rules have social origins, that they are often (though not always) concerned with social or interpersonal relationships and that ideas of moral virtue and good conduct are open to some degree of different interpretation in different societies. But to regard moral values and principles as matters *only* of social agreement based on considerations of convenience is to forget that such agreements may be made by *bad* men as well as *good* men, for wicked or corrupt purposes – the cynical and brutal manipulation and exploitation of others – as well as for the decent and morally respectable purposes of promoting security and justice for all members of society regardless of their station.

Thus we need only to remember that social customs and conventions are themselves susceptible of moral evaluation in order to appreciate that concepts of morality and virtue are not at all reducible to or eliminable in favour of notions of social rule. It also requires to be observed, however, that not all aspects of moral life are anyway bound by rules and not all of them are socially implicated. With this in mind, we may now turn to a consideration of some modern psychological theories concerning moral life and the formation of moral attitudes and dispositions.

6

PSYCHOANALYSIS AND MORAL CHARACTER: FREUD, LANE AND NEILL

In the work of Sigmund Freud – the founding father of psychoanalysis – we encounter what may well be the most significant academic contribution to the understanding of human psychology of the twentieth century. Moreover, like Darwin's theory of evolution and the social–economic views of Karl Marx, psychoanalytic theory – or at least some psychoanalytic terminology – has contributed to the conceptual currency of the modern world; non-academic lay people from all walks of life freely use without any sense of inhibition, terms drawn from the specialised vocabulary of psychoanalysis – repression, ego, unconscious, rationalisation and so on – though often, of course, in more or less a state of ignorance regarding the original context of such terms and of their precise meaning within that context.

In view of this it is somewhat surprising that the views of Freud and other pioneers of psychoanalysis have not had a rather larger or wider impact on the worlds of educational theory and practice than would seem to have been the case. Some attempts do seem to have been made to give educational application to the work of such psychoanalytic thinkers as Anna Freud and Susan Isaacs in British and American universities and colleges but any interest in psychoanalytic psychology among educationalists has in general been largely overshadowed by the attention given to the sort of empirical psychology which constitutes the tradition of psychological behaviourism – the work of Pavlov, Thorndyke, Watson, Skinner and so on.

Arguably this is because the behaviourists have been generally thought to have rather more than psychoanalysts to say about precisely those questions of learning, pedagogy and knowledge acquisition which continue to be of perennial and pressing interest to potential and actual educationalists and teachers. (It is also true, however, that the literature of psychoanalytic theory is generally much harder to read and understand than that of learning theory). My own view, for what it is worth, is that teachers and other educationists have next to nothing to learn from the research work of modern empirical psychologists, the influence of which, where it has been felt strongly, has cast a depressing blight over educational thinking; on the other hand I believe that there is much of value to be learned, by professional educationalists or any other students of human nature who might have a simple interest in coming to understand the human soul, from psychoanalytic ideas, as long as these ideas are handled with some caution.

It is the main purpose of this chapter to show that in fact Freud and psychoanalysis in general have been not entirely without direct influence on both educational theory and practice, although this influence has been greatest, as one might expect, outside the mainstream of conventional state education and the standard contexts of teacher education. Thus the influence has not been extensive, but I should argue that it has been significant at least to the extent that it has been associated with some very exciting experiments and some very distinguished names in modern educational progressivism; in particular with a tradition of radical educational thinking whose most conspicuous representative was probably the late A. S. Neill, headmaster of the famous experimental school Summerhill.

The tradition in question, moreover, extends backwards at least to Neill's teacher and friend Homer Lane and forwards to R. F. McKenzie[1] and it is still very much alive and well in the work of other progressive educators in Britain and America. Shortly, then, I shall offer a brief account of the main ideas of Freud, but I am concerned with these ideas only to the extent that they have influenced the kind of educational thinking which informs the work of men like Homer Lane and A. S. Neill; in particular, of course, I am interested in the psychoanalytically influenced provenance of some quite extraordinary views about moral education and the formation of moral character, to be found in Lane and Neill.[2]

In order to appreciate why the influence on such distinguished progressives as Lane and Neill was from the direction of Freud and psychoanalysis rather than any other direction of psychological theory it is in the first place only necessary to note the profoundly common concerns which these educational progressivists shared with psychoanalysts of a Freudian persuasion. Just as Lane and Neill were preoccupied with the behavioural problems of disturbed and maladjusted children, then, so Freud and other pioneers of psychoanalysis were concerned with the problems of those diagnosed as mentally ill or unbalanced – hysterics, psychotics, neurotics, obsessionals and other patients with particular problems of adjustment to normal or everyday life.

Thus psychoanalysis is a response to circumstances of primarily practical and clinical concern; it begins not as a product of purely disinterested theoretical speculations which are susceptible of proof or disproof by specially designed laboratory experiments, but from the urgent requirement to offer help and relief to real people undergoing genuine distress. The theoretical speculations of psychoanalysis, then, have a certain *ex post facto* quality – they represent largely an attempt to justify or explain in some principled way certain procedures or techniques that have proved reasonably effective in therapeutic contexts; perhaps this goes some way towards explaining their rather conjectural and provisional status.

By now, of course, there is a fair amount of common knowledge among educated people concerning the precise nature of the problems which interested Freud and the general procedures and strategies he adopted in response to them. Working with certain hysterical, neurotic and obsessional patients, Freud was faced with the difficulty of identifying the causes and treating the symptoms of a range of aberrant dispositions which impeded his patients' effective and efficient functioning in everyday life. The forms of behaviour in question were usually of a kind that would make perfectly good sense as appropriate responses to certain easily imaginable normal circumstances but which made very little sense as they occurred in the everyday lives of Freud's patients. Washing one's hands, for example, is a completely rational action to engage in before sitting down to tea after planting out the lettuces, but washing one's hands every five minutes regardless of whether or not they're dirty seems not in the same way to add up to reasonable behaviour.

Likewise, returning to the house to check whether one has locked the door on the odd occasion is reasonable enough, but checking whether one has switched off the gas for the twentieth time within an hour would appear to indicate the presence of some deep-seated anxiety which cries out for rather more than a conventional explanation. Freud was so struck by the inappropriateness and the inadequacy of the reasons given by sufferers from these conditions to explain why they did what they did, that he coined the expression 'rationalisation' (more often than not commonly misused) as a psychoanalytic term of art to characterise such forms of spurious reason-giving.

By appeal to what sort of explanation, however, could the causes of such wayward or deviant behaviour be identified? For although the actual reasons offered by those in the grip of such behaviour were clearly inappropriate and could not be accepted on their face value as real reasons, the behaviour in question did yet seem to be purposive or goal-directed rather than just arbitrary or haphazard. Thus Freud came to the conclusion that hysterical and neurotic symptoms were indeed psychologically directed – they *were* the expressions of intention and guided by purposes – but the reasons for the behaviour were *unconscious* rather than conscious. (It has been pointed out on numerous occasions, by the way, that Freud did not so much invent the concept of the unconscious mind as inherit it from earlier thinkers – including perhaps the philosopher Schopenhauer[3].)

Mentally disturbed patients, then, could have no control over the various behavioural symptoms of their psychiatric disorders so long as their behaviour lay under unconscious rather than conscious control. Freud's problem was thus twofold: first, to explain how certain forms of apparently purposive or goal-directed behaviour could have come under the control of reasons and motives concerning the nature of which the agents responsible appeared to know nothing at a conscious level, and second, to gain some access to the realm of the unconscious mind.

Again, it is well enough known that the early pioneers of psychoanalysis, including Freud himself, first experimented with hypnosis as a possible path to the unconscious, but Freud was not greatly successful in the employment of this technique. This, then, required the development of the other strategies or techniques that have since come to be associated with psychoanalytic therapy – free association, the interpretation of dreams, the analysis of early recollections and so on. Generally, however, psychoanalysis does affirm the reality of the unconscious construed as a network or constellation of psychological associations and fixations which may nevertheless become accessible through analysis to those undergoing therapy.

Such large and impressive works of Freud as *The Psychopathology of Everyday Life* and *The Interpretation of Dreams* attempt precisely to identify the principal sources of clues to the actual operations of the unconscious in the waking and dreaming lives of patients – slips of the tongue and pen, regular and recurring mistakes in routine performances, selective memory with respect to names of people and places and terms for common things and so on.[4] Many of these 'mistakes' as well as most of our dreams, according to Freud, may be construed as symptomatic of purposeful attempts to fulfil or express (by proxy) wishes or states of desire that the conscious minds of individuals would find otherwise quite unacceptable.

But why this inner prevarication? Why do certain wishes and desires have to remain hidden in this way, apparently cut off from the conscious mind of the individual? Why is it that they express themselves in such a bizarre variety of oblique ways ranging from (Freudian) slips of the tongue in relatively normal people to the hysteria, neurosis and obsession of those who are diagnosed as suitable cases for psychiatric treatment? Freud's answer is essentially that the mental states which make up the unconscious mind express wishes, wants and desires which were at one time conscious but were banished to the unconscious level as a direct consequence of certain psychic conflicts. For Freud, then, human mental life can be viewed as a kind of battleground between relatively distinct psychic forces or sources of motivation which are not readily reconcilable by the individual.

The two principal antagonists which are locked in the psychic power struggle for the control of human identity and personality are what Freud calls the id and the ego; whereas the id is the locus of the largely innately given primitive instinctual wants and wishes of the individual, the ego represents the rational capacities of a person which dispose him towards a true or at least reasonably sensible view of reality and of what it is practical to aim for with respect to that reality. These two sources of individual inclination are bound to conflict because there will inevitably be some sort of gap between a person's instinctual wants, natural appetites and so on and what a person must come to accept in this hard world as reasonable for him to want.

Moreover, it should by now be clear that the discovery of this potential for conflict within the human psyche is by no means, of course, original to Freud, since it is the cornerstone of Plato's moral psychology and it is certainly also acknowledged in the moral philosophies of Aristotle and Kant. The originality of Freud consists rather in his ingenious account of how this conflict is resolved for good or ill with respect to the development of human personality and mental health. Indeed, the difference between the psychologically 'normal' person and the one who is mentally 'ill', should not be construed in terms of either the presence or absence of such psychic conflicts which are in fact unavoidable aspects of any human experience; it is rather to be understood in terms of how well or badly individual human beings are able to cope with these conflicts in their own particular circumstances.

But what is the precise character of the particular conflicts in which Freud is interested? He came to the conclusion that the conflicts mainly responsible for the subsequent development in adulthood of mental illness had occurred in quite early childhood; thus it seemed to him to be crucial for psychoanalytic therapy to re-establish an adult patient's contact with his earliest memories of the frustration or denial of expression of his childhood wishes, desires and impulses. Freud held that the character of a human individual is formed for good or ill at three or four main stages or phases of psycho-physical development which begin shortly after the birth of the child (some later psychotherapists came to hold that critical character-forming events also occur at birth and even before) and continue until pubertal developments at adolescence.[5]

Inclined to a wider or more liberal interpretation of the term 'sexual' than had previously been usual, Freud also held that the critical periods of individual development identified by him, were all of a fundamentally sexual nature; that is, all the traumas he identified as likely to influence the formation of an individual's character at any of these stages appeared to involve some denial or frustration of childish desires, instincts or needs for some kind of physical or sensual pleasure or gratification. The first natural source of pleasure or gratification which occupies the centre of attention in the early life of the child is the breast of the mother at the stage of suckling; it is reasonable enough to suppose that the mother and the warmth, security, affection and nourishment that she provides is the first source not only of satisfaction and comfort but also of physical stimulation that the small child encounters.

Thus the inevitable and unavoidable weaning of the child away from the breast is liable to be experienced as an event of some emotional and physical trauma by the child who has now somehow to come to terms with the reality or fact of a great loss. The so-called oral stage (at which 'erotic' satisfaction is achieved via the mouth) represents the child's first real encounter with the harsh reality which will continue to impede the uninhibited fulfilment or satisfaction of his basic desires and impulses. Thus if the process of weaning is not conducted with some sensitivity and understanding with respect to all this, the child is apt to be left not only with a feeling of loss but also with unexpressed infantile desires which may be repressed by the conscious mind to become a future source of unconscious conflict or anxiety.

Much the same applies, according to Freud, to the subsequent anal and genital stages in the development of the child. The anal stage is essentially that at which the process of toilet training occurs and at which allegedly the source of quasi-erotic pleasure experienced as gratifying by small children involves elimination via the bowels or bladder. Again, in relation to this process and these pleasures, children have to come to terms with a reality in which toilet activities are circumscribed by various social rules which dictate their performance at certain specified times and places and the procedures by virtue of which children are acquainted with these constraints may, especially if harsh penalties attend rule-infraction, be experienced as traumatic.

At what Freud labels the genital stage matters are even more critical, however, for the child's appreciation at this time of sex differences and of his or her emerging sexual identity together with a natural curiosity about these matters often leads to certain immature expressions of sexual exploration and experimentation which may bring the whole weight of the masturbation prohibition and associated parental disapproval crashing down on the child. It is precisely at this stage, for example, that many children acquire the common mental association of any form of sexual interest or activity with what is to be regarded as dirty, shameful or unclean – an association which may persist into later life in the form of quite serious personal and sexual maladjustment.

It is also close to this time, in the view of Freudians, that a crisis occurs in the psychic life of the child which outweighs all the others in its potential for deep personal trauma. Freud construed the classical Greek myth of Oedipus as a symbolic or allegorical representation of what he took to be a universal theme in the story of the personal and sexual development of individuals – at any rate, of male individuals (though the classical myth of Electra was supposed by Freud to map a corresponding theme with respect to female sexual development). He held that a concomitant of the male child's discovery of his sexual identity at the genital stage is a certain intense focus of love and affection on the mother as a source and object of erotic desire and a corresponding concentration of hostility and resentment towards the father as an obvious rival for the mother's attention.

In short, like Oedipus, all little boys fall in love with their mothers and incline (whether or not they know it) to the destruction of their fathers (likewise all little girls fall for their fathers and want to get rid of their mothers). Freud believed that the outcome of this conflict or the quality of its resolution is crucial to subsequent adult development and the future of an individual's mental health. A relatively successful resolution of this conflict or crisis on the part of a male child consists in the internalisation of the resentment generated towards the father (in this case, on the Freudian account, for fear of punishment by the father in the specific form of castration) and the creation out of this process of a moral conscience or super-ego which embodies precisely all of the values of paternal authority (including presumably the incest-prohibition). With the successful formation of the moral conscience in the form of the super-ego the male child is now prepared, having endorsed the incest taboo, for a stage at which the erotic desire he once felt for the mother can be transferred in due course to another more appropriate female.

This final adjustment, however, awaits the negotiation by the young person of the so-called phallic stage of puberty which occurs during adolescence; the phallic stage represents the last crucial hurdle before the child makes the full transition to adult life and, with good fortune, the establishment of a mature and loving sexual relationship with another appropriate person. A failure to negotiate any one of these stages satisfactorily, however – particularly the Oedipal crisis – may well occasion the kind of traumas which result in the repression of unfulfilled longings for various kinds of infantile satisfaction which may persist into later life. Moreover, as the repression of unsatisfied longings or desires into the unconscious life of the individual is ever a very precarious and uncertain way of dealing with frustrated instincts and impulses, the risk of those suppressed states of unfulfilment breaking out in adult life in the form of neurotic or hysterical symptoms is quite considerable.

The theory of infantile sexuality is employed by Freud as a basis for speculation about the psycho-genetic origins of a wide range of commonplace and not especially neurotic traits of human personality and character. Since each one of us has been required to run the gamut of crises just identified with variable success, we will all exhibit to some degree the characteristic expressions of oral fixation (a passion for smoking cigarettes or sucking mints) or anal retention (a disposition towards over-fastidiousness or hoarding things) and so on – though we should not on that account be considered psychologically 'ill'. Of course, Freud is most interested in those whose failure to negotiate the crises he has identified has been so drastic or pronounced as to issue in the range of behavioural disorders we are accustomed to associate with neurosis or mental illness.

It is also reasonably clear that for Freud such psychiatric disorder is held to be represented, among other conditions, by a range of particularly sexual deviations or perversions included in which are homosexualty, paedophilia, bestiality and a wide variety of fetishist obsessions. Nowadays, of course, there would be strong resistance from some quarters to the idea that homosexuality is a perversion, let alone a form of psychiatric illness, but since Freud's view is certainly that it is the former, it seems likely that he also regarded it as a case of the latter. His basic position, then, is that the sexual perversions clearly represent individual failures to have adjusted properly to the frustration of those predominantly erotic forms of childhood desire which he identifies in his theory of infantile sexuality.

What is generally characteristic of infantile expressions of sexuality is that they are egocentric and auto-erotic and what is precisely characteristic of the various crises which the child confronts at each of the different stages of auto-erotic sexuality is a demand that he give due recognition to a public domain of social and moral principles, obligations and expectations which lies beyond his privately experienced world of personal self-satisfaction; thus if the child is to mature as a person fit for full engagement in social life he has to acquire some respect for the public world of interpersonal values, to come to terms with those with whom he shares that world and to develop some capacity for responsible adult love in that world. This is what the neurotic has typically failed to do; he has clung instead to basically infantile forms of auto-erotic pleasure like a child clinging to an old teddy bear and if his infantilism does not express itself in deviant sexual behaviour (the unproductive and sterile sexual cul-de-sac of homosexual or fetishist activity for example) it may well be exhibited in some form of neurotic or psychiatric illness.

Thus for example Freud recognises in his important *Essays on Love* a curious but widespread form of sexual maladjustment in men which he attributes to a failure to negotiate the Oedipal crisis satisfactorily; that of men who cannot give appropriate sexual expression to those with whom they have fallen romantically in love and who cannot love those with whom they are able to express themselves sexually. According to Freud, this is just because for some men real love always means something very like the early love of the child for the mother in relation to whom sexual relations were forbidden by the incest taboo; in that case, however, any object of sexual desire cannot also be the object of the original true love but only some form of infinitely inferior substitute.

Here, of course, it is necessary to consider Freud's ideas only to the extent that they have influenced certain rather peculiar views about education in general and moral education in particular associated with those modern progressive educators we mentioned earlier. Perhaps the most powerful and direct influence of Freud himself on progressive education during this century was on the thought and practice of that colourful and charismatic figure Homer Lane whose work with juvenile delinquents in Britain and the USA in the early years of the century was to have such a profound influence on the shape and direction of experimental schooling beyond the conventional state system. Those who have written about Lane[6] are usually anxious to point out that he was foremost a practitioner in the field of education rather more than a theorist, but the surviving fragments of Lane's writings collected under the title *Talks to Parents and Teachers*[7] present a remarkably coherent perspective on education which is both insightful and profound (as well as sadly neglected); in fact, they represent an interesting and fruitful union of practical commitment and experience with considered theoretical reflection and speculation.

We must be brief concerning Lane's practical educational work but one or two events of significance in his life which shaped his general outlook should be noted. He began his educational career as a fairly conventional teacher of woodwork in New England but it was not long before he became interested in the education or reclamation of difficult and delinquent children – what would nowadays be called 'young offenders'. His early work amongst such youngsters around the area of Detroit soon convinced him that a punitive approach to the treatment of problems of delinquent and anti-social behaviour with such as those for whom he was working was largely futile and self-defeating.

What precisely he perceived in juvenile delinquents was a kind of dismal personal and social alienation which appeared to be based mainly on a lack of self-esteem; in fact, children who sought for self-assertion, identity and power in the activities of the gang did so only because they experienced a deep sense of inadequacy and worthlessness as individuals. Such familiar authority figures as parents, teachers and policemen were perceived by these children merely as negative sources of hostility and repression which required to be responded to at every opportunity with appropriate gestures of resentment and rebellion. Lane came to recognise, however, that the essentially resentful and nihilistic attitudes that had been built up in these children could hardly be contained, let alone cured by further punitive measures. What seemed to be required instead was some method by which their deep suspicion and hatred of authority might be eliminated or at least eroded and which might build up self-esteem and get rid of the sense of personal inadequacy of these youngsters.

The fundamental idea which was to inform Lane's various responses to this problem centred around the importance of self-government. Difficult and delinquent children failed to respond in anything other than a defiant or compliant way to the demands of external authority; moreover, they were unable to perceive the discipline which that authority attempted to impose on them as anything other than an expression of rejection and hostility and so Lane had to find a way of introducing into their lives a self-discipline and self-determination which was free from such negative associations. In the first place he embarked upon a policy of diminishing the containment aspect of reformatory life and eroding the custodial role of those in charge of the young inmates so as to increase as far as possible the degree of freedom and responsibility the detainees had for the running of their own lives.

As far as possible the young inmates of detention centres were to be required to prescribe and abide by their own rules of conduct with the minimum of adult interference and independently of the influence of anyone who might be perceived as a representative of external authority. This was the method that Lane tried first in the so-called Ford Republic in Detroit and later elaborated in the Little Commonwealth in Dorset – an experiment which can be fairly regarded as a blueprint for the work of A. S. Neill in his rather better known progressive school Summerhill.[8]

In the course of instilling self-government in anti-social, delinquent and often violent young people, Lane had to discover some way of undermining precisely those negative and destructive attitudes towards society at large which lay at the root of their aggressive and hostile tendencies; he required a way of destroying the strong association in the minds of these children of authority with what is to be rejected or resented. He saw that, given their general conception of authority, any further punitive measures on his part in response to their rebelliousness would serve to do little other than confirm that conception on the part of the delinquents, merely reinforcing their view of authority as a negative force. Thus Lane, anticipating some of Neill's later tactics at Summerhill, often employed some rather unorthodox strategies in order to undermine or defuse tendencies to disruptive and anti-social behaviour.

Thus, when a gang of particularly disruptive children tried by means of various kinds of mayhem to turn the Little Commonwealth into a free-for-all, Lane refused to react by punishing them and instead joined them in their lawless behaviour thereby soon, as he put it, 'spoiling the fun'. Denied an external authority towards which they could direct their hostility and resentment, the children's rebellion quickly lost its point and Lane was able to turn the collective energy of the group to the more constructive task of self-government. A. S. Neill's later unorthodox practices at Summerhill of rewarding children for lying or stealing were inspired by and based on fundamentally the same intuitions about deviant human behaviour as Lane's apparently paradoxical methods of treatment in the Little Commonwealth.

Far from being expressions of mere eccentricity or perversity the irregular methods of Lane and Neill were founded on a good deal of close observation of human psychology and behaviour; it seems clear that both these educationalists were quite shrewd as well as sympathetic observers of others and that both of them were possessed of a quite uncanny and most uncommon instinct for judging the right thing to do in any circumstances of personal or emotional confrontation. It is clear that Lane deeply understood delinquent children and that he had a remarkable capacity for seeing beyond unprepossessing appearances or exteriors into the depths of seriously unhappy and tormented young hearts. He saw that the lack of self-respect or esteem on the part of such youngsters was all too often simply the result of the psychological and physical abuse they had suffered at the hands of others; mostly they were more sinned against than sinning.

Thus the trick of 'spoiling the fun' by removing from their lives the oppressive image of external authority was part and parcel of what he also called 'the breaking of constellations' – the deep association of ideas that held problem children in the thrall of instinctual negative reaction to whatever they perceived as an expression of repressive authority. In fact, Lane's 'constellations' – the association in some children's minds of the idea of authority with those of abuse and rejection – were clearly of a very similar nature to the association of sex with sin which occurs, according to the account given by Freud, as a result of certain kinds of prohibition and repression during some processes of the early socialisation of the child.

Lane's eventual discovery of Freud provided him with an

authoritative source of theoretical reflections or speculations which appeared precisely to support and confirm his own views as these had emerged and been tested in the fires of practical experience. Freud's attempted explanations of and observations concerning the origins of certain psychiatric disorders – neurosis, hysteria, obsession, sexual deviation and so on – also seemed to be applicable with some slight adjustment to the kinds of attitudinal and behavioural disorders in which Lane was interested. Thus the key notion which links the theoretical work of Freud with the practice of Lane and other progressives is that of *repression* viewed as the psychological mechanism which is responsible for the production of certain negative mental states and dispositions.

What we discover in the few fragments of Lane's writings which are available to us is a sketch of an extremely insightful theory of child development accompanied by a body of advice to parents, teachers and other child handlers about how that child development should be wisely managed, which seems unmistakably to be derived from and inspired by Freud's theory of infantile sexuality. To be sure, Lane's critical periods of child development do not exactly or chronologically match those of Freud and he is interested in a rather broader range of aspects of development than feature in the theory of infantile sexuality, but otherwise the comparison seems unavoidable.

Like Freud, Lane believes that his stages mark qualitatively different critical periods of adjustment to the demands of reality which need to be negotiated with great care if the child is not to suffer serious psychological damage resulting in later behavioural problems; moreover, his critical periods also resemble Freud's in being categorised by reference to different objects of childish preoccupation. Lane's stages are as follows:

i   Infancy (from birth until about three years of age); a stage characterised essentially in terms of the child's earliest efforts to gain some psychomotor mastery or control over its immediate environment and also by a certain preoccupation with largely sensual sources of pleasure and gratification.

ii The Age of Imagination (from two or three years of age until about seven); during this stage the world of the child consists in a largely personal and individual exploration of fantasy and imagination in terms of which he attempts to cope with and compensate for his feelings of insignificance and powerlessness in relation to others, especially adults.

iii The Age of Self-Assertion (from about the age of seven until about eleven); Lane calls this stage 'the period of greatest activity, mental and physical, in human life'.[9] It is characterised by the beginnings of a true development of the social instinct, but even more by a great need on the part of the child to express his independence of parents and other 'authorities' which is often manifested in the form of much apparent rebellion, 'naughtiness' and wilful disobedience.

iv The Age of Loyalty (first, a stage of transition from about eleven to fourteen; then the stage of adolescence until about seventeen). In the early transitional part of this phase the child requires to free himself finally from the immature interests and preoccupations of the earlier stages so that a 'synthesis' and redirection of earlier energies and instincts may be achieved for pursuit of the higher goals of adolescence and beyond. By the end of adolescence the individual should have formed some developed capacity for responsible social interaction and co-operation with other people.

With respect to the treatment of children at each of these stages, however, Lane counsels extreme caution. Thus in his essay on infancy Lane devotes much space to emphasising that there is nothing more frustrating and discouraging to the baby during its first attempts to master and control its immediate environment than the mother who persists in interfering with what she regards as help, attention and assistance leaving the child with nothing to do for itself, no challenges to overcome and no way to test its own will or exercise its powers of agency. Again, in his chapter on the age of imagination, Lane advises against the dangers of construing the childs fantasies as deliberate lies and of responding to them with inappropriate censure or punishment; but he also warns against too much encouragement and indulgence of the child's fantasy life which can fixate him in an unreal world of infantile make-believe.

In relation to the even more crucial age of assertion he observes that although it is undoubtedly dangerous to attempt by means of heavy-handed discipline to break the child's spirit in response to his naughtiness or disobedience, it is no less dangerous to let him have all his own way because a child definitely requires a secure framework of sensible and reliable authority and order as a context for his efforts towards rational independence and self-sufficiency. Lane, then, holds that there are, corresponding to each critical stage of child-development, two respects in which parents and teachers can go wrong in responding to the child's needs:

> Two rules of good conduct for parents may here be set down: first, always discover a new interest for the child's activity before making any attempt to correct a fault through which his activity is finding outlet; second, remember that if it is harmful to say 'Don't', it is no less harmful to do too much for the child, and to take all initiative from him in his play or in his dressing or in all the other activities of the day.[10]

In cautioning against establishing in the child a state of impotent dependence upon the parents from whose authority he must eventually emancipate himself if he is to mature into a self-reliant adult capable of entering into satisfactory and fulfilling relationships beyond the family, it seems that Lane's view is influenced again by Freud. For like Freud he sees such independence as threatened not only by hostile repression but also by the indulgent, over-possessive and spoiling parent who cannot let the child alone and who seeks to secure and perpetuate his bondage by fostering dependence – doing everything for him and granting all he asks. Just as much harm may be done by never saying 'no' as by always saying 'no':

> With too much dependence on mother goes an equal degree of irritability against mother; this will later be repressed into the unconscious mind, but it will be a dominant motive of adult life. It is a constant problem with a baby how much to coddle it, how much to help it to be independent. The great principle is to make the wrong thing very easy for the child to do and the right thing difficult, as it is the fighting against difficulties which charms the child.[11]

According to Lane, the emergence of self-determination is possible only given genuine opportunities for the child to exercise its own will in solving problems and overcoming difficulties. The child requires to learn to stand on its own two feet, but this will happen only if it has genuine occasions for discovery and experiment in which there is a real risk of failure as well as opportunity for success, for if it is to learn to do what is right, correct or effective it also needs room to make mistakes. The freedom presupposed to self-determination is precisely threatened, however, by *two* sorts of restriction on the child's activities; by excessive censure and prohibition which deprive the child of the inclination to act by discouraging him and undermining his confidence, but also by excessive interference and intrusion in the child's affairs in the form of too much attention or indulgence.

It is not just prohibition and discouragement, then, that threaten to curb the natural development of self-determination, but also spoiling and indulgence, and for *the same reasons*; that both spoiling *and* prohibition frustrate the child, leaving him with nothing to do and no room for the exercise of genuine decision and action. Repressive prohibition and spoiling are alike in that they both conduce to the inhibition of positive freedom on the part of an individual. Thus Lane generalises certain points of Freudian theory; he extends application of the concepts of repression and so forth beyond the restricted sphere of sexual life and intimate personal relations, in the interests of understanding a rather wider range of problems of human life and conduct. It is beyond reasonable doubt, moreover, that Lane's application of concepts of repression to the analysis of the problem child had a crucial influence on the theory and practice of A. S. Neill, probably the most famous of all progressive educationalists of our time. Lane's influence is apparent, for example, in Neill's well known observation about freedom and license:

> It is this distinction between freedom and license that many parents cannot grasp. In the disciplined home, the children have *no* rights. In the spoiled home they have *all* the rights. The proper home is one in which children and adults have equal rights. And the same applies to school.[12]

In brief, three general theses about the nature of education and human conduct can be distilled from that well-known selection of Neill's writings which were published under the title *Summerhill*:[13]

i   The difficult child is the child who is unhappy. Tendencies to anti-social and self-destructive behaviour have their origins in deep psychological disturbances and conflicts.

ii   The psychological conflicts in question are susceptible of something like a psychoanalytic interpretation and are largely if not exclusively caused by unnecessary repression of the child; by unwarranted prohibition and censure particularly in matters of the expression of sexual instincts and interests.

iii   The psychological conflicts and hence the resultant anti-social expressions can be eliminated or to a considerable extent remedied by the removal of prohibitions in an atmosphere of love, understanding and freedom.

Thus Neill also largely follows Lane in his view of the cure as well as the diagnosis of the problems of the problem child, though there is much more of an attempt in his later work to free himself from the very heavy emphasis on Freud and psychoanalytic theory in general which is so self-consciously present in the writings of Lane. But both Lane and Neill believed that the general form of the answer to any question about why so much hate, resentment and hostility appear to enter into the attitudes of many young people as they approach adulthood is that they did not experience the right quantity or quality of love and support in their early years. Both held that this lack of love could be experienced by children in at least two forms – either as overt repression, neglect or abuse or as spoiling or indulgence which can be construed as just another form of neglect or abuse. As Neill says:

> Parents who overdo the giving of presents are often those who do not love their children enough. Such parents have to compensate by making a show of parental love, by showering expensive presents on their children much the same as a man who has been unfaithful to his wife will lavishly buy her a fur coat he can't afford.[14]

For Lane and Neill, then, the solution to the problems of problem children consists in extending to them love, trust and under-standing – in showing them that one is 'on their side'. The love required for this task should not be construed as a matter of mere sentimentality or weakness, however, since it requires very great very great self-sacrifice, determination and patience on the part of the educator and Homer Lane was eventually to be destroyed by the effort and risk that is the cost of completely expressing such love.[15]

The precise method through which both Lane and Neill attempted to 'cure' problem children involved the promotion of responsible freedom on the part of the child – the exercise of self-determination via self-government in the Little Common-wealth and Summerhill – a new kind of education which attempted to avoid the dangerous and destructive extremes of force and repression on the one hand and spoiling and license on the other. Inevitably some critics have judged both experiments to be no more than disastrous and chaotic failures (though Summerhill is still with us as a going concern) but equally others have been impressed by the work of both Lane and Neill and with the extent to which they do appear to have had considerable success in mending broken young lives.

Indeed, in the present context we should be wise to heed the most important general moral lesson which progressive educationalists like Lane and Neill have to teach us – that it is possible to identify a range of life-distorting influences in relation to the experience of children which do not fail in a significant minority of cases to have a warping effect on adult moral and social development. If we are honestly concerned with arriving at a true understanding of the nature of moral virtue, then, we cannot deny the fact that vice begets vice and that children who are unwanted, unloved, neglected and abused (or alternatively smothered with possessive attention to the point of what we call spoiling) will inevitably have had their potential for the development of more positive moral dispositions seriously jeopardised. Since they are also thereby unlikely to have acquired any propensity or inclination to treat their own children any better than they were themselves treated, the vicious circle of lovelessness and moral distortion is thus perpetuated.

The psychoanalytically influenced work of Lane and Neill is of considerable interest in drawing our attention to a range of circumstances or conditions which undoubtedly can contribute causally to the inhibition of moral development, especially in relation to the emergence of certain altruistic or other-regarding attitudes; it goes a considerable way towards explaining something of the origins of vicious, spiteful and anti-social behaviour. In this connection it is interesting to discover that Neill identifies one agency of negative repression in the form of much traditional or conventional moral, social and religious instruction; conventional moral education was a frequent target for Neill since he clearly felt that much conscious or unconscious parental resentment and irritation towards children was often expressed in and hidden behind moral prohibitions.

I have deliberately set out in this chapter to offer as charitable an account as possible of the contribution of Freud, Lane and Neill to our understanding of the development of moral life – especially since more negative views may be easily enough found elsewhere.[16] It is crucial to conclude this section by emphasising, however, that although Freud, Lane and Neill may be understood as having much to tell us about the way in which moral development is inhibited or impeded, they have relatively little to tell us about the circumstances in which moral virtue actually flourishes. It may be necessary for the emergence of certain altruistic or other-regarding sentiments that a child's early experiences are not wholly warped or distorted by certain forms of repression, abuse or neglect, but mere freedom from such conditions alone does not necessarily culminate in the altruistic dispositions in question; likewise parental love may assist the growth of virtue but it does not suffice for it.

As all the philosophers we have so far considered agree, moral virtue crucially involves *freedom* and that freedom either for good or ill cannot be logically accounted for in causal terms. As Socrates and Plato recognised all those years ago, whereas some individuals have survived the most brutal and vicious environments to become good men, others have turned out badly following the greatest possible advantages. To be sure, if we wish to do all in our power to assist children to grow up capable of worthwhile and decent lives involving warm and positive relationships with others, we must try to ensure that their earliest experiences are supportive and loving, but we must also beware of being seduced by psychoanalytical views or by any other form of psychological theory into believing that human environments and circumstances might be arranged in such a way that we might be able to exert a *causal* influence for good or ill on the shape of human conduct. Bearing in mind this point we may now proceed to the next chapter.

7

COGNITIVE GROWTH AND MORAL DEVELOPMENT: PIAGET AND KOHLBERG

The status of psychoanalytic theory in scientific terms is notoriously problematic, for since its findings in particular cases appear to depend rather heavily on the interpretations and judgements of individual psychoanalysts they do not seem to be readily susceptible of empirical confirmation. All the same, of course, it is quite reasonable to value psychoanalysis as a profound source of psychological insights whilst rejecting the idea that it does have the character and status of an empirical science; we have merely to recognise that there are many important forms of human wisdom and enquiry, expressed, for example, in religion, poetry and fictional literature, which are great sources of moral and psychological insight though they cannot on any account be considered sciences. In fact, the truth may well be that the standard procedures of natural scientific enquiry are not the most promising or fruitful for yielding psychological understanding and insight.

Still, those kinds of psychology which have had the greatest influence during this century on the academic study and the conventional institutionalised practice of education have been those which have aspired to precisely the standards of scientific precision and objectivity to which the natural physical sciences are often supposed also to aspire. In general, I suspect that the greatest academic impact on the theory and practice of education during the present century has come from that tradition of empirical psychology known as 'learning theory' or alternatively as 'behaviourism' and which is associated with a host of famous names in psychology beginning with Pavlov and proceeding via Watson, Thorndyke, Hull and Guthrie to Skinner and beyond.[1]

Behaviourism or learning theory was itself an 'objectivist'

reaction to certain nineteenth century 'subjectivist' forms of psychology which relied methodologically on the 'introspection' or 'inner' cognition of the subject's private experiences as a basis for public reports on the nature of such experiences. To many interested in psychology this procedure appeared to be quite hopelessly unscientific since it clearly left no room for the independent confirmation (or disconfirmation) of any of the results of such introspective experiments. More seriously, it occurred to many scientifically inclined students of psychology that the method of introspection rested anyway on a simple conceptual mistake (of a Cartesian kind) about the nature of the human mind.

In the manner of Aristotle rather than Plato, then, the learning theorists were to insist that the human mind is not adequately understood as a private sphere of largely 'inner' ideas, but is rather better construed as a repertoire of dispositions to various forms of overt conduct. Thus to acquire or possess knowledge or understanding of a thing is not to form or acquire some mental image of it, rather it is to learn to *do* certain sorts of things. Precisely what is characterised by such terms of our ordinary psychological or 'mentalistic' vocabulary as 'intelligent', 'voluntary', 'thoughtful', 'deliberate', 'spiteful', 'insightful', 'jealous' and so on is just *behaviour* and thus the study of the mind is just the study of behaviour.

It is clear enough, of course, why this strong emphasis on the publicly observable aspects of knowledge acquisition attracted the immediate attention of educationalists with their primary interest in questions about how individuals learn and how best teachers might assist them to learn. Psychological behaviourism, then, had a considerable influence on those American philosophers of the pragmatic school who were interested in education – notably John Dewey and his followers – and a powerful behaviourist influence on American philosophy has persisted to this day.[2] The learning theorists naturalistic view of knowledge acquisition as the growth of individual repertoires of behaviour was perfectly consistent with Dewey's own philosophical psychology which construed knowledge as an essentially active and pragmatic matter and W. H. Kilpatrick's 'ways of behaving' were equally easily adaptable to the construction of a new topic or enquiry centred conception of the school curriculum.[3]

Unfortunately, however, this approach to understanding knowledge and learning as the acquisition of behavioural dispositions rested largely, among psychologists themselves, on a very narrow conception of the nature of behaviour. This is nowhere clearer than at the birth of behaviourism where Pavlov is interested in hardly more than the ways in which the biological mechanisms which control some of the automatic reflexive responses of animals (for example, the salivation of dogs) might be modified or manipulated through the introduction of artificial stimuli (for example, salivation in response to the conditioned stimulus of the sound of a bell). To be sure, in subsequent learning theory this limited conception of behaviour is rather less conspicuous since such theorists as Thorndyke and Skinner do build the conditioning process upon the less mechanical and more voluntary responses of animals;[4] through instrumental and operant conditioning they have shaped the behavioural responses of creatures by exploiting their natural unconditioned motives towards such reinforcers as food, liberty and so on. It cannot be denied, then, that there is a significant degree of voluntariness behind the animal learning in the experiments of later behaviourists that there was not in the case of Pavlov's dogs.

Nevertheless, these differences between the earlier form of classical mechanical conditioning and the later forms of instrumental and operant conditioning are philosophically far less significant than the similarities and continuities. What we meet in the work of mainstream theorists of the behaviourist tradition of empirical psychology of this century is an *associationist* view of learning and knowledge acquisition which, whatever its relevance to non-human animals, does not seem to promise a satisfactory account of how knowledge acquisition occurs in the case of rational human agents. In fact, modern behaviourism has a direct ancestry in the British empiricism of the Enlightenment which we have already briefly described.

As we have seen, David Hume thought that our knowledge of the world was constructed precisely by means of the psychological association of atomistically conceived elements of experience called 'impressions'; our idea of causation was to be understood primarily in terms of the acquisition by human beings of a habit or disposition to expect that what we had connected in the past – the sight of fire and the feeling of heat, for example – could be expected in the future. The behaviourist view of learning of modern times is predicated on essentially the same assumption – on the idea of an habitual association of stimulus and response; if what an animal does on some particular occasion leads to a reward or a pleasurable experience it will repeat the behaviour in the expectancy of some further reward or reinforcement.

Now Kant criticised the epistemological programme of the empiricists as essentially incoherent; far from it being the case that we form the idea of causation from the habitual linking of elements of experience, the idea of causation is presupposed to any such intelligible linking – nothing could count as intelligible or meaningful experience apart from the idea of causation. A roughly related criticism can be made of modern learning theory. According to behaviourist learning theorists, learning is a matter of the habitual association of responses (construed as items of behaviour) with environmental stimuli, so that our conduct comes to exhibit certain regularities conducive rather than otherwise to human survival. This association is held to be of a primarily 'natural', biological or mechanical character such that some eminent modern behaviourists, Skinner for example, have denied we have any need for a special 'mentalistic' terminology of thoughts, judgements, intentions and so on to characterise human learning;[5] learning is just the natural or manipulated modification of behaviour in response to environmental circumstances and pressures.

But to what extent is it correct to describe such behaviour modification as learning in the way this term is largely understood in human educational contexts? To be sure, it would be a mistake to deny that human agents often conduct their affairs according to something like the processes of habituation which the learning theorists describe – if we all had to reflect consciously on everything that we do instead of relying on habit, custom, reflex and other forms of more or less automatic behaviour, few of us would get through a normal day. But this fact should not be allowed to obscure for us the point that even what we do unreflectively and habitually has *sense* for us in the context of the narrative in terms of which we characterise our lives – a narrative we *understand* or at least seek to understand in terms of various norms, principles and values which have distinct significance for us.

What the account of learning canvassed by the behaviourists precisely lacks is any theory of *meaning* or of what it is to acquire an *understanding* of anything whatsoever. It is clear enough that we can employ behaviourist methods – techniques of conditioning – to equip children with 'correct' repertoires of behaviour in relation to many familiar modes of human activity and conduct. In the learning of an ethnic or folk dance, for example, we could employ a schedule of reinforcement which might be successful in conditioning children in the effective performance of the appropriate steps and gestures of the dance. It is also clear, however, that this can be achieved in the absence of anything that might be reasonably well described as having taught the children ethnic dance, for this requires that we should also have communicated something of the human value, meaning or significance of the dance to them.[6]

To the very considerable extent to which education is crucially concerned with the promotion of understanding, with assisting children to invest what they do with some meaning, purpose or significance, it is not at all clear that any part of the entire tradition of behaviourist learning theory has much of a contribution to make to explaining how this occurs; it is not at all clear what bearing the learning theorist's notion of a 'behavioural response' has on the question of the educational initiation of children into meaningful human enterprises or worthwhile forms of life. Since education is concerned with the understanding of human practices and conduct, it concerns the promotion of rational thought and agency, of behaviour which is both *interpreted* and directed towards some particular goal or purpose. Learning theory, on the other hand, appears to be a science of *uninterpreted* behaviour, of human movement construed as little more than a sequence of physical events.

Now since this is clearly in general the case of learning and behaviour as these are understood by the behaviourists, it is also going to be the case in particular of moral learning and moral conduct.[7] On the behaviourist account moral learning can amount to little more than the habituation of children to certain prespecified patterns of conduct regardless of how the agent in question feels about them. Thus the criteria whereby we might judge into what patterns children ought to be conditioned could only be based on considerations about what we as the behaviour shapers wanted or what was generally considered acceptable in a given social context.

But at best this construes moral behaviour as no more than a matter of blind conformity to a given set of social conventions and at worst the entire business of securing the conformity of children in this way could be regarded a little more than a matter of pure indoctrination. If virtuous or moral conduct is to be understood as all the great moral philosophers have tried to understand it, as conduct deliberately and freely chosen in the light of practical reason, behaviour for which an agent might be reasonably praised, blamed or otherwise held responsible, clearly no coherent conception of the nature of moral life and conduct is available within the terms of the behaviourist account.

In the light of these considerations, it should hardly occasion much surprise that the main reaction within modern empirical psychology to the behaviourism of the learning theorists has come from the direction of psychologists conspicuously influenced by Kant who have also wanted to say a great deal about the nature of moral learning and understanding. In general, then, the psychologists of the so-called 'cognitive' school (to some extent also the beneficiaries of psychological insights discovered by the earlier school of 'Gestalt' psychologists[8]) are concerned initially to question the associationist basis of the behaviourist account of learning and then to provide some positive account of their own of the nature and growth of understanding, particularly of the way in which rational human agents come to order the elements of their experience and formulate rules and principles.

One of the best known and most influential of all the cognitive psychologists is of course Jean Piaget, whose pioneering work has had a significant impact on the thought and practice of educationalists in relation to the problem of the nature of the growth of understanding in general. It is to Piaget's account of the growth and development of *moral* understanding, however, that we must turn our all too brief attention now.

Piaget will be remembered primarily by those who have some acquaintance with educational theory for the idea that knowledge and understanding in any given field of human enquiry or endeavour is something which increases or develops not just quantitatively but *qualitatively*. The predominantly empirical–

associationist account of learning offered by the behaviourists makes it appear that the growth of knowledge is merely an incremental or accumulative process – largely a matter of the enlargement of a repertoire of responses to stimuli. For Piaget, on the other hand, the growth of knowledge and understanding concerns qualitative changes in the way we come to structure and interpret empirical experience, and his work represents an impressive systematic attempt to chart the various developmental stages of such understanding from childhood to maturity.

Like Kant, then, Piaget believes that the business of understanding understanding is a matter of identifying and describing the various general principles, rules and categorial judgements in terms of which human beings make sense of their experience, and like Rousseau he thinks that this is a process of development from a childhood which has its own ways of seeing, thinking and feeling. Piaget's more particular views about the nature of moral growth and development require to be understood in the light of these assumptions of his about the growth of knowledge and understanding in general.

Enshrined in Piaget's general account of the development of knowledge and understanding is the idea of a progression from relatively subjective and perception-based forms of understanding towards ways of thinking and perspectives on experience which are more objective, principled and abstract. Unsurprisingly therefore, his account of the development of moral reasoning and judgement charts a somewhat analogous progress from the subjective, via the objective, to the abstract. Piaget's *The Moral Judgement of the Child* is concerned to investigate the child's conception of the nature of moral rules and moral motivation but he begins by examining children's conceptions of rules in general; he starts by inviting children to reflect on the nature of rules in a non-moral context – as they govern the conduct of the simple child's game of marbles.[9] Where do the rules of a game come from? What exactly invests them with authority?

Piaget discerned a marked difference between the responses of younger and older children to these questions. The younger children of the ages corresponding roughly to Piaget's developmental stages of intuitive and pre-operational thinking exhibited attitudes of largely unquestioning obedience and respect for the rules taking them to have absolutely binding authority and force. By contrast, the older children of ages corresponding to later stages of Piagetian development – concrete operations and beyond – regarded the rules as far less absolutely fixed and binding and more of a conventional or custom-made nature; for them the rules possessed no special mystical significance beyond their practical utility in relation to the smooth-running and efficient conduct of the game.

Likewise, in investigating the criteria employed by children during their formation of moral judgements and decisions, Piaget discovered that the element of deliberate intention in conduct to be assessed as virtuous or vicious weighed much more heavily with older children than with younger ones; for younger children the gravity of a misdeed was to be judged more in terms of the weight of consequences. Thus, whereas for younger children the accidental destruction of a whole set of crockery would constitute a more serious moral offence than the malicious destruction of a single piece, for older children the deliberate act of vandalism with respect to a single item was more culpable than the accidental large-scale destruction.

Yet again, the attitude of younger children to justice and punishment in general seemed to differ significantly from that evident among older ones. Young children inclined rather more towards a kind of retributivism in their attitudes to punishment as an appropriate response to breaches of justice; punishment was necessary to restore the balance in the moral order which a violation of justice had upset. For the older child, however, punishment appeared to have the rather more utilitarian function of deterring others from similar breaches of justice; but it was held to have no special value or importance in its own right.

From Piaget's investigations, it would appear that children's judgements about what is morally good or bad, right or wrong, just or unjust and so on do undergo some kind of transformation or evolution in the course of a reasonably normal child's development. The general inflexibility which informs the attitudes of the younger child towards rules, motives, justice and punishment Piaget generally refers to under the heading of *moral realism*. He takes it largely as a sign of moral immaturity that moral rules and principles are accorded an absolute and inviolable status and as indicative of moral progress that moral rules and principles come to be regarded as in some sense a matter of human convenience and thus open to some degree of adjustment or negotiation.

The general moral perspective of the older child is often characterised by Piaget as a morality of co-operation or reciprocity. In fact, as paradoxical as it may sound, the moral realism of the young child – his firm belief in the absolute objectivity of moral rules and principles – is held by Piaget to be a direct result of the child's subjectivity or egocentricity. The same inability to distinguish the subjectively experienced 'self' from what is objectively 'out there' in the world which affects the young child's judgements of physical conservation in his theoretical reasoning, coupled with the limitation of the child's social contacts to the sphere of parents and immediate family, makes it extremely difficult for him to recognise the possibility of any point of view, moral or otherwise, which might be significantly and radically different from the heteronomously given one which informs his own perspective.

It is precisely with the growth of a greater appreciation of objectivity which occurs as a result of developments in his theoretical reasoning, together with the opening up of the child's social world in terms of greater possibilities for exchanges of opinion and intellectual disagreements with others beyond the family, that a greater appreciation of other points of view and of how human practical affairs and moral conduct might be otherwise or more beneficially organised overtakes the child. For Piaget, then, the moral realism of the younger child itself evolves from a more inchoate or anomic state of infantile experience and activity in which no responses of a principled nature are to be discerned in the child's earliest behaviour.

Moreover, the occurrence of the period of moral co-operation and reciprocity is also for Piaget just a signpost on the road to the development of a still more adult condition of moral autonomy at which the individual will no longer merely subscribe or conform to ready-made moral principles and conventions but be capable of rational self-legislation in moral matters; thus the ghost of Kant's autonomous moral legislator stands over Piaget's *The Moral Judgement of the Child*. In short, complete progress in Piaget's account of the moral development of the individual is from an indiscriminate egocentricity to a rational, independent and flexible attitude to moral issues which is rooted in a respect of the moral law and driven by an altruistic concern for the good of others.

But, of course, it is possible to raise many questions and objections to this general story of Piaget's. In the first place, for example, what appears to be masquerading as objective empirical research of a hard scientific character into the evolution of children's moral judgements is clearly of a highly interpretative and value-laden nature; Piaget's account is loaded with assumptions of a generally philosophical kind about what constitutes an advance or progress towards a state of maturity in moral thinking and some of these assumptions are highly questionable. It is possible, for instance, to question whether moral realism viewed as the belief in the absolute objectivity of moral rules and principles is, as Piaget sees it, a primitive stage of moral evolution, since very many of the greatest moral philosophers have counted it as a moral advance on a contractual or reciprocal view of moral principles to regard them as having a universal nature or absolute force. (Clearly Kant, who is principally Piaget's inspiration in all of this, would have been among such philosophers.)

But one can also question whether moral realism as Piaget conceives it should be reasonably regarded as a stage in the evolution of moral thought at all, since no genuinely *moral* perspective would seem to be possible under the conditions of subjectivity or egocentricity which Piaget seems to associate with moral realism. Indeed, in his own work on moral education Durkheim makes the striking observation that it is not strictly correct to describe the attitude of a small child who is incapable of even acknowledging the rights and claims of others as 'egocentric' or self-centred just because there is precisely no condition under which he might be appropriately described as anything else.

Since as applied to the small child, then, the term 'egocentric' fails to mark any meaningful contrast with 'altruistic' or 'unselfish', it is obviously being used by Piaget in a sense quite other than that which it normally has in ordinary contexts of moral discourse. Above all, however, Piaget's account appears to be committed to a particular moral–philosophical position the general outline of which becomes clearer as we turn to the elaboration of it to be found in the work of Lawrence Kohlberg;

we may thus postpone further criticisms until after we have considered the general form of Kohlberg's theory.

Although it is only fair to remark that Kohlberg's theory of moral development does differ in a number of crucial details from Piaget's, it is also no great distortion to view his account as basically just an elaboration of Piaget's conception of moral judgement and reasoning as processes which gradually evolve through various stages from childhood to maturity. In fact Kohlberg adopted a roughly similar methodology to Piaget in the course of his empirical enquiries[10] – he asked children what should be done in certain circumstances of moral dilemma in order to try to identify qualitative differences between the sorts of reasons given by children of different ages for one decision or another.

The most widely known of the problems posed to children was that of the man whose wife was dying of cancer and who could not afford to buy the drug that would save her life or alleviate her suffering; the children were asked whether it would be morally right in these circumstances for the husband or some family friend to steal the drug from the person who had discovered and manufactured it. In another example children were asked whether it was right for people to help runaway slaves in the American Civil War when slaves were regarded as the legal property of their masters.

By analysing the various responses of children to these questions, Kohlberg claims to have identified six main stages of moral development organised into three principal levels or categories of moral thought or judgement. At the first level of moral thought the child's judgements exhibit the tendencies towards moral realism already observed by Piaget; moral values are invested with an objective status and they are treated by the child as something entirely external to him to which he can only respond with total reverence and compliance.

The child's moral reasoning at this level moves through two main stages. At the first stage – called by Kohlberg the stage of obedience and punishment orientation – the child's responses are expressed essentially in a desire not to rock the moral and social boat, to avoid punishment and to keep out of trouble at all costs. From this first stage, however, the child moves to the second at which he will seek to do what is generally presented to him as right or acceptable, in the hope more of securing praise and rewards than of avoiding punishments. Kohlberg terms this stage that of naive egoistic orientation – the child's behaviour is motivated by little more than a hedonistic drive towards self-satisfaction.

The second level of moral judgement to which children should naturally proceed after the first two stages once again corresponds reasonably well with Piaget's stage of co-operation and reciprocity. At this level children are great respectors of accepted convention because conventions, customs and traditional ways of doing things are held to represent and enshrine good form and good order. During the first stage of this level, then, children are orientated less to pleasurable rewards and more to the approval of other people; the motive or intention for which a given action is done is also more important to the child so the very idea of seeking to please assumes greater moral significance. Kohlberg calls this the stage of good-boy orientation.

From here, however, the child should proceed to what Kohlberg terms the authority and social order maintaining orientation at which the ideas of respect for authority and doing one's duty for its own sake assume moral significance. Generally at this second level it appears that the child has advanced to some understanding of the way in which moral rules contribute to social co-operation and social cohesion but to a large extent he is still a conventional conformist in his attitudes to moral rules and social duties and he remains inclined to a largely unquestioning obedience.

This largely conformist attitude to moral and social roles is held to undergo a transition at level three at which the child acquires a deeper appreciation – also noted by Piaget in his enquiries into the moral reasoning of the older child – of the contractual and negotiable aspects of morality. Stage five, or the first of the stages of level three, Kohlberg calls that of contractual–legalistic orientation and it precisely involves a grasp of the idea that many moral and social rules possess much of the character of agreements and contracts which may be open to negotiation or modification if changed circumstances lead to the loss of previous benefits to one party or another. Thus at this stage, according to Kohlberg, children come to the recognition that moral rules have the nature of man-made laws or conventions.

161

The last and highest stage of Kohlberg's developmental scheme, however, is that which he refers to as the stage of conscience or principle orientation. At this point the individual is supposed to be able to recognise that true allegiance to morality may not be to existing moral and social rules or contracts but rather to principles which override these and which are arrived at as a result of independent rational reflection via something like the process of moral universalisability. This is the very same stage that many educational philosophers and psychologists refer to as that of rational moral autonomy, the stage at which an individual moral agent should be able to construct his own set of self-accepted moral principles and prescriptions to which he can appeal in the name of conscience in any circumstances of moral uncertainty or indecision.

For Kohlberg, as well as many others, this sixth and final stage of orientation to autonomous conscience and principle is the ultimate goal of moral development and full moral maturity cannot be regarded as having been achieved until this stage has been reached. Thus Kohlberg, like Piaget, regards the process of moral development as evolutionary in character; the later stages of development may only be reached or achieved by first passing through the earlier stages and once a later stage has been attained genuine or full regression to an earlier stage is hardly possible.

Kohlberg also argues that his stages of moral development are cross-cultural; he has set out to demonstrate the respects in which moral values and judgements are not relative or local to particular social circumstances but universal and invariant across all cultures. In this respect his work does seem to reinforce quite powerfully the idea which has also been canvassed by the prescriptivist philosopher R. M. Hare – that in understanding the nature of moral thought and action, it is the logical form of the reasoning and judgement that matters rather more than the content. What equally interests Hare, Piaget and Kohlberg, then, is the nature of the reasons which people give for making moral judgements of one sort or another and the criteria they employ for judging this way rather than that.

Thus it doesn't matter so much *what* people believe – whether, for example, they regard abortion or capital punishment as right or wrong – what matters more is *why* they believe a given thing and what sort of reasoning they use to support their moral conclusions. But, of course, this may seem to be in many respects a quite perverse or bizarre view of moral reasoning, for surely the only really intelligible purpose that moral reasoning might be seen to have is to arrive at conclusions which are right rather than wrong or true rather than false; our judgements in moral matters, it will be said, do not have the goal of exhibiting valid or invalid reasoning but that of guiding us towards conduct which is morally correct.

To be sure, then, there would appear to be deep philosophical problems about this view of moral reasoning which we have touched on in earlier chapters and to which we shall have to return below. Before this, however, it is worth asking in relation to the features of moral development which Kohlberg claims to be invariant across cultures and universal in nature, why this should be so? Is this really a conclusion to which Kohlberg comes by empirical enquiry; is it indeed something that *could* be confirmed by empirical enquiry? In fact, this seems unlikely. Only an investigation of all cultures past, present and future (including those of rational beings on the worlds of Arcturus and Sirius) would show *empirically* that Kohlberg's account of moral development was universal in scope. But given the sheer impossibility of ever completing such an investigation, would Kohlberg be content to treat his theory as a mere tentative hypothesis?

I think it is reasonably clear that Kohlberg does not regard his account as just a provisional hypothesis but rather as something in the nature of a necessary truth about the form that the evolution of individual moral judgement must take. In short, there is an ineliminable *a priori* dimension to the character of both Piaget's and Kohlberg's purportedly empirical investigations into the growth of moral reasoning. For a start, it is rather difficult in the case of Piaget–Kohlbergian type enquiries to make much sense of the idea of raw observational data upon which scientific judgements might be based or from which generalisations might be derived. On what evidence, after all, are their conclusions about the nature of moral development based? On the replies to their questions of small children. But the replies of small children, like those of primitive tribesmen, cannot be taken at face value without due regard to the motives behind those replies; since the children might want to please the enquirer, to mislead him, or they might simply not understand what he is asking, their replies will obviously be susceptible of a wide range of possible interpretations.

These considerations among others point to the unavoidable conclusion that Piaget and Kohlberg's observations concerning the development of moral thought cannot be directly derived from uninterpreted data and are in fact based on philosophical assumptions, highly debatable ones at that. It is therefore difficult to avoid the conclusion that what Piaget and Kohlberg have presented to us in the form of objective scientific enquiry into the nature of moral development is really little more than a very contentious philosophical theory in empirical disguise. Moreover, of course, given the normative character of the subject matter with which the enquiry is concerned, it is difficult to see how things could be otherwise.

These suspicions are further confirmed by the remarkable degree to which, in particular, Kohlberg's observations about moral development are entirely consistent with such relatively recent post-Enlightenment views in the liberal tradition of analytical philosophy as prescriptivism; the founder of prescriptivism R. M. Hare has in fact written in terms of warm approval of Kohlberg's work as largely supportive of his own. But again, as we have seen, Hare was greatly influenced by Kant and all of Piaget's work on genetic epistemology, including his writings on moral development, are explicitly and deeply inspired by Kant.

The fundamental idea which ties all of these views together, of course, is that moral maturity consists chiefly in the development on the part of an individual of a capacity for rational self-legislation with respect to the formation of moral values; the main goal of moral education is thus essentially to promote this capacity by encouraging pupils to frame their own rationally consistent code of moral principles so that their lives may be lived in the light of a conscience responsibly informed by such principles.

Now obviously the first point to be observed about this is that the philosophical perspective to which Piaget and Kohlberg appear to be committed here is one that has serious rivals. As we have seen, for example, Kohlberg considers the stage at which children regard the existing moral conventions of society in a contractual light, as the best available way to protect and uphold the interests of all parties to the social contact, to be a lower stage of moral development than that at which individuals act according to principles which are independently formulated and self-legislated in the name of autonomy. But as we have seen, Hobbes held a contractual view of the nature and origin of social and moral rules and it is not unreasonable to suppose that the interests of human justice (which Kohlberg holds to be the supreme moral value) might be better served by large scale observance of conventional codes of conduct than by the widespread promotion of independent perspectives and initiatives (especially as, on the admission of prescriptivists, we cannot be certain in advance that all autonomous agents will universalise identical or interpersonally consistent prescriptions). Moreover, not just Hobbes but many present day contract theorists seem to think in this way.

Again, as we have already observed, Piaget included among the elements of what he called moral realism a belief in the absolutely objective nature of moral rules and principles which he regarded as at a lower stage of moral evolution than that at which moral rules are considered to be contractual or conventional in nature; but many if not most of the great moral philosophers of the past (including Kant himself) would appear to have taken a different and opposite view. To be sure, none of these observations about significant rival positions to that of Piaget, Kohlberg and prescriptivism guarantee that their view is wrong, but they do point to their being wrong as a distinct *possibility*. There are further considerations of a more compelling kind, however, which point more directly to the conclusion that the philosophical perspective which is presupposed to cognitive moral development theory is mistaken.

We have already alluded to some of the general philosophical problems with a view of morality which construes its highest expression or goal to be the development of a capacity for the rational universalisation of self-accepted prescriptive principles. First, the very idea that morality or moral principles are somehow a product or expression of individual will is problematic for much the same reason that viewing morality as a product of God's will or the will of society is problematic; it just does not seem reasonable to suppose that it is entirely up to the individual to decide whether murder or adultery are morally right or wrong, permissible or impermissible in any circumstances.

For the conscience or the will of an individual to be morally

165

effective with respect to the formulation of moral prescriptions, then, it requires to be an informed conscience or will – but the tradition of post-Enlightenment liberal thought about morality as represented by the line which reaches from Kant to Hare leaves very little in the way of content for the will of the individual to be informed by if he is to be regarded as truly acting morally rather than otherwise. That is because to act morally, in the view of Kant and his philosophical heirs, is to act autonomously – independently of conventional moral influences – rather than heteronomously or under the influence of views that are not truly one's own. Thus the modern autonomist account of moral life and moral conduct is one with plenty of form but not much substance.

In fact, Kohlberg explicitly rejects what he rather derisively terms the 'bag of virtues' approach to moral education which emphasises the deliberate promotion of a diverse range of character traits – honesty, self-control, courage, tolerance, benevolence and so forth.[11] This seems to be because he regards the promotion of such character traits as a rather haphazard and unsystematic affair which fails to address itself to the real question of the transmission to the individual of the understanding of fundamental principles which should underpin any genuine conception of moral life and conduct. But though one may agree that some conception of practical knowledge or wisdom as informed by rational moral principles must lie at the heart of any coherent view of moral conduct, to exclude from one's account of that conduct any reference to those qualities of moral character we call virtues is to throw out the baby with the bath water; for it is only by reference to such familiar qualities as considerateness, generosity, sincerity, temperance and so on that we can give any real content to the notions of moral thought and conduct.

In fact, as we have already noticed, Aristotle's account of moral life hinges crucially on a particular conception of practical reason or wisdom, but the relation of that wisdom to moral life is explicable only in terms of the way in which it informs the various moral virtues of courage, temperance, justice and the like, in so far as these are independently demonstrable as generally conducive to individual and social human flourishing. We are able to make sense of the role of practical wisdom in moral life precisely to the extent that we are able to see how it informs the moral virtues and how the possession of these dispositions enriches or ennobles human life. To omit any reference to the virtues in our account of morality *in favour of* a theory of moral reasoning or to conceive some topic-neutral process of moral reasoning as offering a route to understanding morality alternative to one which makes reference to moral dispositions is simply incoherent.

Another regrettable consequence of this attempt to cut moral reasoning loose from any substantive conception of moral life as exhibited in a particular range of moral virtues or qualities of character is that the relationship of moral thought to feeling and conduct becomes rather obscure if not totally mysterious. First of all, it would appear that an account of the nature of morality which focuses pretty well exclusively on moral reason and judgement can hardly be either sufficient *or* necessary to comprehend all that we should ordinarily take to be implicated in moral life and conduct. For one thing, as Aristotle points out, those acts which are truly virtuous are those which are performed as a truly virtuous man – a man of sound practical wisdom – would perform them; but this is not to say that a small child or an educationally sub-normal teenager who performs a small act of kindness to someone else in the conspicuous absence of a consistent and thoroughly worked out set of universalised prescriptions (by which criterion we are all, I suppose, backward) has not behaved in a morally commendable way.

In fact the *only* reason for regarding such actions as of less value than those which occur as a consequence of a consistent system of rational principles would be one which asserts that sound reason rather than right feeling is the overriding criterion of moral value – but this begs the question. It is also clear, however, that someone who does have a well-worked out and consistent system of prescriptive principles can nevertheless fail to act in a morally appropriate way due to the familiar enough conditions of *akrasia* and failure of nerve. As Aristotle also appears to have thought, then, moral principles whether they are universalised or not do not appear to be enough for appropriate moral action; the principles which inform practical wisdom, in order to be morally effective, require embodiment as the rational aspects or expressions of those steady and settled states of character we call the moral virtues.

It seems, then, that the most conspicuous problem about the accounts of moral life and growth offered by such cognitive development theorists as Piaget and Kohlberg is that they are weighted far too greatly towards the intellectual or rational aspects of morality; they fail to do sufficient justice to the motivational and affective dimensions of moral conduct. We need not go so far as to agree with Hume's view that reason is utterly impotent to move men to action, to see that Piaget, Kohlberg and the various advocates of prescriptivist-like views fail to show quite how moral wisdom or reason is related to the motivational aspects of moral life as these are expressed in familiar ideas of will and character.

It is also clear that these ideas themselves cannot be adequately explicated without reference to notions of feeling, passion or emotion. Again, for Aristotle reference to feelings – to either the control or the expression of them – is a crucial element in any reasonable or coherent account of the moral virtues; but once again the moral development theorists are almost completely silent on these topics. As we shall proceed to try to show, it seems that this omission is quite disastrous to any satisfactory account of moral life.

We cannot, for example, reasonably hope to explain that feature of moral experience we call courage in terms of some such prescription as 'always act so as to behave confidently and resolutely in dangerous circumstances', since as Aristotle again pointed out, such action is consistent with motives, attitudes and passions which are anything but courageous. More seriously still, however, we cannot adequately explain many of the most highly valued altruistic elements of moral life in terms of the universalisation of prescriptions. The complaint has often been made against Kant's account of altruism and benevolence that it seems gross and absurd to value a charitable act performed from duty or obligation above one performed by an agent moved by kindness or compassion. And despite the fact that some degree of caricature of Kant's viewpoint is doubtless involved in this way of stating it, the point is well made that it cannot be correct to assess the moral worth of an action *exclusively* in terms of rationally determined obligations and to view the altruistic passions and sentiments as having no value at all.

To be sure, an appropriate and effective act of charity should properly be performed in accordance with principles legitimated by sound practical wisdom; but for it to count as a genuine or sincere act of charity it should also be done in the appropriate spirit or be motivated by the right sort of inclination. A person who acts with all the appearance of charity or generosity but from a sense of duty through which he successfully manages to stifle his feelings of resentment or irritation, is hardly being charitable at all.

8

MORAL DEVELOPMENT IN PROGRESSIVE AND TRADITIONAL EDUCATIONAL THOUGHT

In the light of the different theories of morality and moral education that we have considered in this and the previous section, it may be worthwhile to look here at how these relate generally to some themes and perspectives in the philosophy of education as such. An obvious place to start, though it is no place to end, is by considering a familiar distinction of educational philosophy which has in the course of time become rather clichéd – the distinction between so-called educational traditionalism and educational progressivism.

In many respects, I believe that this distinction stands just as much in need of demolition as the equally influential analytic–synthetic distinction in mainstream epistemology and metaphysics and I am convinced that its effects on educational thought and theory have been almost as harmful.[1] The distinction has in fact already been attacked on the grounds that it is far too crude and inadequate to express the rich variety of interesting educational views and perspectives that it is philosophically possible to profess, but without reneging here on my own previously published comments on this topic[2] I shall first try to discover what it is about the distinction that educational philosophers seem to have found so difficult to abandon. What differences of perspective, if any, on questions of education in general and moral education in particular might the distinction be said to express?

As always, it is worth starting from the plausible observations that others have made concerning the distinction in question. And since it is arguable that the most stimulating, fruitful and insightful work to have emerged in educational philosophy over

170

the last quarter of a century has followed in the wake of the philosophical contribution of R. S. Peters, we might do little better than to begin with the view that he appears to have taken of the progressive–traditional dichotomy. In fact we find the main statement of his view of this matter in *The Logic of Education* co-written with Paul Hirst almost twenty years ago.[3] In this work it is suggested that whereas traditionalism is essentially a doctrine which emphasises aims and content in education to the exclusion of methods, progressivism is a perspective which focuses on methods to the exclusion of content.

From this point of view it could be held that traditionalism and progressivism, far from being radically opposed doctrines, are in fact susceptible of reconciliation (Hirst and Peters use the term 'synthesis') in terms of a new philosophy of education which combines a traditionalist defence of the curriculum with a progressivist conception of learning and pedagogy.[4] It would also appear that what Peters and Hirst take themselves to be propounding in *The Logic of Education* is the general outline of some such composite theory.

The main trouble with this rather simple interpretation of the progressive–traditional distinction, of course, is that it cannot be correct or, at any rate, that it is difficult to give any clear sense to it. What, for example, is a progressivist conception of educational methods? When one considers the range and diversity of past and present day educationalists who have been categorised as progressivists, it is very difficult to identify any set of teaching strategies or methods that might be held to represent a distinctive body of progressive pedagogy. Indeed, the teaching methods adopted at A. S. Neill's famous experimental school Summerhill were criticised by the official educational inspectorate precisely for being insufficiently innovative and for exhibiting an approach to education which appeared too formal and conventional; yet it would clearly be odd to classify Neill as a traditionalist on that score alone.

So it is not just that there would appear to be no single conception of the development of pedagogy common to all who have been labelled 'progressives', it is also that some renowned progressives do not seem to have been much interested in pedagogy at all. Similar things are true, however, of the relationship between traditionalism and the educational content of the curriculum. Quite clearly no common view of content is discernible among all who have been justly called traditionalists; different criteria of educational value have led to the justification and defence of different sorts of content by educationalists in utilitarian and non-utilitarian traditions and quite different curriculum theories have been upheld in the liberal educational tradition by conservative traditionalists such as G. H. Bantock and liberal traditionalists like John White.[5]

But, more seriously, some of these traditionalists have been *more* interested in questions of learning and pedagogy than has a progressive like Neill, just as Dewey – often called a progressive – was just as much interested in questions of the content of the curriculum as any traditionalist. It is much too simplistic, then, to characterise the traditional–progressive distinction in terms of different emphases on content and methods in education. By the same token, moreover, other common attempts to explain the distinction are also too simplistic. It also seems false, for example, to characterise traditionalism as teacher-centred and progressivism as child-centred since many if not most traditionalists have had important things to say about the active role of the child in learning and for many progressivists the teacher has a prominent and distinctive role to play in promoting learning on the part of the child.

How, then, has the distinction between traditionalism and progressivism assumed importance as one that marks a genuine difference between educational–philosophical perspectives? In fact the proper route to a true appreciation of the ideological opposition expressed in the traditional–progressive dichotomy is to be found by careful reflection on the various views about society, morality and moral education that we have so far considered in this work. Generally speaking, then, the difference between traditionalism and progressivism with respect to educational theory is expressed in different conceptions of human nature, of society and of the way in which human nature is reconciled to the demands of society by the processes of socialisation and education.

Thus, though it is not really very helpful to try to express the idea of progressivism in terms of a primary preoccupation with pedagogy, it is not too wide of the mark to associate tradition-alism with a focus upon content. For the simplest way by far to characterise educational traditionalism is in the sort of terms in which Matthew Arnold did conceptualise education in *Culture and Anarchy*; as essentially the transmission of certain worthwhile features of culture from one human generation to the next. The fundamental idea which underlies traditionalist thinking is that education properly construed represents the systematic initiation of untutored human nature into the highest wisdom, traditions, values and customs of a civilised human society – into, as Arnold put it, 'the best that has been thought and said in the world'.[6]

The basic idea of the traditionalist is, then, that the progress if not the very survival of human society and civilisation depends upon the compulsory socialisation of the child into the knowledge and values of the tribal group; since human nature in its raw state leaves something to be desired, an education or initiation into civilised social values can only represent an improvement in the human condition. What sort of an improvement this is supposed to be is expressed quite vividly for traditionalists in the observation by R. S. Peters himself that the small child is 'a barbarian at the gates of civilization'.[7] The view which underlies this remark is, of course, quite clear – that unsocialised human nature is somehow suspect, indecent or untrustworthy; that in the absence of a proper induction into civilised social values via a satisfactory or at least adequate education, it is only to be expected that human individuals will grow up coarse, crude and cruel, with little consideration for anyone but themselves and for anything other than the satisfaction of their own animal lusts.

Now, of course, it is hardly necessary to look far in order to discover a direct ancestry for such views in the history of moral and social philosophy, for in considering the political philosophy of Thomas Hobbes we encountered elements of just this kind of thinking – precisely the view that man in a state of nature is egotistical and self-seeking and generally indisposed towards any concern for the rights and interests of other people. That being so, the only path to salvation or redemption lies in some sort of social contract whereby men may be brought into a state of relatively harmonious social co-operation with their fellow human beings.

On Hobbes' view, it is clear that the initiation into something like co-operative social and civil values which the social contract requires is as much for the purpose of curbing or limiting men's anti-social desires and inclinations as it is for making them in any sense better; on this view it seems that rational or enlightened self-interest is the most in the way of individual salvation that we are entitled to hope for. All the same, most of the basic assumptions that we find deeply embedded in educational traditionalism are of a fundamentally Hobbesian kind; untutored human nature is by and large to be construed in terms of self-interested and non-social inclinations which stand in dire need of social checks and restraints via imposition of the rules and laws of civilised society. Thus education construed as the organised systematic initiation of the individual into such social codes is regarded as the principal route to the relative *improvement* of the human condition.

If it is not inappropriate to link some of the basic themes of educational traditionalism to certain classical conservative political and social theories and perspectives like that of Thomas Hobbes, it may be more easy to appreciate the precise respects in which Rousseau, the great-grandfather of educational progressivism, is opposed both to traditionalism in his educational philosophy and to Hobbes in his social and political philosophy. For Rousseau, as we have already indicated, took a quite different view of the nature of the relationship between unschooled human nature and so-called civilised life. Against Hobbes and others, he argued that the individual in a state of nature or, at least, in a state of being prior to the emergence of civil society, was far from being self-interested and anti-social and was in fact naturally disposed towards co-operative and harmonious social coexistence with others of his kind.

Indeed, rather than to regard man as naturally ignoble or debased and as only redeemed by social existence in civil society, it is nearer the truth in Rousseau's view to regard him as originally endowed with a range of essentially benevolent dispositions which are liable to become corrupted as a result of the change in his economic and social circumstances which occurs when he makes the important transition from a primitive nomadic hunter-gatherer culture to a more settled form of civilised life. Viewed in this light, however, right education becomes not so much a matter of imposing traditional social values and beliefs on children for their own good, as of shielding them from the potentially corrupting influence of most of these values and beliefs. Thus a large part of the proper education of children must consist in what Rousseau calls *negative* education; it must be a matter of protecting the young from the potentially indoctrinatory effects that follow from so much conventional education.

From this point of view, it appears even more ironic that some modern educational philosophers have represented progressivism as essentially a doctrine about methods, since one of the points upon which many past and present progressivists have continually insisted is that we should as much as possible avoid doing very much at all in the way of a positive interventionist pedagogy. For many progressivists, the child is to be left largely to his own devices, to learn from his experience in circumstances which will require the free use of his reason for the solution of basic practical problems. In due course a natural or God-given sense of justice or fairness combined with a benevolent disposition towards others which has not been warped by the selfish and possessive values enshrined in the social practices of most so-called civil human communities will enable him to construct a principled code of conduct conducive to a respect for the rights of other people as well as his own. These ideas or something like them, it should be emphasised, are to be found expressed in the thought and practice of many modern educationalists of a progressive turn of mind, not just in the work of Rousseau.[8]

It would appear that there is a genuine difference of perspective discernible between so-called traditionalist and progressive educationalists, then, but it is one that does not seem to have been very precisely identified by many of the theorists who employ these terms. It is not that whereas traditionalists are interested in content progressives are more interested in methods, or that whereas progressives are child-centred – whatever that means – traditionalists are teacher or subject-centred. Rather more complicatedly it is that traditionalists and progressivists hold somewhat different views of human nature, of society and of the way in which education should be properly viewed as adapting or fitting the individual to society.

In short, to the extent that both traditionalists and progressives regard conventional education as a matter of initiating children into the accepted values, knowledge and practices of their culture, they disagree about whether this is to be construed as a *good thing*; whereas the traditionalist sees this as a matter of improving or civilising the child, the progressivist will view this largely as a matter of his corruption or indoctrination. Of course, it is still by no means true that one can neatly classify every significant contributor to educational philosophy and theory according to the terms of the traditional–progressive distinction – John Dewey for one is an extremely ambivalent figure notable precisely for his own vehement rejection of the dichotomy – but many of the great educational thinkers can be relatively easily accommodated to the distinction as we have just characterised it.

Again, the possibility of classifying educational theorists in this way does not adversely effect my earlier observation that the distinction is not a particularly useful one from a conceptual point of view since it is not otherwise adequate to express the much richer available variety of interesting and significant educational perspectives; it is thus ultimately not really very helpful or illuminating to regard a given view as traditional or progressive. All the same, it is of some interest in the present context to observe that according to the interpretation of the traditional–progressive distinction that I have just given, Peters and Hirst come out quite clearly and unambiguously on the side of traditionalism since they subscribe to an essentially conservative view of human nature and the role of socialisation – it is worth noting here that Peters is also the author of a respected commentary on Hobbes[9] – and to an explicit culture-transmission or initiation model of education.

But not only do Peters and Hirst emerge clearly as traditionalists according to the above analysis of the traditional–progressive distinction, it is also clear that they do not on that analysis succeed in reconciling the terms of the dichotomy by the construction of some educational view which transcends it. And it should also be reasonably clear why they do not contribute in any way to the reconciliation of the two viewpoints; it is precisely, of course, because the viewpoints thus construed are not clearly susceptible of reconciliation. To be sure, one can avoid the problems raised by the traditional–progressive distinction by denying – as, for example, Dewey does – that it has any genuine significance or status; but once one admits that the distinction does express certain genuine differences of philosophical outlook of the kind I have just explored, one is forced to concede that the viewpoints in question are well nigh irreconcilable and then it is necessary to take sides.

If traditionalism and progressivism do mean what I have argued they can only mean, then, there can be no real possibility of synthesis of or compromise between one extreme position which maintains that human nature is essentially corrupt and only redeemed by a systematic educational initiation into civilised social values and another which holds that human nature is basically in good shape but stands to be corrupted by an initiation into the conventional traditions and values of civilised society – for obviously, what goes under the name of education from one point of view can only count as indoctrination from the other. It is thus idle to suppose that one has reconciled progressivism to traditionalism by retaining the traditional forms of educational institutions and curricula whilst adopting pedagogical strategies which involve play or discovery; for progressivists of the temper of A. S. Neill or Bertrand Russell,[10] this is only to have liberalised conventional traditionalist education and to have transformed it into something perhaps even more degrading, manipulative and indoctrinatory.

Thus if it is true that the familiar traditional–progressive dichotomy does express a definite and identifiable difference between two philosophically reputable perspectives on human nature and its relation to social life – if it gives expression to two diametrically opposed points of view – we cannot reasonably sit on the fence in our educational thinking with respect to this distinction and it would appear that we have to make some sort of choice. If it is not logically possible to identify a position of compromise between the ideas that corrupt human nature requires to be redeemed by initiation into civilised life and that on the contrary innocent human nature is vulnerable to corruption by such initiation, we must side with one view or the other. Or must we?

Let us first see how some of the social and psychological theories of morality and moral education that we have already examined stand with respect to the traditional–progressive distinction. As we have characterised it, traditionalism is essentially the view that education is concerned with the transmission of a given human culture from one generation to another – it represents the systematic socialisation or acculturalisation of the young with respect to the customs and values of their social group. It is clear from the start that this idea accords perfectly with that sociological tradition of thinking about education in general and moral education in particular which stems from Durkheim.

As we have already seen, Durkheim held precisely that moral education constituted the improvement or civilisation of a basically wayward and unruly human nature via explicit initiation into principled codes of human conduct which could be identified and determined by rational reflection on the actual empirical circumstances of human social and moral life. For Durkheim there is not even the problem that has so painfully exercised moral philosophers both before and after him of establishing how the moral principles expressed in familiar statements of duty and obligation are to be rationally derived from or related to the empirically observable circumstances of human interpersonal conduct. In fact, for him, the rules of behaviour generally observed and encouraged by society just *are* the source of any principled duties and obligations we ought morally to recognise.

Thus for Durkheim morality is exhibited in any conduct of an essentially self-controlled and altruistic kind which an agent engages in as a result of something like his voluntary rational endorsement of or acquiescence in those codes of behaviour which are generally accepted by other rational agents in his society. To be sure, of course, this entails a certain degree of cultural and moral relativism – what looks reasonable to go along with in one set of social, political or economic circumstances may not look so reasonable in another; but generally speaking it is reasonable to endorse any social or interpersonal rules which appear to facilitate harmonious and co-operative relations between most of the members of a given society.

And though it is probably true that many if not most modern educationalists of a liberal traditionalist persuasion would want to criticise Durkheim for taking a far too conventionalist or social relativist view of the nature and origins of human social and moral practices in particular and a far too structural functionalist view of human society in general, there is hardly any room for doubt that his views sit quite easily and comfortably with the particular view of traditionalism that we have given in this chapter. Generally speaking Durkheim also takes rather a dim view of undisciplined human nature and although it is doubtful

178

whether he would be prepared to go quite so far as Hobbes, he seems committed in his *Moral Education* and elsewhere to the view that without the checks and constraints provided by an externally imposed code of morals, human nature stands in real danger of going to the dogs. It is not really possible to doubt therefore that Durkheim's views fall very much on the traditionalist side of our interpretation of the progressive–traditional dichotomy.

Turning now to the views we considered in the chapter on Freud, Lane and Neill, I suspect that we have to draw a distinction. For although we were concerned in that chapter to forge certain links between the thought of Freud and that of some modern progressive educationalists, to demonstrate the line of descent of the views of Lane and Neill from the theories of Freud, there are also important differences of outlook which require to be recognised here and which were on at least one occasion explicitly acknowledged by Neill himself:

> The fundamental difference between the Freudian school and Reich is simply the one I am examining now; Reich believes that life isn't evil, that the unconscious isn't a devil, that all individual and social evils are manmade, made by interference in the life process.[11]

Now whatever the degree of looseness here in Neill's interpretations of Freud and Reich, a real enough difference is nevertheless discernible between the views of the founder of psychoanalysis and his progressive educational 'followers'; educational progressivism and classical psychoanalytical theory do appear to be somewhat at odds over the question of the basic disposition towards good or evil of human nature. Whereas for Freud and other pioneers of the psychoanalytic method a certain degree of repression of the natural instincts and their redirection or rechannelling via the defence mechanisms would appear to be regarded as a necessary part of individual adjustment to the demands of civilised life, such repression seems to have been viewed by Neill as an essentially destructive force in the life of the individual, fundamentally inimical to the development of a healthy and well-integrated personality and character. To a certain extent, as might be expected, Lane occupies a position somewhere between Freud and Neill on this question, but he must ultimately be seen as moving away from Freud in Neill's direction.

179

In both Lane and Neill, for example, we find a quite clear expression of the view that human nature is basically good and becomes bad only through the effects of this, that or the other environmental influence. On the other hand, Freud's view of human nature inclines to a pessimism which finds expression in the idea that the psychological conflict between the id and the ego is an inevitable consequence of the unavoidable confrontation between the individual's subjective instinctual desires and the requirements of civilised life the result of which is bound to be at best a certain degree or level of anxiety or neurosis and at worst sexual maladjustment or actual mental illness. In general, then, it would appear that Freud inclines towards the conservative and pessimistic view of human nature as it tends to be found on the traditionalist side of the progressive–traditional dichotomy.

In Lane and Neill, however, we encounter an unequivocal commitment to the idea of the basic goodness of the individual which is an enduring feature of the progressivist educational tradition reaching at least as far back as Rousseau. One could not find a clearer modern expression of the idea that unschooled human nature is basically in good order but stands to be corrupted by the influence of diseased civilisation than one finds in these two progressives but one also finds it wedded to a peculiarly modern theory – the psychoanalytic perspective of Freud and others on the nature and consequences of the encounter between individual subjectivity and social reality. The view of Lane, however, is that this encounter does not inevitably have to result in a conflict which is necessarily damaging or disadvantageous to the individual's instinctive nature; *Talks to Parents and Teachers* is certainly a cautionary work which sets out to warn of the dangers of various kinds of psychological mismanagement of the child, but it is also a profoundly optimistic work in which Lane clearly believes that a state of happy compromise *can* be achieved in child-rearing between the satisfaction of natural instinctual desires and the demands of social reality.

The idea of sublimation as a defence-mechanism, for example, seems to be construed by Lane rather more positively than it is by Freud and other psychoanalytic theorists. In fact Lane explicitly maintains that anti-social or generally negative behaviour is just the misuse or the misdirection of instinctual energies which should be channelled in more positive directions; he regards growth towards human maturity as essentially a question of transcending the infantile preoccupations of childhood so that the instinctual drives which originally assumed a childish expression can later be invested in more serious human enterprises involving more constructive goals.

It is in this connection, of course, that Lane regards adult interference in the form of parental prohibitions on the expression of childish instincts and interests as often doing far more harm than good, since far from eliminating the behaviour that they set out to extinguish, the prohibitions merely succeed in fixating that behaviour.[12] Consequently, Lane urges that one should always discover a new interest to capture the child's energies before attempting to correct a 'fault' through which the energies are seeking a negative outlet. Thus the sublimation of instinctual energies in forms of activity other than their 'original' ones which is for many psychoanalytical theorists merely a defence strategy against neurosis – the redirection of sexual energy into artistic creativity, for example – is for Lane just part of the normal process of human development towards individual maturity.

To be sure; it is also clear enough from the details of Freud's very morally conservative account of sexual development and sexual perversion that he too believes that the road to individual maturity lies in a certain altruistic transcendence of immature auto-erotic forms of infantile sexuality, but he also seems to think that this is purchased at something of a cost to the individual in terms of general psychological equilibrium; somewhat paradoxically, many of the forms of life and conduct which are characteristic of adult maturity are seen by Freud to have their origins in the defence mechanisms – in the early attempts of individuals to cope with infantile frustrations.

On the contrary, however, Lane seems to have believed that the 'sublimation' or redirection of instinctual psychological energies along more positive channels can occur only given that the child does not remain in the grip of any states of ungratified desire or carry forward any undue frustrations into later life. For Lane, the 'breaking of constellations' – the destruction of certain psychological associations, for example, of negative feelings with the idea of sexuality – is a precondition

181

of the forward movement of the child towards a mature and constructive deployment of his instinctual energies.

Neill wholeheartedly follows Lane in this general point of view and in so doing he moves even further away from any position of orthodox Freudianism; in fact, much of his work at Summerhill was concerned precisely with what Lane referred to as the dissolving of constellations. More or less, Neill's view is that, like the sleeping princesses of fairy-tales, many children – especially those who have undergone or suffered a conventional education and upbringing – need to be freed from enchantment before they can aspire to fulfilment via mature engagement in any worthwhile human enterprise. This is because they are the victims precisely of evil spells cast by wicked parents and teachers – spells which have fixated them on childish obsessions with infantile expressions of sexuality or with whatever else has been represented to them as forbidden and therefore as of the greatest possible interest. Until such a time as children can be released form these negative forms of bewitchment, it is not possible for teachers to consider realistically how they might be educated in a more positive way.

Hence the most striking and conspicuous features of the school experience at Summerhill – those in which the difference between this most famous of progressive schools and more conventional educational institutions is most marked. First and most obviously, there is the absence of compulsion, especially in relation to the *requirement* that children should learn anything. In the context of Summerhill this is chiefly a psychologically remedial measure – for children who have not been subjected to a conventional compulsory education proper motivation towards learning is not really a problem. According to Neill, compulsion to learn itself inhibits learning by the formation of a reaction against the compulsion. Thus for Neill the removal of compulsion is rather like Lane's joining the outlaw gangs in their delinquent activity and spoiling the fun – it is a way of undermining authority as a repressive force and of eliminating a source of impotent inhibition.

Then, of course, there are Neill's 'P.L.'s' or private lessons in which children are invited and encouraged to air their anxieties in a free and open way. To be construed essentially as informal psychotherapeutic sessions, the private lessons are once again directed at the dissolution of those repressive constellations which hold children in thrall and obstruct their progress towards the higher goals of mature human life. All these features and others place Neill alongside Lane squarely on the progressive side of the traditional–progressive dichotomy as we have interpreted it.

So far, it seems that whereas Durkheim and probably Freud fall on the traditionalist side of thought about human nature and social and moral development, Lane and Neill belong clearly in the progressivist camp; but what of the so-called moral developmental theorists Piaget and Kohlberg? In fact, there is a considerable degree of ambivalence and unclearness about this since there are clear intellectual and historical associations between the cognitive developmentalists and both the main traditions of educational thought we have been considering in this chapter. It is clear enough that Piaget and Kohlberg belong to a line of intellectual ancestry which stretches all the way back to Rousseau, and the general goal of rational moral autonomy which lies at the heart of the developmental theories of the modern psychologists is also that which is argued by Rousseau in *Emile* to be the main aim of education.

There is also much in the developmental ideas of Lane and Neill which sits comfortably enough with Piaget and Kohlberg – especially the notion that the principal route to moral maturity consists in the transcendence of the condition of egoism in favour of the development of a perspective which enables children to grasp the principled nature of morality via an appreciation of the social–contractual character of moral and social codes. Moreover, Lane has, like Piaget and Kohlberg, a complex and detailed theory of child development.

But although Piaget and Kohlberg have a great deal to say on the topic of moral reasoning and judgement their views are in many ways much less complete and complex than those of Lane and Neill since they are almost completely silent on questions of the emotional and motivational side of child-development – particularly about the development of those conditions, in which Lane and Neill are very much interested, under which children can develop wrongly through the acquisition of anti-social and other negative attitudes. Thus, in the absence of anything much in the way of an account of the healthy or not so healthy development of moral and social motives and attitudes, it is rather difficult to see quite where the moral developmentalists stand on the question of the basic disposition to good or ill of human nature; consequently it is also difficult to trace a clear route from them to the sort of progressivism which is clearly exhibited in the work of Rousseau.

Moreover, it is also clear enough that the empirical work of Piaget and Kohlberg has been used to support views concerning the development of morality of a much more traditionalist temper; R. S. Peters, for one, has commented favourably on the work of the moral developmentalists in the context of developing his own essentially liberal traditionalist conception of education.[13] And in fact it is not at all hard to understand how this should be so. Basically, the developmental theories of Piaget and Kohlberg support very rationalist accounts of the idea of moral growth. Since they construe moral development as essentially a matter of a child's grasp of various kinds of moral rules, they are, at least in principle, more consistent with interventionist accounts of moral education than with the non-interventionist accounts to be found in the progressive tradition from Rousseau to A. S. Neill.

It has sometimes been said in criticism of Kohlberg that his theory is rather *too* developmental and doesn't give sufficient weight to the role and influence on moral growth of explicit moral teaching; but it is fairly easy to see how specific pedagogical and curricular strategies might be developed on the basis of a theory like Kohlberg's to facilitate precisely the sorts of development of moral understanding that are envisaged in his account. Basically, then, Piaget and Kohlberg do appear to view moral development as a matter essentially of the promotion of rational moral autonomy via the mastery of rules and principles; moral conduct is fundamentally rule-governed conduct which occurs when human behaviour is regulated in accordance with principles of interpersonal conduct which constrain individual self-interest in favour of the promotion of the general interest. So though little is explicitly said as such in moral development theory concerning the basic disposition towards good or evil of human nature, implicit in the theory is the idea that this nature requires to be controlled or regulated in the interests of the group or society as a whole.

Even if modern moral development theory can be regarded as reasonably faithful to the Kantian tradition which holds that natural human inclinations are not necessarily either good or bad in themselves then – that it is indeed only conduct which follows from a rational grasp of the moral law that is truly susceptible of genuine moral appraisal – it still seems that a view of morality as in many respects contrary to human nature and inclination is nevertheless enshrined in it. At any rate, it appears that modern moral developmental insights of a Piagetian or Kohlbergian kind exhibit sufficient ambiguity to be easily enough accommodated by either a progressive or a traditional conception of the evolution or emergence of morally principled individual conduct.

Despite the ambiguity discernible in the positions of Piaget and Kohlberg, then, it still might seem possible to divide different moral and social theorists into two distinct categories according to whether they fall on the one side or the other of the progressive–traditional distinction. And if that distinction is held to be a reasonably sound one conceptually, then it might also seem that we are faced with a choice between two different and fundamentally irreconcilable conceptions of human nature and its relation to society and moral life. One of these positions maintains that human nature is largely disposed – through original sin perhaps – to self-interested and anti-social attitudes which require to be controlled externally by imposed law or internally by the inculcation of a conscience informed by principles of altruistic self-control; the other maintains that human nature is essentially inclined towards benevolent and co-operative attitudes towards others which stand in danger of corruption or perversion by certain forms of negative interference – psychological repression and social indoctrination. Which of these perspectives are we to endorse as the correct one?

In fact, we should be extremely unwise, I think, to opt for either of these entrenched perspectives – especially in the extreme forms in which they have sometimes been stated – for clearly human nature is a much more complicated phenomenon than many traditional theories have allowed. It seems clear enough that some traditional social and political theorists – perhaps Hobbes for one – have rather overweighted the case against human nature as selfish and anti-social, though they have been right to remind us that there are many natural human dispositions of a negative character which require to be restrained or controlled in the general interests of individual and social wellbeing. All the same, however, it is also clear enough that human nature could not be *exclusively* selfish and anti-social, because if men entirely lacked any sort of inclination towards fellow-feeling and co-operation it would hardly be possible for them to enter into the kind of social contract which makes some sort of moral life (albeit construed as enlightened self-interest) possible.

But clearly again, the reaction towards extreme conservative–traditional views of human nature on the part of some social theorists of a more progressive or romantic temper (and it is actually doubtful whether Rousseau should really be included among these) has often been equally extreme and unrealistic; it is just not reasonable to portray human nature as innocent of or untainted by *any* negative, destructive or selfish qualities and to characterise human society or culture as almost wholly negative and corruptive in its moral influence on the individual. Once again such an extreme position is hardly consistent; on the one hand it supposes that negative social environmental influences are so pervasive as to lead to the total moral corruption of innocent human nature but on the other hand it envisages some non-environmentally influenced source of inclination to goodness which might free human beings for the exercise of a true altruistic morality in the context of that very environment.

Certainly, some modern formulations of what we have characterised as the traditionalist and progressive perspectives on human nature and society do appear to be overstated. Without doubt the contributions of Lane and Neill to our understanding of what can go wrong in the upbringing of children to cause aggressive and anti-social attitudes have afforded valuable insights into the origins of human deviation and wickedness. But these insights only partially explain human hostility and aggression, they do not contribute much at all to the explanation of altruism and benevolence and in general it seems likely that the work of Lane and Neill with problem children led them to exaggerate or overemphasise the adverse affects of parental prohibitions and social conditioning.

On the other hand, some traditionalist educational theorists have often come close to suggesting in the manner of the moral developmental theorists that the inculcation of moral principles or rules constitutes something like a *sufficient* condition of moral development and moral education; that, for example, an intellectual grasp of the principle of respect for persons may be sufficient to enable children to cultivate a real love and respect for other people. Lane and Neill help to show precisely why the grasp of such a principle is unlikely to have such a miraculous effect and how some attempts to inculcate such a principle might even have precisely the opposite effect. [14]

If this chapter has a moral, then, it is the fairly obvious one that human nature is a quite complex and complicated source of dispositions of both a self-interested and an altruistic, an aggressive and a benevolent, kind and that the way human beings are individually constituted is not susceptible of any easy explanation in terms of either nature or nurture. The lesson is that if our thinking about moral education is to be practically helpful then we cannot afford to take sides over the question of traditionalism versus progressivism because *both* of these perspectives on human nature are essentially false. It is not the case, as some recent educational philosophers would have us believe, that traditionalism and progressivism represent two educational emphases or two fragments of a single account of education which require each other for completion.

Traditionalism and progressivism are not doctrines about educational content and educational method which are both true but incomplete, they are doctrines about human nature and society which are both *false* and which require to be replaced by a more subtle and complicated picture of the relationship between human nature, morality and society.

Any realistic view of moral virtue, then, must be one which clearly recognises that human nature exhibits both negative aspects which require control and restraint and positive aspects which deserve to be cultivated. It is with an attempt to sketch such a more realistic account of the relationship between human nature and moral virtue that we shall now be concerned, amongst other things, in the next section.

Part III

VIRTUE, REASON
AND EDUCATION

9

VIRTUE AND PASSION: SELF-CONTROL AND EXPRESSION

So far, in previous sections, we have been concerned to examine the views of certain important theorists, both philosophical and empirical, on the nature of moral life, virtue and education. We have also drawn attention to serious difficulties about most of these views, however, difficulties based less often on their downright wrongheadedness and more often on the one-sided or limited nature of their perspectives on moral life and experience. I *do* believe, to be sure, that many modern accounts of the nature of moral wisdom or practical deliberation are quite simply mistaken, based as they are on a wholly unattainable ideal of pure or disinterested moral rationality, and I shall return in this section to a full consideration of this problem. But there is nevertheless a great deal of truth to be encountered in most of the views that we have so far considered – in Durkheim's view of the social origin and character of human moral life, in the Freudian-influenced views of Lane and Neill on the origins of much perverse and anti-social behaviour, in Piaget and Kohlberg's view of the importance for moral education of the promotion of certain capacities for rational judgement and so forth.

The trouble with such views is not so much that they are entirely in error as that they are in too great haste to locate the idea of moral development in some particular aspect or other of moral life and experience at the expense or to the exclusion of all others; they are all thus in a certain sense *reductionist*. For Hume and the emotivists (in their rather different ways) the crucial element in human moral life is to be found in the idea of feeling or sentiment, for Kant it is the idea of a universal law of reason, for Durkheim it is that of society, for the prescriptivists and the

191

psychologists of cognitive development it is the notion of moral self-determination, for certain educational progressives the idea of freedom from repression is crucial and so on.

Now certainly, as we have also seen, Aristotle attempted to elucidate the nature of moral life and to give an account of moral virtue principally in terms of the idea of a state or disposition of human character, but for him a state of character is a complex entity which, far from being reducible to or explicable in terms of either feeling or reason or self-determination or the social character of individual human existence, in fact requires reference to all these aspects of human experience. The *Nicomachean Ethics* contains important though obviously not final discussions of the place of all these aspects of human nature and moral experience – feeling, reason, self-control and weakness, the social character of moral life and the rest – in the constitution of those states of character ordinarily called virtues.

Like any great philosopher, Aristotle bequeathed as many problems as he attempted to solve, but the present work rests solidly on the view that the general moral–psychological approach which he adopted in his *Ethics* – the general strategy of attempting to understand moral life via some account of the logical structure of those complexes of human character and disposition called the virtues and of their place in human social life – is the most promising one available. To this extent the approach of the present work, like that of Aristotle, is *naturalistic* in a manner that has not been generally fashionable in modern moral philosophy until fairly recently.

Of course, this is not at all to deny that accounts of moral life must deal inevitably in certain *idealisations* in relation to human experience – with the realm of what morally *should* or *ought to be* rather than with what simply *is*; unlike social evolutionists, for example, I do not believe that whatever conduces to the survival of the fittest is to be appropriately regarded as right or good in human affairs.[1] It is to insist, however, that what may properly be regarded as right or good for human beings in moral terms requires to be clearly related to considerations about the needs, interests and desires that such beings are accustomed to have as biological and social creatures. (It is also, moreover, to see *these* aspects of human existence – the biological and the social – as crucially related; man's biological nature places certain definite limits or constraints on the character of what he can reasonably want as a social creature, whatever society he belongs to.)

It is for this very large reason that I believe that no satisfactory account of moral wisdom or deliberation can be given that does not show clearly what relation such deliberation bears to the proper *satisfaction* and not just the frustration of such natural human interests, desires and inclinations, and that is also why I find Aristotle's account of the nature of moral reason, as I shall shortly argue in greater detail, more illuminating than any other. In particular, I do not believe that Kant's view of the nature of moral rationality succeeds, precisely because of the sharp wedge that it drives between the ideas of moral judgement and natural inclination.

At any rate, I am inclined to the view that Aristotle's approach to understanding virtue and moral life is in general sufficiently fine-grained, exhibits the appropriate degree of complexity, to provide the right sort of model upon which a reasonable picture of moral experience – and hence of the right direction of moral education – might be constructed. Thus although in the following pages of this work I shall largely pursue my own reflections on the basic nature of the moral virtues in my own fumbling way, I shall also try to acknowledge something of much the same complexity that Aristotle himself recognised about the topic in his own work.

At the end of the chapter on Piaget and Kohlberg, then, I argued that no ultimately satisfactory account of the nature of moral virtue and moral life could be provided in terms of the development of rational judgement alone because moral life also requires to be characterised by reference to feeling and will; that is to say, some account has to be given of the way in which the virtues are informed or impeded by natural human sentiments and inclinations and also of the manner in which men are motivated (or disinclined) towards moral conduct. It seemed to me then as now that no fully satisfactory perspective on these matters can be generated from a consideration of the nature and provenance of moral reason alone.

In the chapters of this section I shall attempt to say something – by no means all that requires to be said – about these three main aspects of moral life and virtue; I shall try to provide rough perspectives on the nature of passion, motivation and reason in relation to the development and conduct of the moral virtues which will, I hope, have clear enough educational implications. In the final chapter I shall offer observations of a rather more general nature concerning questions of moral objectivity, subjectivity and relativism as these obviously affect considerations of moral education. Clearly, anything that I have to offer on these questions must ultimately be inadequate to the demands and the scale of the task from every conceivable point of view; the most I can hope for is that the discussions I shall provide may at least stimulate further and more able work in what I see as urgent as well as interesting directions.

First, then, the rest of this chapter is to be devoted to an examination of the nature and place of natural human feelings, inclinations and sentiments in human moral life via a consideration of the views of some distinguished recent philosophers on precisely these questions. My main quarry here is a widespread negative view of the role of feelings and instincts in human experience which we have encountered on numerous occasions already and which almost certainly has its source in classical and early modern accounts of the nature of morality.

Probably the first and perhaps the worst culprits in relation to this idea, then, were Socrates and Plato who seem to have taken the view that virtue consists largely in the suppression or denial of natural instincts and feelings which are to be construed for the most part as little more than sources of temptation towards self-destructive or anti-social behaviour. Thus, as far as we can see (though, of course, we are accustomed to viewing Socrates only through the eyes of Plato) the moral philosophy of these two great Greek philosophers was somewhat coloured by certain manichaean or dualist tendencies to regard the soul viewed as a potential source of moral goodness as susceptible only to corruption and perversion through its association with the lower nature of the physical body. Socrates and Plato would seem to have been among the very first to give human feelings and instincts a rather poor philosophical press.

To be sure, we encounter a significantly different view in Kant who is not in principle opposed to natural human inclinations and who clearly recognises that there are human feelings of a positive and beneficial as well as a negative and destructive kind. Nevertheless, *moral* conduct is for Kant that which follows from an individual's acknowledgement, via the proper exercise of rational practical deliberation, of the overriding demands of the moral law in relation to which his natural fellow feelings for those he assists through his charity or benevolence are neither here nor there; natural feelings are largely irrelevant to and have no significant role to play in human moral life.

It is only in the work of Aristotle that we encounter a view according to which natural human feelings and instincts enter into the practice of the moral virtues as essential elements – a view which tries to show how morally unsatisfactory conduct may follow from a defect of feeling just as much as from an error of judgement (as, for example, when a man behaves recklessly rather than bravely through a defect of due fear or caution). Aristotle, however, also gives an account of how feelings enter into the practice of the virtues which is not just, like Plato's, an account of the control or *suppression* of feelings. I shall now address this question of the relation of virtue to feeling via a consideration of the views of some more recent moral philosophers, however, and only indirectly in relation to Aristotle.

As a place to begin I shall attend first to the account of virtue offered by the philosopher G. H. Von Wright in a chapter of his work *The Varieties of Goodness*.[2] Although Von Wright's account is characteristically clear and insightful, I believe that it goes wrong, though there is much to be learned from the way it does go wrong. In his discussion, Von Wright turns first of all to Aristotle whom he calls 'the master philosopher' with respect to the topic of virtue, and although he is critical of Aristotle for allegedly regarding virtues rather too much by analogy with technical skills, he nevertheless proceeds to find much that he is able to endorse in the basic Aristotelian account. I shall forbear from tracing the considerable extent of my own agreement with his arguments concerning what the virtues are not, however, and I shall attend to his discussion after the point where having rejected views of virtues as skills, habits and features of temperament, he applauds Aristotle for identifying the moral virtues as *traits of character*.

Now, Aristotle, of course, went on to say that 'virtue, then, is a state of character concerned with choice, lying in a mean . . . this being determined by a rational principle'.[3] Von Wright finds the idea that virtue is concerned with choice of very much more interest than the doctrine of the mean, and it is to the nature of the choice with which virtue is allegedly concerned that he gives considered attention. Characteristic of choosing virtuously, he maintains, is that the good of some being, the choosing agent himself or some other person or persons is in question:

> To have another helping of a delicious dish is tempting, but may cause indigestion. Here *temperance* is needed for choosing rightly. Or if I provide myself with a third helping, some other person at the table may be deprived of the possibility of having a second helping. Then *consideration* is required.[4]

Aristotle, of course, spoke of virtuous choice being in accordance with a *rational* principle and this, as Von Wright observes, brings intellectual virtue into the general Aristotelian picture in the form of *phronesis* or practical wisdom. In order to choose rightly, then, a kind of knowledge – practical knowledge – is needed to help determine what is good or bad in particular circumstances requiring human decision. But Von Wright also maintains that the Aristotelian ingredients of state of character and choice in accordance with principles of practical wisdom need supplementing with a further notion – that of 'an emotion or feeling or passion' – in order for a complete account of virtue to be given. For, in general, according to Von Wright:

> Action in accordance with virtue may (thus) be said to be the outcome of a contest between 'reason' and 'passion'. . . . In the case of every specific virtue there is some specific passion which the man of that virtue has learned to master. In the case of courage, for example, the passion is fear in the face of danger. In the case of temperance it is lust for pleasure.[5]

In Von Wright's account, virtues are largely a matter of the subjugation in accordance with rational principles of unruly passions or emotions which, were they allowed to govern the conduct of men, would produce self-destructive or anti-social consequences – drunkenness, lasciviousness or injury to others. In looking for a name that might serve to characterise the virtues in general, Von Wright lights upon 'self-control' and he maintains that something like this may have been associated with the Greek word *sophrosyne*. He goes on to argue that the exercise of a particular virtue probably requires some susceptibility to the sort of temptation that the virtue in question characteristically shields one from. Thus no man insensitive to pleasure could truly be described as temperate, no one not subject to amorous passions chaste and, more strongly no one who had never experienced fear could possibly be described as courageous.

Now, in the very apt phrase which he uses to praise Aristotle, it seems to me that Von Wright has himself hit the nail on the head by introducing the idea of 'an emotion or feeling or passion'[6] as an essential ingredient in a satisfactory account of the nature of virtue, but it is precisely over the way in which he introduces it that one may begin to have serious reservations about his account. For although as we have seen, there is a certain intuitive appeal about the rather Platonic idea that basically virtue may be understood in terms of a fundamental *struggle* between reason and passion, difficulties soon appear when this notion is closely examined.

In fact, trouble arises as soon as we recognise that although Von Wright's account of the operation of the virtues for the most part fits the sort of examples he is inclined to give, it does not fit other examples at all well. He shrewdly discerns that there are several different ways of classifying the human qualities we ordinarily call 'virtues' and in relation to this he introduces two important distinctions. First, according to whether virtues are concerned with acts or forbearances (doing or refraining) he maintains we may distinguish traits like 'courage' on the one hand from what he calls the 'ascetic' virtues of chastity and temperance on the other. Second, he draws attention to another crucially important distinction between self-regarding virtues such as courage, temperance and industry, and other-regarding virtues such as consideration, helpfulness and honesty.

But clearly these distinctions cut across each other and they straightaway suggest a possible four-fold classification of: (1) ascetic self-regarding virtues (chastity); (2) ascetic other-regarding virtues (patience); (3) non-ascetic self-regarding virtues (industry); and (4) non-ascetic other-regarding virtues (charity). In view of this four-fold classification, however, it does not appear possible, merely by reference to the name of a virtue, to assign it to one category rather than another or to only one in particular. Clearly, for example, courage may be regarded as an ascetic or a non-ascetic virtue depending upon the manner and circumstances of its exercise. But there would appear to be dimensions of a quality like courage – that it may show itself in inaction as well as in action and in the bearing of our own sorrows as well as in suffering on behalf of others – that might incline us to include given instances of it under any one of the four just mentioned classifications. The point of most pressing importance for the moment, however, is that Von Wright's general account of virtue as the government of unruly passions fits what he calls other-regarding virtues far less well than those he calls self-regarding, though it doesn't fit all of the latter comfortably either.

As Von Wright observes, then, the courageous man is not he who experiences *no* fear in dangerous circumstances (for such a man would be simply foolish or reckless), he is the man who keeps his fear under reasonable control; and, likewise, the priest who observes chastity may well be a man who is required to control quite powerful sexual feelings. But the same element of self-control would not appear obviously to enter, for example, into charity or considerateness. If a selfish or inconsiderate person changes his ways to become unselfish or considerate in his dealings with others, it is not clear that there is any specifiable passion or emotion that he has learned to keep under control. Von Wright appears disposed to *define* virtue as *inter alia* the prudent control of an unruly passion or emotion and it would appear therefore that he would also define that which is contrary to a given virtue, let us call it the corresponding *vice*, as the akratic failure to control the passion or emotion in question.

Thus courageous and cowardly men have something very specific in common, for what is present in both cases is a state of fear. Again, chaste and lascivious men have feelings of sexual arousal in common, the difference being that whereas the chaste man controls them, the lascivious man seeks their wanton and promiscuous exercise. Von Wright is fairly insistent concerning the importance of this passion-subduing element in virtue maintaining, for example, that it is doubtful whether anyone should be called chaste if he is not prey to sexual temptation. So a rough generalisation of Von Wright's account would be that for every virtue, there is some unruly passion or emotion and some corresponding vice, such that whoever exercises the virtue controls the passion, and whoever doe not control the passion is prey to the vice (excluding, of course, circumstances of legitimate uncontrolled passion, for example, the marital discharge of sexual obligations). Particular separately identifiable passions and emotions, then, are the elements in common between virtues and their correlative vices – a ravenous appetite for food and drink, for example, would be what temperance and gluttony have in common.

Concerning charity viewed as an other-regarding virtue, however, the mean-spirited or uncharitable person who undergoes a change of heart to become generous-minded or charitable should no longer feel anything in common with his former self in his present state of charitableness. If, converted to his new attitude towards other people, he longer acts spitefully against them or engages behind their backs in assassination of their characters, we do not suppose that he is suppressing his former malicious feelings towards them but rather that he harbours such feelings no longer. Indeed, were a man who appeared to have changed his character and his attitudes towards others in this way, to betray in various small ways that he was still nursing spiteful feelings towards his fellows, we should no longer credit him with a change of heart but rather add hypocrisy to our original estimate of his mean-spiritedness.

Now this appears a pertinent sort of observation in relation to most of the virtues Von Wright calls 'other-regarding', but it also seems to apply too in the case of some of the self-regarding virtues. A person who was formerly vain or arrogant, for example, and who has now acquired modesty or humility has, by changing his ways, entirely repudiated his former vain self *and* the feelings that attended his vanity; consequently we may say with reasonable confidence that a person who is suppressing feelings of vanity or arrogance, however successfully, is not one of whom it may be truly said that he possesses the correlative virtues of modesty and humility. In short, progress from vanity, *hubris* or arrogance to modesty or humility requires a complete change of heart and not merely the control or suppression of a passion or emotion.

In her discussion of the notion of virtue the moral philosopher Philippa Foot observes that Aristotle appeared to be sensitive to something very like the distinction we have just indicated:

Adapting Aristotle's distinction between the weak-willed man (the akrates) who follows pleasure though he knows, in some sense, that he should not, and the licentious man (the akolastos) who sees the life of pleasure as the good life, we may say that moral failings such as these (vanity and worldliness) are never purely 'akratic'. It is true that a man may criticise himself for his worldliness or vanity or love of money, but then it is his values that are the subject of his criticism.[7]

According to Foot there is an essential element of false judgement in some vices and moral failings and, therefore, right judgement would appear to be an essential constituent in the corresponding virtues; as we have indicated above, the considerate person who was once inconsiderate and the modest man who was once vain have not come to be able to control inconsiderate or vain feelings so much as they have been converted to a new view of life or change of attitude towards themselves and others. But by this observation we are brought, I think, to recognise yet another and perhaps rather more important way of classifying virtues than those indicated by Von Wright – one that acknowledges a fundamental distinction between virtues that are largely a matter of self-control and those in which, speaking vaguely for the moment, self-control matters less than the right direction of attitude, value and feeling, and in which the need for self-control might even be a sign that the virtue is not fully present. The particular class of virtues which are not a matter of self-control that I wish to consider in this chapter, I shall refer to as the virtues of *attachment*.

Now, this class of character traits I wish to distinguish from the virtues of self-control as the virtues of attachment includes such other-regarding attitudes as unselfishness, considerateness, sympathy, benevolence, kindness, generosity, courtesy, respect, charity and possibly patience and tolerance, as well as such self-regarding virtues as modesty and humility. I say 'possibly patience and tolerance' because these virtues do appear to be consistent with a degree of self-control; occasions upon which patience and tolerance are exercised may well be ones that call for the control of a certain level of irritation or anger. All the same, it is arguable that if a person who regularly appeared patient had always to suppress powerful feelings of anger or irritation, it would be better to describe him as a person trying to be patient than as a patient person.

It may also appear irregular to label such self-regarding virtues as modesty and humility 'virtues of attachment', but since such conditions do imply a serious estimate of one's own worth in relation to others, and a serious consideration of other people thereby, they do fall, so I believe, into the same category as the virtues of charity and respect. And that category is mainly distinguished, so the argument has so far run, by the absence of the kind of inner struggle that according to Von Wright characterises such virtues of self-control as courage, temperance and chastity; genuine considerateness, sympathy or charity cannot coexist with inconsiderate, unsympathetic or uncharitable feelings. But if, in these cases, there is no struggle between reason and passion, what becomes of my insistence that Von Wright made an important point in the introduction of 'an emotion or feeling of passion' into his account of virtue?

In fact I do believe the notion of feeling or passion to be an essential ingredient in a satisfactory account of any virtue but it seems to me that Von Wright was mistaken in introducing it as an inevitable party to conflict with reason. As already noticed, virtues like considerateness, sympathy and charity are matters of attitude and value, and as such to be explained not merely in terms of the beliefs and judgements held by those who exhibit these traits but also in terms of the emotions and feelings of the individuals in question towards the objects of their attitudes and values. To have sympathy for another person, then, is not merely to observe his plight but also to care about it, and genuine charity follows not just from recognising that others need one's help but from feeling enough for them to want to assist. The point of crucial importance, therefore, is that whilst 'an emotion or feeling or passion' is just as important a feature of a virtue of attachment as a virtue of self-control, it is not in the former case engaged in a struggle with reason but is joined in alliance with it; reason and passion in virtues of attachment do not face one another in confrontation but face rather in the same direction. In the case of virtues of self-control, virtue results when passion is subdued by reason and vice follows from reason's defeat by passion; but in the case of virtues of attachment, the correct attitudes consist in believing *and* caring for the right things in respect of the good and well-being of others.

A rather more formal way of making the point might be to say that whereas in the case of virtues of self-control passion is related only *externally* to reason, passion and reason are related *internally* in the case of virtues of attachment. That is why it is impossible, rather than just difficult, to identify by name a specific emotion characteristically associated with inconsiderateness or vanity that the considerate or modest man might be said to be controlling, since the feelings can only be named after the vices which, *ex hypothesi*, the man with the correlative virtues does not possess. In short, whereas there is in the case of the courageous man a *separately* identifiable emotion fear which the cowardly man can also be said to possess, there is not necessarily in the case of the considerate man a separately identifiable feeling that the inconsiderate man should also be said to possess.

But, it may be objected, are not also the virtues of attachment inevitably a matter of self-control and discipline, since surely it is a fact that human beings care first for themselves and only secondly for others? Consistent with his general account of virtue Von Wright, for example, argues for this logical difference between self-regarding and other-regarding virtues: that whereas in relation to the former it is necessarily the case that one will want to do what is in one's own interests, it is only contingently the case in relation to the latter that one will want to do what is in the interests of others. If self-interest on the part of human beings is natural like the appetites for food and sex, then, caring for other people may only come with the kind of conscious and deliberate self-discipline associated with the virtues of self-control.

It is arguable, however, that although it may well be the case that the virtues of self-control require the imposition of strict discipline upon our more violent and unruly passions of fear and anger and upon our natural physical cravings and appetites for food and sex, there is no compelling reason to suppose that caring only for ourselves at the expense of others is natural in the sense that our sexual and other appetites are. In fact, the most casual consideration of human psychology and society would appear to present much evidence to the contrary. In relation to the facts of human psychology, Foot puts the point in a fairly extreme way:

It is possible, for example, that the theory of human nature lying behind the traditional list of virtues and vices puts too much emphasis on hedonistic and sensual impulses and does not sufficiently take account of less straightforward inclinations such as the desire to be put upon and dissatisfied or the unwillingness to accept good things as they come along.[8]

Now certainly, as Foot suggests, it cannot be doubted that there are many people who would make a virtue of self-martyrdom as well as not a few who appear to take a perverse delight in being abused or trodden on by other people. It is arguable, however, that such attitudes represent aberrations or perversions of human nature rather than qualities of any moral significance, that properly construed they hardly afford evidence of anything other than man's fundamental susceptibility to corruption and that on no account anyway should they be mistaken for anything resembling the altruistic virtues.

Indeed, if self-martyrdom is viewed as a method of getting one's own way or deriving personal gratification by causing others to feel guilty (as it very often is) and a readiness to suffer ill-treatment at the hands of others is understood as an expression of masochism, then there is nothing in these attitudes that is basically at variance with a self-interest conception of human nature. So although Foot successfully makes the point that human inclinations and motives are a good deal less uncomplicated than self-interest theorists often suggest, since human beings are frequently driven by purposes that explicitly conflict with their best interests, her point does not quite touch the heart of what is wrong with the self-interest theory. It seems to me, however, that in his work *The Virtues*, Professor Geach does state the crucial point clearly enough:

It is . . . sophistical to write as if the alternatives were moral virtue for its own sake and selfishness. Men are so made that they do care what happens to others; quite apart from respect for Duty, that is the way men's inclinations go. And Hume pointed out in a passage quoted by Mrs Foot, that it is precisely our concern for others that may tempt us not to observe justice; say, to divert to B money justly due to A, because A is a miser or profligate whom the money could not benefit, whereas B could benefit greatly.[9]

It does not, then, require the conduct of callous and cruel experiments depriving baby monkeys of their mothers[10] to show that human beings and at least some of their nearest mammalian relatives are social animals; and that to be a social animal is to need others of one's kind and to have an interest in and a care for their welfare in addition to one's own. Because man is a social creature, then, the other-regarding virtues of attachment, of caring, sympathy, charity and consideration for others, since they join him in harmonious and co-operative social relations with others of his kind, are as much needed by him as the self-regarding virtues of self-control. But whatever basis there might be for comparison between human qualities of sympathy, charity and consideration and non-human animal bonds of attachment, the former are *virtues* rather than instincts and it is important to emphasise that they should not be confused or simply identified with the feelings and sentiments that underlie them.

On this, we would do well to recall that what Aristotle said of the virtues in general very much applies to the virtues of attachment in particular – that 'Neither by nature, then, nor contrary to nature do the virtues arise in us'.[11] We should agree with Aristotle, I think, that none of the human qualities that have been referred to as 'virtues' in this paper are to be regarded as innate endowments; neither self-control nor consideration for others is a faculty like sight or an instinct like suckling. Of course, it could be said that the virtues of self-control are 'contrary to nature' in a way that the virtues of attachment are not, since they precisely involve, unlike the latter, the restraint or suppression of many of the 'natural' passions, desires and appetites of men. It is in this sense, at any rate, that those moral philosophers who have largely identified morality with self-control have regarded it as contrary to nature.

But the human qualities of goodwill and benevolence that we have identified as virtues of attachment are not contrary to nature in this sense, for although a human individual does not arrive into the world already in possession of qualities of care and consideration for others, such qualities do not appear, so we have argued, to be contrary to or in conflict with certain aspects of his nature as a developing social being. The virtues of charity, consideration and sympathy, then, are entirely in agreement with those positive feelings, inclinations and sentiments respecting the interests of others that men should come to feel, if nothing goes wrong, as social creatures. But possessing the virtues is clearly more than just feeling certain feelings since a virtue is 'determined by a rational principle' and the identity of individual virtues would indeed appear to depend upon the precise nature of the practical wisdom that informs them. But this now gives rise to a serious problem concerning the precise role of reason or rational principle in virtues of attachment.

It might be said, for example, that if, as on Von Wright's account, the role of reason with respect to such virtues as courage and temperance is to help control or subdue unruly feelings of fear and sensual pleasure so that their indulgence does not lead to vices of excess, it is difficult to see how Aristotle's doctrine of the mean could apply to virtues of attachment in relation to which there may be vices of defect but none of excess. The doctrine of the mean is, of course, notoriously difficult to interpret[12] and Aristotle himself betrayed some unease about it; but the clearest cases of its application would appear to be to such virtues of self-control as courage and temperance where recklessness and insensibility respectively may be reasonably well understood as vices of defect and cowardice and profligacy counted as vices of excess.

It is reasonably clear how a man might fall into error by being ruled too much or too little by fear or by submitting too much or too little to sensual pleasure. But if genuine considerateness and sympathy are underpinned by feelings of positive attachment to or concern for others, how could there be vices of excess in these cases and what need therefore of reason to control what appear to be fundamentally positive feelings of an altruistic kind? Surely, the altruistic feelings would be sufficient for the issue of virtuous conduct and there would be no need for any controlling operations of practical reason?

Turning again to Aristotle, we see that he did recognise vices of excess among some of the qualities we have called virtues of attachment. In matters of generosity, for example, he suggested that as well as erring on the side of defect through meanness a man could also err in the direction of excess through prodigality. And it is true that men are criticised for stupid and indiscriminate generosity and we speak both naturally and tellingly of being 'generous to a fault'. Again, Aristotle points to timidity or bashfulness as the excess of modesty (the defect of which is shamelessness) and, as we have seen, Foot mentions cases of apparent extreme unselfishness which seem to stem from a kind of neurotic indulgence in self-sacrifice for its own rather than other people's sake. In *The Great Divorce* one of the candidates for Hell of C. S. Lewis is the pitiful ghost of a mother who in her apparently selfless devotion to her son has clearly mistaken a fierce and uncontrolled possessiveness for legitimate maternal care and concern.[13]

But the trouble is now that such considerations may make it appear that the role of reason in virtues of attachment is not after all essentially different from that it has in virtues of self-control. Reason may again appear to be required to control excessive feelings of modesty, generosity, concern for others and so on, in a way that threatens the collapse of any distinction between virtues of attachment and self-control. I believe, however, that several further considerations serve to show why no such collapse need be imminent.

First: I believe it should be doubted that timidity and possessiveness are in fact cases of excess of modesty and unselfish concern for the welfare of others. Whereas it may reasonably be held to be the same state of fear that is felt and controlled by the brave man and felt but uncontrolled by the cowardly man, it is not clearly the same feeling that underpins either possessiveness and genuine concern for others on the one hand or timidity and modesty on the other. It just does not seem, that is, either that timid feelings are excessively modest feelings or that possessive feelings are excessively unselfish feelings. Perhaps the feelings that accompany timidity or possessiveness might be regarded (psychoanalytically perhaps) as neurotic perversions of modesty or care for others but it might be just as well to regard them as quite distinct sentiments. The role of practical reason in modesty and concern for others would not be to prevent degeneration by excess into the vices of timidity and possessiveness, but rather to judge when and how it was reasonable or appropriate to be modest or concerned for others in their and our own true interests. Thus the role of *phronesis* in these cases, though crucial, is not one of self-control.

Second: in the case of prodigality or being generous to a fault, whilst it seems that this may indeed involve an excess or overindulgence of the sentiment attending genuine generosity, it is not clear again that this case is quite analogous to that of courage and cowardice. Even if it is true that as in the case of courage and cowardliness it is the same passion or feeling that underpins generosity and prodigality, the failures of the prodigal and the coward are not alike in being failures of self-control in Von Wright's sense. For the failure of the coward to control his fear is essentially an akratic failure – a failure of nerve or will; his fear is a negative and destructive emotion that interferes with or deprives him of his powers of rational agency. The failure of the prodigal on the other hand appears to consist less in weakness of will than in error of judgement; the sentiment he feels may be judged positive and constructive enough, he is just unwise in the way he expresses it. It is not so much that like the cowardly man with his fear, the prodigal needs to control his feeling of generosity in the sense of overcoming or weakening its hold on him, but rather that he needs to exercise or express his generosity with greater prudence and caution in accordance with sound principles of practical wisdom.

Third: it just would, of course, appear unreasonable to suppose of very many virtues of attachment that they actually do represent happy compromises between states of excess and defect. Just as, generally speaking, there do not appear to be any nameable vices associated with being too truthful, just or honest, neither would there appear to be specifiable vices associated with being too considerate, tolerant or courteous, though, of course, the same point previously made about the prudent exercise of other-regarding virtues in accordance with principles of practical wisdom applies in these cases too. In these cases too, the role of practical wisdom would appear to consist in determining the appropriate circumstances and manner of exercise for the qualities of character in question, rather than in the control or subdual of the sentiments that underpin them.

In this chapter we have tried to identify some basic logical features of at least two quite different kinds of virtue; the virtues of self-control which largely represent the triumph of right reason over unruly passion or appetite; and the virtues of attachment in which judgements concerning the best interests of other people are attended by appropriate feelings of care and concern for them. For, as Foot has suggested, although it may well be the case that the man who is most courageous is he who has to put the most effort into controlling his fear, having to put a lot of effort into being charitable or sympathetic may well be a clear sign that the virtues in question are not wholly present. It may also be argued that whilst respect for the *principle* of courage is required to act bravely (especially in the face of considerable danger) it is not at all like this with something like caring for others. In fact, I am inclined to argue that far from caring for others because we revere some such principle as that of respect for persons, we revere the principle in so far as we are naturally inclined to care for others.

But both the kinds of virtues we have considered are clearly of importance for human well-being since, both in our own interests and those of other people, we are required to control our more troublesome and anti-social passions and appetites *and* also to create the sort of climate of co-operative and harmonious social relations that is generally promoted via the exercise of such qualities as tolerance, consideration and charity and also presupposed to decent human life.

10

VIRTUE AND MOTIVATION: OBLIGATION AND ASPIRATION

As we have lately noticed, though the moral virtues are by no means concerned exclusively with the suppression of negative feelings, passions and emotions, since they are also concerned with the proper expression of the more positive altruistic sentiments, nevertheless, they involve the general discipline of natural dispositions in ways that may clearly go against the grain of natural human inclination. Becoming just, courageous, temperate, charitable and the rest may well require the inhibition of certain natural human feelings or the control of various basic desires at the cost of considerable hardship and difficulty. In this respect at least, Aristotle's analogy between acquiring a virtue and learning a technical skill[1] seems quite appropriate; whatever the sense of achievement to be gained from learning to play a difficult piece of music on the piano or from having disciplined oneself for the pursuit of some worthwhile charitable project, the process of working oneself up to these accomplishments may well be long, arduous and tiresome, and a person might well wonder in the course of it whether the project is truly worth the effort involved.

And, indeed, moral philosophers have wondered about precisely this question with respect to the pursuit of the moral or virtuous life. For whereas it may be easy enough to see what rewards attend the perfect mastery of a musical instrument – if not the intrinsic pleasure of just playing, then the fame, the money, the foreign travel and the adoration of beautiful women – it may appear less easy to see what a person might gain from a lifetime of self-sacrifice and dedication to others as a good and trusted servant of the community, especially if, as some moral sages are prone to remind us, good or virtuous acts when performed for the sake of an extrinsic reward, even a feeling of self-congratulation, hardly count as virtuous acts at all. What, after all, is the attraction of the lifetime of sacrifice made by parents on behalf of a handicapped child, if they are to be denied even the feeling that they are to be commended for doing the right thing?

In short, one can easily see how it might in the long run pay a man to put a lot of effort into training himself to be an actor, sportsman or musician, but how does it pay him to put the same effort into becoming morally good? Why should a person engage in something so difficult as improving himself morally or becoming more virtuous when so often the only reward of virtue is to be put upon, even abused, by others?

We have seen that one highly influential modern attempt to answer this question simply insists that we should not look for a reward for being virtuous or obeying the moral law as we might reasonably so look in relation to other practical enterprises. We properly engage in moral conduct not out of any desire for personal reward or satisfaction but guided by a rational recognition that we are required so to behave irrespective of our personal desires; not because of what we want but because of what we owe in terms of public duties and obligations. In short, on this view moral motivation is of a quite different order from prudential motivation and the grounds of moral conduct have to be sought in terms quite other than those relating to our natural interests and purposes as human agents.

And, of course, there can be little doubt that, from a moral or any other point of view, obligations provide agents with genuine reasons for action. Many of the actions that we ordinarily perform are done precisely because we have promised or entered into some kind of contract with others to do them and contracts and promises clearly create duties and obligations. Our fulfilment of these duties and obligations is not usually, however, unconnected with what we want. Thus we often (though not always) enter into contracts and make promises because we expect to benefit in certain ways and it is the nature of the case that we stand frequently to harm ourselves as much as others by breaking contracts or reneging on our promises; even if we do not become involved in expensive litigation over such breaches we are liable to undermine the confidence of others in our word and to gain an inconvenient reputation as untrustworthy. Be this as it may, however, the important question for now is whether the idea of a duty or obligation, derived as it is from that of a contract, is sufficient to explain all those features of human association and intercourse which we should reasonably want to regard as moral or as involving ethical considerations.

Clearly, in the social and political philosophy of such early modern theorists as Hobbes, the idea of contract looms large; the moral obligations, duties and requirements which people do recognise on this view, moreover, they acknowledge for the sorts of reasons we have just given – for what they stand to gain from honouring their contracts and what they risk losing from their breach. For many contract theorists, however, society is itself regarded as the product of a kind of agreement entered into by self-interested individuals for precisely prudential reasons and this seems to be a position which is difficult to sustain.[2] For whilst it is relatively easy to make sense of the ideas of obligation, agreement and contract against a background of other more fundamental kinds of human association – ties of kinship, culture, tribal status and so on – it is rather more difficult to make much sense of the idea that contracts might forge such ties out of some kind of pre-social human chaos.

The more serious problem for many philosophers of the later modern period about identifying moral obligations with precisely this sort of contractual obligation is that the commitments thus generated are too prudentially motivated or personally biased to count as moral commitments. For Kant, to commend a man in respect of the fulfilment of his moral duty is to honour him for acting in something like a principled or disinterested way and for rising above his personal desires and inclinations. But in that case the law or covenant from which moral obligations are derived cannot be of either a local or a prudential nature but must be one that has the authority to require the obedience of all agents irrespective of whatever they may or may not have to gain personally from their entry into it.

If, however, the moral law is to motivate men through something other than their natural wants, desires and inclinations it must do so through what is in some sense external to those desires. As many ancient and modern philosophers have concluded in a variety of different ways, then, the only element

211

of human psychology which seems capable of an objective, impersonal and disinterested response to the world of experience is reason; thus on the Kantian view the source of moral motivation must be a rational will which is capable of discerning a universal and impartial moral law and which recognises that law as the ultimate authority in human practical affairs.

So starting from the idea of morality as the fulfilment of a duty or obligation rather than the pursuit of one's personal interest one moves to the notion that duties and obligations are created by the existence of some sort of covenant or contract. But since moral obligations cannot be generated by the merely prudential and self-serving contracts of mundane human practical experience they must be the product of a law or contract which is not of this world – the Kantian moral law which arises from the very idea of rational agency itself and from which, via the notion of universalisation, it is held that all significant human moral obligations can be derived.

But it seems to be reasonably clear from Kant's own illustrations that they cannot. In the *Groundwork* Kant examines particular instances of four important categories of moral duty which he believes can be derived from the idea of the moral law by universalisation.[3] First, he distinguishes between duties towards others and duties to ourselves and second, between perfect and imperfect duties. The distinction between obligations owed to others and obligations to oneself appears reasonably straightforward – I owe it to other people to do the best I can to promote their welfare but I also owe it to myself to do much the same on my own behalf (even though or especially because my own welfare may involve something I do not personally want like going to the dentist).

The rather cloudier distinction between perfect and imperfect duties seems to be between those moral obligations which require a specific practical response and those which allow me some freedom of expression with respect to fulfilling the duty. Thus Kant offers as his example of a perfect duty towards others the requirement to keep our promises – in order to fulfil this duty I am required to keep precisely those particular promises I have made to others. Regarding the imperfect duty towards others of benevolence, on the other hand, it is not required that I should be benevolent to this or that particular person in some specified way, only that I should be benevolent to some person or persons in some way on some occasion or another. Likewise, a perfect duty towards myself is the duty never to take my own life and an imperfect duty to myself is the requirement not to waste my talents; although it is specified that it is my own life that I should take care to preserve it is not laid down which of my talents I should seek to develop and presumably there is some scope for choice here.

Still, concerning these four categories of practical human conduct and the precise examples of them that Kant gives, I think that most people would agree that they all have genuine moral significance; that is to say, most people's moral intuitions would incline them to the view that *some* sort of moral failure – some defect of character, degree of wickedness or variety of irresponsibility – is involved in cases of promisebreaking, misanthropy, suicide and squandered talent. But Kant appears to believe that the rational procedure of universalisation will show precisely what this is in each of his cases – it will demonstrate clearly that it is somehow rationally self-defeating for a person to will that all might break their promises, fail to exhibit benevolence, take their own lives or waste their talents.

There are very many difficulties about the notion of universalisation, not least that unless it is checked by certain arbitrary restrictions it is possible to characterise any action whatsoever in such a way that the universalisation of it might appear reasonable from some point of view. What is of even greater significance in the present context, however, is that universalisation will not clearly do what has been asked of it – to demonstrate what is morally obligatory – in at least three out of four of Kant's cases, for the simple reason that any moral incentive we may have as human agents to be benevolent, talent-developing or life-preserving is not at all naturally expressed as a matter of duty.

For a start, the very idea of a duty to oneself is notoriously problematic if not just downright nonsensical. There are, to be sure, self-regarding virtues about which we shall shortly have much to say; but to feel rightly that it is a defect of character on my part, a consequence of inertia, apathy or spinelessness, to fail to develop my God-given talents, is merely to acknowledge that I am not making as much of myself as I might. Precisely nothing is added to my recognition that I am failing through indolence to realise some potential human good by saying that

I am reneging on some *duty*. This is all the more so to the extent that the potential human good that I am failing to realise is a matter of *self*-development and in Kantian terms there would appear to be nothing beyond personal interest – nothing in the notion of the moral law – that would require such self-development.

Precisely nothing, then, is added to the thought that this is something I should be doing to better myself or preserve my own life by my saying to myself, 'You have a duty to do this', and no peculiar compulsive force enters into my character by my silent utterance of these words. The simple point is, I suppose, that the ideas of duty and obligation are relative to those of contract and covenant and these are essentially notions of interpersonal or public agreement. Thus, since I can make a promise to John Doe or a covenant with my greengrocer I can have certain obligations to them, but I cannot in the same way, if at all, create a contract between me and myself which would generate a genuine obligation to myself.

But again, whatever I may be inclined to bestow on other people by way of benevolence is not comfortably characterised as a duty or as something that I am obliged to do. Actually a good deal depends here on what Kant precisely meant by benevolence, but if it means being charitable or kindly disposed to other people rather than merely being inclined to assist or co-operate with them in their various enterprises, then it seems clear enough that much of the moral value we ascribe to benevolence is in recognition of its supererogatory features – the extent to which it goes beyond mere duty, exceeding rather than merely observing the letter of the law. It is precisely this consideration which has contributed an air of paradox to the Kantian observation (despite the more charitable constructions that some have tried to impose on it) that there is something rather more morally admirable about the man who performs a charitable act out of a sense of duty and against his own natural disinclination to do so, than there is about another who does so merely out of a natural love for his fellow men.

But, of course, though it may indeed be more morally admirable to do certain things from a sense of duty than from a love of doing them (sentencing a man to a term of life in prison, for example) benevolent acts would not seem to be numbered among these. Here it seems that the perfectly correct recognition that the virtue of benevolence or charity is not merely a matter of natural inclination has been wrongly construed as meaning that it should not involve natural feeling or inclination at all, only a rational acknowledgement of duty; but this is just false.

Kantian sympathisers have been inclined to defend the idea of benevolence as a duty justified in terms of rational universalisation by construing it as essentially an injunction to help or co-operate with others whenever required; on this view it does indeed seem incoherent to will universal nonco-operation since that would precisely serve to undermine those contractual aspects of human social life upon which we all depend at some time or another. This makes willing unbenevolence appear to be, like willing universal nonpromisekeeping, a case of sawing off the branch upon which one is sitting; to will that no one should ever assist his fellows threatens to undermine a social practice upon which we all depend for individual and social survival. There are, however, at least two serious problems with this view. The first is that on this interpretation of matters, Kant has offered a prudential justification for what he maintains is a moral practice and the second is, quite simply, that a contractually defined notion of assistance or co-operation just is *not* benevolence.

In fact, it would appear that the only morally significant practice which Kant comes near to justifying through the idea of universalisation is that of promisekeeping. On the face of it, promisekeeping does appear to have the character of a covenant to which we are all required to be party as rational members of a human community (something which, in turn, we have not much choice about) and which commands our assent so long as we wish to continue as members of such a community. From this viewpoint it does seem to be rationally self-defeating to will it as a universal law that no one should honour or be sincere in the making of promises since in any society in which this was generally willed life would be not so much intolerable as impossible. Be that as it may, however, it is still possible to regard Kant's justification of promisekeeping as standing matters rather on their head.

For it is still not so much the case that promisekeeping is justified on the grounds that it is not rational to will that no one should make sincere promises; it is rather that it is not rational to will the making of insincere promises precisely because of the indispensibility and centrality of the institution (convention, contract or what you will) of promisekeeping in human social life. We may make this general point by observing that as human agents we are not moral in order to be rational but rational in order to be moral; the proper view of the nature of practical wisdom or reasoning is that it is instrumental to the ultimate goal of individual and social human life of being moral or virtuous. Thus small children quickly grasp the point and importance of making and securing promises (as well as the advantages of making lying promises) long before they have any real grasp of notions like universalisation. Kant seems to argue as though the moral value of promisekeeping is underpinned by the rationality of the practice whereas in fact it is really the other way around.

It is also arguable, however, that although when I keep my promises, thereby respecting the practice of promisekeeping, I am engaging in conduct that has a contractual character, I am nevertheless not normally doing something that I should readily *describe* as honouring the institution of promisekeeping but rather something I would call paying the gas bill, respecting Anne's confidence, settling my gambling debts, returning a favour and so on. Whereas, then, I will normally have a particular reason (moral or otherwise) for acknowledging an obligation in any of these or a thousand other circumstances the one thing that I do not normally have or require a reason for is keeping my promises in general. I will have reasons good, bad or indifferent for keeping this promise or breaking that one but not for keeping promises *as such* which is merely a general presupposition of contracts moral and otherwise rather than a motive for keeping a particular promise.

Consequently, despite the fact that to make a particular promise is to contract into some agreement which we need a reason to break, if not a reason to keep, the practice of promisekeeping is not itself a contract which can generate particular obligations and duties construable as motives for action. So even in the case of Kant's final category of perfect duties towards others such as the requirement to respect promises and contracts, it seems that this places no particular duties or obligations upon the rational agent. I may be bound to meet this obligation or that one depending on the precise circumstances of the agreement under which I have placed myself but neither the existence of the social practice of promisekeeping nor my recognition that it is a sensible practice actually *constrains* me as a rational agent to keep promises as such.

In fact, it is arguable that to believe that the moral status with respect to the social contract of the practices of promisekeeping and truthtelling is crucial or overriding to the extent that we are thereby provided with a firm reason why promises should *never* be broken or lies *never* told is a dangerous piece of moral superstition which was well exposed by Plato in the early part of the *Republic*.[4] To be sure, lying and promisebreaking are always morally reprehensible and should be avoided as a matter of principle – but not at all costs; not if the occasional lie can save the life of another person or a breach of promise, the destruction of the state.

Anyway, the upshot of all this is that although contracts, duties, obligations and promises do provide us with valid reasons for behaving in this, that or the other way aptly describable as moral, they do not provide us with the only reasons of a moral sort there are. A man may be commended in moral terms for courageously enduring a painful illness or for his selfless charitable work with down-and-outs although his reasons for such conduct are not founded on any recognition of duty or obligation. Moreover, it is instructive that Kant, the philosopher who sought more than any other to ground moral conduct in the idea of duty, does not clearly succeed in this task in relation to any of his own chosen examples. Any prohibition against suicide or exhortation to develop one's talents cannot be clearly grounded in a duty to oneself (though, of course, the prohibition against suicide might be grounded in a duty to *others*) because the idea of a duty to oneself is far from coherent, we are simply not *obliged* to be benevolent towards others and although Kant may well be right that it is generally rational to keep one's promises and to will that everyone else should too, that does not seem to turn promisekeeping into a duty in the way that my making a marriage vow obliges me to love, honour and obey my wife.

The principal problem about the observations of Kant and some of his followers on the moral law and the obligations to which it is alleged to give rise, is that they trade in notions which are too far abstracted from the actual sorts of circumstances in which real obligations and duties are normally generated. In attempting to locate the moral law at some point above and beyond those specifiable human interests, purposes and roles in the context of which duties have their rightful place, Kantians fail to show how their moral imperatives might reasonably engage with anything we could conceivably regard as genuine human motivation. So whilst it is relatively easy to see why a man might acknowledge a duty or a responsibility towards his wife and children, it is less easy to see why he should recognise an *obligation* to keep his promises as such – whether or not, that is, he considers keeping promises to be a good thing.

But whatever we may think of the knotty problems of promise-keeping, Kant's more obvious failure to ground the moral motives of benevolence, self-development and self-preservation in the idea of duty or obligation is most instructive. In fact Durkheim, who was often severely critical of Kant, nevertheless, subscribes to an ethics which is even more uncompromisingly deontological than Kant's and which forces him to recognise quite clearly the overwhelming difficulties about basing the virtues of benevolence and self-regard on the idea of a duty. As we have seen, Durkheim regards morality as precisely a matter of the individual's recognition of the duties which he owes as a member of a given society; not so much to the other members of that society, but to the *idea* of society as such – to its laws, customs and conventions.

Consequently, since he sees morality as purely a matter of social duty and obligation, he is quite clear, unlike Kant, that little in the way of moral value or significance can be attached either to what people do for themselves or to anything that they might do for others which goes beyond the call of duty. Anything that we do on our own behalf is presumed to have a prudential more than a moral character and charitable action which goes beyond what is expected of us is to be regarded as having *aesthetic* rather than moral significance (apparently because it is prompted by feeling more than a rational sense of duty.)[5]

Although it is clear enough that all of this follows from something hardly distinguishable from the Kantian way of thinking about morality, it also embraces conclusions that Kant was clearly unwilling to accept. As we have seen, for example, despite his view that morality requires to be sharply distinguished from self-interest, Kant was clearly concerned to

218

preserve the view that there are self-regarding virtues – virtues which concern self-development and the preservation of one's own life and so forth. We have seen, however, that the only way in which Kant can accommodate such an idea in his ethical system is by appeal to the dubious notion of duties to oneself – dubious because since the ordinary notion of a duty is that of something publicly owed to some other person or some external institution, there is some obscurity about the idea of being obligated to oneself.

But the problem is even more serious than this, since it is not just that it is difficult to view the self-regarding virtues as duties, but also that in the general context of Kant's moral philosophy it is well nigh impossible to see them as relevant to moral life at all. It has often been observed that the fundamental idea at the root of Kantian universalisation is that of simple reciprocity or reversibility – the tit-for-tat moral principle of the golden rule as expressed in 'Do as you would be done by'.[6] On the face of it this sounds like a positive enough injunction to help others wherever and whenever possible in circumstances in which were we similarly placed we should also wish to receive the assistance of others. The trouble is that combined with the liberal Kantian principle of respect for persons, the requirement to respect the autonomy or freedom of other people, the golden rule is susceptible of the rather more negative reformulation 'Do *not* do unto others what you would *not* have them do unto you'.

In fact this slight recasting of the golden rule is of the very highest consequence because whereas the positive formula, if it can be combined with some principle of benevolence (though as we have seen benevolence seems to be only doubt-fully universalisable in Kantian terms) is quite consistent with helping people who have some trouble helping themselves, the negative formula tends to counsel non-interference in the affairs of others out of respect for their personal integrity, no matter how diminished that may be. What am I to do about the alcoholic down-and-out who is clearly set on a short road to his own destruction? I can try to straighten him out on the grounds that what he is doing to himself appears not to be conducive to the goal of human flourishing and that if he cannot help himself then someone else should help him. But this clearly involves a certain attitude of condescension and of paternalistic disrespect for his freedom of choice in relation to the way he wishes to live his life. If he wishes to drink himself to death then that is surely not my business. I should not like it if he tried to interfere in my affairs, so why should I interfere in his? Thus, derivable from the basic idea of reciprocity combined with the principle of autonomy is the fundamental liberal principle that the only real offence against morality is an unwarranted and illegitimate interference in the affairs of other people – a principle codified by the nineteenth-century utilitarian thinker John Stuart Mill[7] and widely subscribed to by moral philosophers of the liberal tradition ever since.

The problem, however, with this overall perspective on the nature of moral life and experience – the view that all significant moral transgressions come down to unwarranted interference in the affairs of others or to some failure of the democratic spirit with respect to other people's choices about how they wish to live their lives – is that it cannot give much real content to the idea that there are self-regarding virtues for which people may be praised and blamed which is not broadly utilitarian in character or does not measure personal moral failures exclusively in terms of their adverse effects on others. To be sure, suicide or alcoholism may be deplored on the grounds that they devastate the lives of other people besides the drunk and the suicide, and buried talents may be regretted because they are unproductive of so much potential human good to others, but nothing much of *intrinsic* moral disvalue may be attributed to idleness or alcoholism. If a man wants to spend all of his days drunk or lying in bed and this does not seriously inconvenience other people, then that is his own affair and no one else's – the liberal perspective has no power and little inclination to pass judgement on his personal choice of life-style.

But whilst this basic liberal principle of live and let live seems eminently reasonable and tolerant from a philosophical point of view, it would yet seem to fail to do full justice to our ordinary moral intuitions and experience. For in fact we do as part of our common moral experience pass judgement not only on the respects in which people are prone to violate the rights or intrude upon the personal space of others, but also upon the ways in which they fail, deceive and abuse themselves even when such abuses have no noticably adverse social consequences. We do regard it as a shortcoming of a moral kind when a man neglects to realise his potential and use the gifts and abilities he was born with through sheer laziness, apathy or a failure of resolution. We often consider it to be not merely ludicrous but also a matter for moral reproof when a person allows himself to become blown up with vanity or conceit over a piece of not especially well-deserved good fortune. Again, it may be regarded as a moral failure when a person oversteps the bounds of reasonable social drinking to seek total escape from reality in drugs or alcohol or allows himself to become obsessed with pornographic or sadistic fantasies.

We deplore these states of affairs even when they do not seriously inconvenience other people because we regard such conditions as hardly conducive to a decent, well-balanced and healthy human life; these personal defects of cowardice, laziness, apathy, vanity, intemperance, conceit and perversion are offences precisely against the self-regarding virtues of courage, industry, commitment, humility, self-control, modesty and purity. They are vices or failures of moral character not primarily because they adversely affect or involve failures to fulfil obligations towards other people but because they sour and corrupt the life of the individual whose vices they are and prevent him from becoming all that he might be. There is nothing, moreover, at all extraordinary about the view of matters that we are currently taking – the names of the virtues and vices in terms of which we evaluate individual lives are simply the common conceptual currency of (any) everyday moral experience; what is rather more extraordinary is that there appear to be modern moral perspectives which do not seem to regard it as especially a matter for moral judgement (but rather perhaps of personal taste) whether a man lives his life self-indulgently, conceitedly or impurely rather than otherwise, just so long as he doesn't, so to speak, frighten the horses.

But just as the present view of the moral significance of the self-regarding virtues would appear to be somewhat at odds with the basic tenets of modern liberalism so, of course, were most of the philosophers of classical antiquity, particularly Socrates, Plato and Aristotle. To mark the contrast as sharply as possible we may begin with a brief rehearsal of the relevant ideas of Socrates and Plato. It is clear enough then, that both these Greek philosophers had a reasonably clear view of moral value as something directly attributable to the personal lives of individuals irrespective of the overt or public effects or consequences for pain and pleasure of their actions on other people. As we have seen, in Plato's *Gorgias* and other early to middle period dialogues, an important analogy is pressed between the health of the body and the health of the soul; wickedness or injustice is held to be to the soul as physical disease is to the body and Socrates maintains that just as it is better for a man to be cured, even painfully, of his bodily infirmity than it is for him to continue to suffer a deterioration in his physical health, so it is better for the unjust man that he be corrected or punished for his wickedness in the larger or long term interests of his moral or spiritual health.[8]

In short, Socrates and Plato hold to a conception of the moral value of the individual which is founded upon an idea of the health or well-being of the soul; the important point to grasp here is that if the unjust man is to be punished it is in his *own* interests and in so far as it might effect a change of his heart or bring him to see the error of his ways – punishment is for the good of the offender rather than a matter of retribution or deterrence. Of course, Socrates and Plato do place a high value on social or public order and justice but for them social justice is related *internally* to justice within the individual – it is just the public expression of personal virtue; there may be true justice in social and political terms only if there is true justice or virtue in the hearts of individual citizens (or at least of the rulers of those citizens). One might say that for them, the virtue or goodness inherent in individual lives has a certain logical priority over goodness or justice at the social and political level.

It is reasonable so to express matters, however, only so long as one is quite clear that for Socrates and Plato the soul is not something private and incorrigible to be sharply contrasted with something public and social. To be sure, the soul is private and personal to the extent that it is in terms of souls that moral agents are individuated – a person is directly responsible only for the state of his own soul – but it is also social and political to the extent that the virtues and vices through which souls manifest themselves are dispositions to conduct apt for public expression in everyday contexts of human association. Broadly, to speak in Socratic–Platonic terms of the soul of a person is to speak of the character of his life, and the quality of that life – whether it is courageous or cowardly, charitable or spiteful, drunken or sober and so on – is something which has both personal and private, public and social dimensions and implications.

Unlike the modern liberal perspectives which appear to drive a wedge between the private and the public, hiving off the moral aspects of a person's life exclusively into the public domain of other-regarding duty and obligation, the Socratic–Platonic view makes no such division and recognises an intrinsic connection between personal character and public morality. For the Greeks, then, it is reasonable to expect men to be just with respect to affairs of state only if they are temperate and self-controlled as private individuals since public injustice is just large-scale intemperance. It is sensible to expect them to be loyal and faithful to their country only if they have some grasp of filial piety and eschew adultery because genuine patriotism is just personal and familial loyalty writ large.[9] It is reasonable to expect statesmen to be politically above corruption only if they are beyond greed and lust as private individuals and so on. In general, a man may be expected to exhibit other-regarding virtues and to acknowledge duties and obligations towards others only if he also possesses self-regarding virtues and is capable of exhibiting some degree of excellence or integrity in his personal moral life.

But it is also important to grasp that there is no particular order of priority here for Socrates and Plato between the self- and other-regarding virtues – it is certainly not the case, for example, that the self-regarding virtues are to be valued only in so far as they contribute to the promotion of virtues of a more other-regarding, public or social kind. For them, all the moral virtues of courage, temperance, justice and so forth, whether or not they benefit others or are of benefit only to the individual himself, are of the highest value because they are all aspects of what it means to live well as a human being. Part of living well is, to be sure, that a man keeps his word, acknowledges his duties and fulfils his obligations to others; but it is only a part, because if he does all of this and yet leads a life characterised by vanity, self-deceit, intemperance and impurity, he is not living well in any reputable sense.

Socrates and Plato, then, have a very unmodern conception of moral virtue and value which is not just rooted in or narrowly confined to notions of other-regarding public duty and obliga-tion, and they would have insisted that for a man to fail morally is more than just a matter of his reneging on his social contracts; it is for him to fail to achieve a certain quality of spiritual life which is only partly exhibited in his observance of obligations. We have already observed, moreover, in what that quality of life consists. The crucial difference between the just or virtuous man and the unjust or vicious one is to be expressed essentially in terms of the relationship of the reasonable or rational aspect of human nature to the unreasonable, appetitive or passionate part.

The just or virtuous man, then, is he in whom reason rules the passions in accordance with some vision of or some degree of clarity concerning the form or idea of the good; by contrast the unjust or wicked man who is enmeshed in a relentless, indiscriminate and unprincipled pursuit of his basic sensual passions and appetites in the name of which he will commit any crime or cruelty resembles nothing less in his slavery to the passions than a leaky cauldron in constant need of replenishment. The important point that Socrates and Plato are here making is that the wicked man is not just a criminal (or potentially so); he is also a *victim*; he is in a certain kind of bind from which no true human fulfilment, satisfaction or happiness is to be derived.

Just as for Socrates and Plato the public life of virtue and justice is the natural outcome or expression of the freedom from the passions which follows from the individual's submission to the authority of reason, so the external life of injustice, wickedness and depravity is a reflection of an inner bondage to the basic passions and appetites. Thus, on the Platonic view, wickedness and injustice are to be regarded as symptoms of a gross ignorance of the nature of the good as this stands to be discerned through the proper exercise of reason or wisdom; freedom from the ties that bind us to the passions and appetites is thus an enabling state of affairs – it liberates us for the life of virtue and justice which is absolutely presupposed to any genuine conception of human well-being or flourishing.

Now, as we have also seen, Aristotle departs significantly from Socrates and Plato in his general view of the proper relationship of moral reason to the feelings and passions; he believes, unlike them, that feelings are crucially implicated in the moral virtues to the extent that the virtues may be regarded as in a large part just disciplined (rather than suppressed) feelings. We have also in this work generally preferred Aristotle's account of moral virtue and reason to that of Socrates and Plato. But against the moral prophets of modernity Socrates, Plato and Aristotle stand united on this fundamental issue: that the dispositions characteristic of the moral life are self-regarding as well as other-regarding and that it is generally speaking as much in the interests of the moral agent as of other people that he engages in moral conduct.

Thus the moral perspective of the philosophers of classical (Greek) antiquity has been described as an ethics of *aspiration*[10] as opposed to an ethics of *obligation* because for all these great ancient Greek philosophers it would seem that once a man has been properly educated to understand what the life of virtue is really about, there can be very little mystery concerning why he should want to pursue that life to the very last ounce of his strength. From this point of view it may be seriously doubted whether the Greeks could really understand the precise problems that modern philosophers have raised about the nature of moral motivation.

It *would* be clear to them, of course, how a man might aspire to the virtuous life and yet fail, because the cultivation of the moral virtues is difficult and requires much self-discipline; there are numerous and varied respects, then, in which a man might not come up to the mark or not be made of quite the right stuff for the achievement of those human excellences called virtues. This is hardly more difficult to understand than that a man might aspire to be a distinguished pianist but lack either the talent or the energy required, or that another might want to be successful as a rock-climber but lack the nerve. What is to the Greeks much less comprehensible, however, is that a man should understand fully what the life of moral virtue involves and yet not have any aspiration towards it.

Of course it is possible for a person to understand fully what is involved in piano-playing or rock climbing and yet not want to engage in these activities – precisely because not everyone is interested in rock climbing or piano music. But in what clear sense is it possible for a person to comprehend clearly what the life of moral excellence – of courage, justice, wisdom, temperance and the like – entails and not want to be courageous, wise, just and so on, for this would be to prefer the human conditions of cowardice, ignorance and injustice which are rightly despised as inferior by all rational men. It is common enough, of course, for a man not to want to follow this particular courageous course of action because he is afraid (though his being afraid would anyway be a condition of his being courageous) – just as it is likely that a man with an aching tooth will fear the visit to the dentist – but it is hardly possible for a man to want to be cowardly rather than courageous in roughly the same sense that it is hardly possible for a man to prefer a decayed tooth to a healthy one.

What would appear to have occurred during the modern period at least since the philosophical contribution of Kant is the creation of a conceptual opposition between morality and self-interest which would have been well nigh unintelligible to the Greeks. Acting from self-interest has come to be identified with something like acting *selfishly* in contrast with acting with regard to others which has been identified with the entire sphere of morality. But for the Greeks – Aristotle, for example – the self-regarding conduct which is exhibited in the practice of the moral virtues is precisely opposed to acting selfishly and it is regarded as entirely consistent with action on behalf of others. A *prima facie* self-regarding virtue such as courage or temperance is, after all, a social and public quality which is of benefit to the *polis* in general as well as to the agent himself; a man is a better man who is more successful in his personal enterprises for being courageous, but other men also benefit from his friendship and allegiance.

The life of moral virtue is thus a life of personal *and* public excellence which requires the firmest discipline of those wayward selfish inclinations which so often impede a man's progress towards being all that he should wisely want to be. But if that is the case then there ought to be little that is difficult to grasp about the connection between morality and self-interest; a sensible man regards it as in his own interest and therefore wants to be wise, courageous, just and temperate, because only a fool would wish to be ignorant, cowardly, unjust and a glutton.

Socrates, Plato and Aristotle, then, try to teach us that the virtues are those excellences which all free and rational men should want to profess; thus virtue ought not to be regarded as a matter of obligation so much as aspiration. But in this respect the modern period has precisely further confounded the problem of moral motivation by construing morality not just as a matter of other-regarding *as opposed to* self-regarding qualities, but also by identifying morality well nigh exclusively with the realm of duty and obligation. To be sure, duties and obligations represent an important aspect of our human social experience and they are inextricably woven into the fabric of moral life – but they are only part of that fabric. Particular duties and obligations come upon us with the roles we naturally assume by our belonging to the general web of human association in other ways – as sons, fathers, friends, lovers, compatriots, employees and so on.

However, I owe certain debts of filial piety first and foremost because that man is my father and I am his son and in general that means a good deal more in terms of human moral intercourse than stands to be expressed through the idea of a duty. The duties I owe to my father and mother are to some extent laid down for me by convention but the constraints that I truly acknowledge are in the light of what they have already freely given me in terms of love and care. Thus, obligations, duties and contracts acquire authority in human affairs only against the background of human ties which are not matters of duty and obligation; moreover, whereas these other ties possess the power to generate the duties, the duties have no power to generate the ties.

A duty or obligation, then, is something that is imposed on individuals in certain specific contexts of human social life – it is often a timely reminder to them of what they owe for what they have been given. Human nature needs such reminders, of course, because it is ever inclined towards backsliding and ingratitude. But it is a gross distortion to attempt to construct an entire account of moral life upon the notions of duty and obligation. If one does, not only does it become hard to see, as we have noticed, how a self-regarding quality like temperance might count as a virtue, it also becomes difficult to view such other-regarding dispositions as benevolence or generosity as virtues when they celebrate conduct which is not strictly required by law or covenant.

But why should a man want to give freely of his own wealth or possessions to others if he is not *required* to do so by some moral duty or obligation (such as a universalisation of the idea of charity or justice)? The problem with this question is that it

precisely presupposes or reflects the exclusive modern association of morality with what is required by law or duty – with
what is *imposed* (internally or externally) on the individual –
rather than with what the individual might freely aspire to be. In
modern times morality has come to be identified only with what
is onerous, tedious and unpalatable (duties are more often than
not described as 'painful' or 'unpleasant') and the very terms
'virtue' and 'morality' have acquired negative associations,
especially among young people, largely due to the association of
them with obligation and external constraint.

For the Greeks, by contrast, the virtuous man is held up
as someone we should want to be and the wicked or self-
indulgent man is an object of pity and scorn; moral virtue
is crucially a question of self-respect and self-improvement,
a matter of significant personal achievement. To the question
why I should not betray that secret which a friend has told me
in confidence, I might reasonably reply that since I promised not
to tell anyone else, I am bound by a duty (which conflicts
painfully with my desire to gossip). But it is surely just as
reasonable to reply that I should not like to be the kind of person
that betraying that confidence would make me – that there
is just something personally detestable about that kind of
dishonesty.[11] It appears that to a considerable degree modernity
has lost this idea of moral aspiration and self-improvement,
perhaps because it has abandoned the idea that there is a single
purpose to human life or a single route to personal salvation
or perfection; specifically, of course, it has jettisoned the teleological conception of human life and conduct which was so
central to Greek thought.

The reason why the virtues specifically related to the development of the self are no longer clearly regarded in modern
thinking as within the domain of morality is because it is no
longer considered that there is one goal of human fulfilment –
there are very many different lives to be led and no standpoint
from which any one of them might rationally be preferred to any
other. In fact, I suspect that modernity has merely muddied the
waters here as elsewhere. It may well be that we cannot and
should not return to precisely those antiquated metaphysical
conceptions of teleology canvassed by the Greek philosophers
of old,[12] but modernity has not yet shown how notions of
goal and purpose might be eliminated from our theoretical

discourse about human practical (including moral) life and I doubt whether this (for something like Kantian reasons) could be shown.

But even if the notions of goal and purpose require to be retained in order to explicate human moral life, is it reasonable to subscribe as modern men to the idea that there is *one* goal or purpose to which (as Aristotle suggests) all human activity tends?[13] Yes and no. No, in the sense that clearly people differently conceive the ends of human life as Christians, Moslems, Seventh Day Adventists, Communists, Flat-earthers and so on; but yes, in the sense that all must subscribe to a broadly similar conception of how human conduct is best shaped towards the proper achievement of these diverse ends and goals. And as a matter of fact the different advocates of different faiths and doctrines are remarkably agreed about this – that the different ends in question are best secured by agents who lead lives of wisdom, self-control and courage guided by some conception of human justice.[14]

In a fundamental sense, then, the pursuit of virtue transcends the different social ends and goals by which modernity has divided people from each other. Even if it is true that the different social ends and goals of human moral life to some extent shape different conceptions of the virtues (and we shall return to this problem) there is still nothing but sophistry and illusion in the way of believing that the principal moral goal of acquiring the virtues is something that all men should reasonably want. (And it is idle, of course, as well as in poor taste to introduce a problem at this point about the alternative justice and virtue of people like the Nazis; we condemn Nazism precisely on the grounds that it was inconsistent with virtue and justice.)

The problem that modernity has created, however, is to have made all moral motivation an onerous and unattractive matter – a matter of painful duty rather than personal aspiration. It has made it look like a matter of thankless service or bondage to others rather than something that might be viewed as a free expression of all that is best in the human spirit. At the same time that it becomes obscure what morality has to do with self-interest, it also becomes unclear how it might be related to any love or regard for people that goes beyond duty or obligation. There can be small doubt, moreover, that such modern perspectives have had a lamentable influence on many young people today.

229

It is quite true, of course, that there are legions of young people who, with the right outlooks bred into them by good homes and caring parents, continue to perceive what is admirable about virtue through the fog of lies that have been woven about her by the rhetoric of modernity – young people who lead lives of self-respect, decency, sobriety and genuine altruistic concern for those less fortunate. There are far too many others, however, who have been blinded by the rhetoric; who have come to believe that morality is a matter of reluctantly doing one's duty or fulfilling one's obligations where this cannot be avoided and otherwise going to the devil as one pleases. For them morality is to be regarded as no more than a disagreeable constraint, and personal fulfilment is to be sought elsewhere than in a life of aspiration towards the moral virtues. It is to a life of indolence, self-indulgence, vanity, acquisitiveness and cynical exploitation that they turn (and claim as their right) and the moral conceptual currency of the modern world has no power to persuade them that they are not living as they should or becoming all that they might be.

For the Greeks, however, there was a way of living that is right and ways that are wrong; neither Socrates and Plato nor Aristotle showed much trace of irresolution on this matter. A life of spoiled or undisciplined slavery to the baser passions and instincts is mistaken because it is the royal road to rack and ruin, desolation and despair for man both as an individual and as a member of society. And if they were – as I think – basically right then, they are fundamentally still right today. It is nowadays sometimes said that the educator is someone who should remain neutral between different human values, moral or otherwise; that he should leave these for children themselves to choose between. But if it is true that he must leave young people to choose for themselves – which of course it is – it is also true that he is the one person who *cannot* remain neutral.

No one then, can or should profess to be an educator who does not firmly believe that this way of doing things is superior to that, this is true and that is false or that this way of life is to be valued more highly than that. Above all, he is charged with a sacred mission to reveal the true and the better as more attractive than the false and the worse – and this is as true with respect to moral education as elsewhere. Unfortunately this is

230

largely what the modern educator has so often failed to do in relation to the traditional moral virtues; but since, as the Greeks tried so hard to show us, the life of virtue is indeed excellent and admirable, it *can* be done.

11

VIRTUE AND REASON: PROBLEM-SOLVING AND CLARIFICATION

Having provided some discussion of feeling and motivation in relation to the moral virtues it is now necessary to address the difficult question of the place of reason in moral life. What, then, is the role of rational deliberation in human moral life in general and what part if any does reason play with respect to the acquisition of the moral virtues in particular? By way of an initial response to these awesome questions philosophers have sometimes employed a rather threadbare classification of the different possible perspectives on the nature of moral wisdom into two main varieties; in general moral reasoning can be regarded either as a matter of *discovery* or as a matter of *invention*.[1] In short one can, according to one or the other of these two viewpoints, either regard moral reasoning by analogy with theoretical scientific reasoning as a matter of the rational human discovery of an objective reality which has existence quite independently of any human perception or experience of it, or alternatively one may think of moral reasoning by comparison with technological or craft reasoning as a matter of creating or inventing something that had no existence prior to human ingenuity and reflection.

Despite the Socratic exploration of the problem of moral knowledge in terms of certain analogies with technical skills in the early Platonic dialogues,[2] the name of Plato springs nevertheless immediately to mind in relation to the first of these two models. In his mature works, Plato seems to be finally and irrevocably committed to a form of extreme moral realism which is the very epitome of the discovery model. Of course, he expressly denied that moral reality is accessible to human beings via ordinary empirical perception since there are not for him any clear instances of virtue, justice and so on to be observed sensibly in the world of appearance. Thus Plato drove a meta-physical wedge between the world of experience in general and that of our ideas of it, between the phenomenal world of sensible perception and the intelligible world of rational reflection; only via initiation into a sort of intellectual–theoretical or super-scientific form of rational enquiry can a man hope to emerge from the dark cave of illusion and deception into the bright sunlight of absolute moral certainties.

There are familiar difficulties with 'other-worldly' views of a Platonic kind about the origins of moral and other concepts which give rise to reasonable Aristotelian objections that even if there were perfect forms of good, justice and virtue awaiting rational human discovery in some super-sensible world of objective reality, it is difficult to see what real purpose they might serve in the actual conduct of human affairs. Plato, it seems, construes the achievement of virtue or goodness too much in intellectual terms and fails to show satisfactorily how the operations of reason inform the practice of ordinary moral virtue. Is it not possible then to regard our ordinary moral concepts and judgements as corresponding to a more humanly accessible moral reality than the one offered to us by Plato?

As we have already observed, the sociologist Emile Durkheim did indeed formulate a more straightforward, albeit rather naive, version of the discovery model which does avoid the two-worlds difficulty of Plato by the simple expedient of regarding that moral reality to which our moral judgements might reasonably be held to refer as constituted by ordinary empirical facts. The account of moral reasoning offered by Durkheim, then, construes it as concerned precisely with the discovery of *moral facts* understood as a species of social facts; thus the route to moral rationality and the discovery of genuine moral principles and values is held to lie in a kind of empirical scientific reflection on the everyday circumstances of human social conduct.

Clearly, however, Durkheim's project founders precisely because it is insufficiently sensitive to Platonic and other philosophical considerations concerning the normative character of our understanding of human motives and conduct; human thoughts and deeds do not wear their moral values on their sleeves and require to be interpreted as just or unjust, virtuous or vicious and so forth by reference to norms and standards which cannot themselves be directly derived from experience by pure or unmediated perception or straight-forward empirical generalisation. (In fact, Durkheim's own very *a prioristic* conceptions of moral conduct belie his avowed empirical methodology here.)

Like Durkheim, Kant wished to give an account of morality which severs its ties with traditional theological views and conceptions (divine command notions and so on) but quite unlike Durkheim he does not believe that an ethics of moral duty can be derived from reflection on ordinary empirical experience. Rejecting the moral sense views of the empiricist philosophers, Kant held that the moral worth of an action is not to be located in any personal sentiment of altruism for which it might be performed, but rather in the agent's obedience to the moral law for its own sake. For Kant the impersonal or dis-interested exercise of human reason may assist us to discover moral laws and precepts that are true and valid for all rational beings at all times and in all places.

Clearly, Kant's view of moral rationality hardly represents a straightforward case of the discovery model of moral reason, since the categorical imperatives established by Kantian practi-cal reason are not strictly true in virtue of anything that might be held to lie objectively beyond the norms embodied in the imperatives themselves. Since for Kant the objective and uni-versal truth of the various expressions of the moral law is to be decided exclusively by appeal to purely formal considerations of rational consistency and so on, his view does at least enjoy the advantage of avoiding the problems of verification which follow from supposing that if moral judgements are to be capable of truth it must be in virtue of their correspondence to some realm of independent reality either empirical or supersensible.

The trouble is that this advantage is gained at the extremely high price of the complete dissociation of Kant's purely auto-nomous will from any circumstances that might give genuine sense to the exercise of moral choice or preference; the attempt to ground moral imperatives in something entirely distinct from everyday human affairs and interests, in the nature of a reason conceived as abstracted or dissociated from such interests, makes it harder rather than easier to see what might be con-sidered reasonable about obedience to such imperatives and commands. A corollary of this point is that Kant appears to have a rather over-optimistic view of what the formally conceived machinery of rational universalisation might be expected to achieve in the direction of establishing universally valid moral laws and principles; as we have seen, for example, it is more plausible to appeal to notions of rational universalisation in order to try to show the moral value of promisekeeping and other forms of obligation than it is so to appeal in relation to notions of charity or benevolence.

Kant's general position is best seen as a transitional stage between a discovery and an invention model. What prescriptivism mainly leaves behind in Kant is the idea that by universalisation we can establish moral laws and obligations that would command the assent of any rational will in any circumstances. Rather, individual agents are to employ the machinery of universalisation – basically an application of the so-called golden rule – for generating consistent sets of moral principles or rules for the rational conduct of personal moral business. The content of such moral codes, however, is to be provided entirely by the agents themselves; so long as they are consistent and faithful in their adherence to such personally adopted codes of principle, they are free to decide what their content should be. Thus in its full and emphatic endorsement of the importance of personal choice with respect to the formation of moral values, prescriptivism is the very epitome of the invention model of moral reasoning; morality is in a serious sense the free creation of human reason and there is nothing either good or bad but thinking makes it so.

Clearly, however, whatever there is to be said in favour of the emphasis placed by prescriptivism and related doctrines on the contribution that authentic choice or preference as expressed in the form of genuine personal commitment has to make to moral life and conduct, there is little to be said on behalf of viewing moral judgement as a product *only* of such personal choice. For the human will to find appropriate expression in moral action, it requires to be an informed will, one that is able to operate in the light of some understanding or knowledge of the nature of human conduct as a potential contributor to good and ill in human affairs. It is neither reasonable nor desirable, then, that an individual human agent should be encouraged to decide for himself what is to count as harm or wellbeing in human life. Indeed, even if there are fairly extensive grey areas of rational disagreement and uncertainty with respect to particular aspects of moral life it is yet not the case – and it could not logically be so if genuine moral disagreement is to be possible – that murder, torture and child molestation are to be considered right or wrong only on the basis of personal taste or fiat.

In relation to the distinction between discovery and invention models of moral reasoning with which we began, however, some interesting differences of perspective have already emerged from this rough and ready thumbnail survey of some reasonably familiar views concerning the nature of moral deliberation. Roughly, then, whereas for Plato and Durkheim in their different ways such deliberation appears to be conceived more or less along the lines of a scientific or at least a theoretical enterprise, for Kant and such philosophical heirs of his as the prescriptivists morality is essentially a form of practical endeavour and moral reasoning is viewed more as a tool or instrument for the solution of particular practical human problems.

However, both of these general outlooks on the nature of moral reasoning encounter serious difficulties, since on the one hand, it does not appear that moral values or principles are 'out there' awaiting human discovery in some realm of either sensible or intelligible perception in the same way that what is apt to be reported by an empirical judgement is 'out there' , and on the other it seems grossly implausible to suppose that, say, 'child-sacrifice is a vile and abominable practice' represents a genuine moral judgement only to the extent that it expresses my own personal point of view or that of the social group to which I happen to belong. But in the light of these considerations it would appear that any reasonably satisfactory account of the nature of moral deliberation must be one that avoids the difficulties of the discovery and invention models in their extreme or crude forms.

Of course, that there is a fundamental difference to be observed between the two main kinds or types of reasoning – the theoretical or scientific and the practical or technical – in terms of which we have largely here construed the distinction between discovery and invention models of moral reasoning, seems to have been an original discovery of Aristotle's.[3] Unlike Plato, Aristotle did not regard moral deliberation as a species of theoretical enquiry into the nature of some non-sensible metaphysical realm of abstract objects and unlike Durkheim he does not view it as essentially concerned with some kind of quasi-scientific description of aspects of empirical reality; instead, like Kant and the prescriptivists he viewed morality rather as an essentially practical matter and moral reasoning as a form of practical enquiry and discourse. In that case, however, why should we not simply regard Aristotle as just another subscriber to the invention model of moral reasoning? The answer to this question is, of course, because this is anything but the case, for the invention model is merely a misapplication or misconstrual of the important idea that moral discourse is a genuine form of practical rationality.

In order to see how markedly Aristotle differs from all the other moral theorists we have so far investigated concerning the question of the nature of moral wisdom, it is more crucial to recognise the features that all the others have in common, than it is to emphasise the respects in which they all differ from each other. In short, then, despite the marked differences between Plato, Durkheim, Kant and the prescriptivists, what they all have in common is the idea that it is by means of the employment of moral reasoning or deliberation that the ultimate aims, values and principles of moral life are determined or established. Thus Plato held that by the vigorous exercise of dialectic one might eventually gain a direct intellectual apprehension of the eternal and absolute forms of good, virtue and justice; Durkheim believed that one might be able to discern the moral values and principles most rationally appropriate for a given society at a given time by means of a sort of disinterested social–scientific reflection; Kant thought that moral rationality provided a clear route to the discovery of an objective moral law and order of absolute value and the prescriptivists and other modern moral philosophers have held that the individual can invent moral right and wrong for himself via the exercise of autonomous moral choices and decisions.

Each of these theorists in his own peculiar way, then, believes that the most basic and important task of moral rationality or deliberation is that of discerning or establishing the ultimate values and principles of human moral life. I want to argue, however, that it is a mistake to construe the nature of moral deliberation in this way and that it is precisely this mistake which Aristotle was largely successful in avoiding.

At the very start of the *Nicomachean Ethics* Aristotle rejects the Platonic conception of moral enquiry as a species of quasi-scientific or theoretical enterprise and he insists that his aim is not to discover what in some theoretical sense the good means but rather how we might from a practical point of view become good men;[4] thus, from the outset he establishes that the enquiry of the *Ethics* is a form of practical enquiry. But there are many other crucial observations in the *Ethics* in which the further implications of this practical perspective are spelt out more precisely. One of these, which has a direct bearing on our present concerns, occurs in a crucial passage of his work in which Aristotle argues concerning of the nature of *phronesis* or practical wisdom that we do not deliberate morally with a view to determining the *ends* so much as the *means* of moral conduct. And so he suggests that just as a physician concerns himself in his medical practice not with the question whether he should heal but rather with that of how he might heal, so the deliberations of the moral agent should be concerned with *how* rather than whether to act virtuously or well.

Now despite the fact that, as some recent philosophers have warned us,[5] this point is susceptible of some misinterpretation – moral means and ends are for Aristotle related *internally* and not as technical means and ends merely *externally* – I want to argue here for a view of this point which enables us in general to make rather better sense of the idea of moral reasoning than we encounter in any other account. According to Aristotle, it appears that the main purpose to which *phronesis* is directed is that of choosing or at least discerning the course of conduct which represents the most appropriate expression of a given virtue in some circumstances that call for that virtue's exercise. Thus *phronesis* is concerned not especially, if at all, with establishing the credentials of courage, temperance or justice – with justifying these as *bona fide* moral dispositions as Kant, for example, tries to establish the moral credentials of honesty or promisekeeping – but rather with assisting an agent to express these moral responses in a proper way in the right circumstances.

Aristotle's point would appear to be that whereas it is reasonable to call into question this or that proposed way of expressing or exercising a given moral quality of courage, temperance and so forth, it is not likewise reasonable to call into question the moral value of these qualities themselves; we may sensibly ask whether this or that form of conduct is a genuine case of honesty or compassion but not whether honesty and compassion are morally worthwhile – presumably because notions of courage, honesty, compassion and so on are simply constitutive of anything that might reasonably be regarded as a moral life.

But, it might be said, isn't this just a simple mistake about the nature of moral life, values and action? Isn't it just a fact, after all, that people do disagree quite radically about the nature of moral values and the ultimate goals of moral life? Perhaps living when he did Aristotle was simply insufficiently aware of the kind of serious disagreements about the nature of moral values which are so familiar to those children of modernity who belong to so-called pluralist societies. But it would be an expression of mere historical ignorance to suppose that Aristotle was simply oblivious to the sorts of general considerations about moral relativism and pluralism that have been aired in modern times. Aristotle, after all, was a pupil of Plato and would as such have been thoroughly conversant with those works of his master in which the various relativist doctrines of the sophists were criticised by means of arguments pioneered by Socrates. In any event, I believe that Aristotle's point in the *Ethics* regarding the way in which moral deliberation relates to means rather than ends is essentially unaffected by any considerations about relativism and pluralism since, as I also hope to show, it is only at the level of deliberation about means rather than ends that the problems of relativism themselves intelligibly arise. An example might help us to see all of this more clearly.[6]

Suppose that a man who is for the most part happily married is away from home on a business trip and in the course of a drunken spree at an office party he lapses into a single never-to-be-repeated act of infidelity with one of the company secretaries. As a man of firm moral principles and strict conscience he is the following day stricken by guilt and remorse to the extent that he is strongly inclined to make a clean breast of the episode on returning home. What causes him to hold back from confessing everything to his wife, of course, is the sure knowledge that she will be so deeply hurt by the revelation that her trust and confidence in him will be forever undermined. On the one hand, then, the business man fears that if he tries to keep the matter to himself the strain of living in a state of deceit is liable

239

to sour his marriage and make a hell of his relationship with his wife and on the other hand he fears correctly enough that the truth may well be more than his wife can bear. Here we are confronted by a familiar enough kind of moral dilemma concerning which we are hard put to know what the agent should do for the best.

What, however, is the cause of the agent's dilemma in this example? Could it be said to follow, for example, from any genuine uncertainty on the part of the agent about the moral status of the values and principles in terms of which his dilemma is characterised? Is the man in some difficulty because he is unsure whether acts of adultery are to be generally condemned or commended, because he is uncertain whether or not it is wrong to continue in a state of deceit or dissemblement with his wife, or because he is unclear concerning whether there is anything morally reprehensible about wounding the feelings of others by revealing that one has let them down? In fact no such uncertainties require to be regarded as entering into the case, and the agent in question could not if they did be properly said to be confronted by a moral dilemma; he experiences the indecision and uncertainties that he does only on the basis of his certainties that adultery and deception are discreditable and disreputable forms of conduct whereas honesty and compassion are expressions of probity and decency.

But isn't the point precisely that because the agent is unsure what he should do – whether he should be honest with his wife or spare her sufferings – he is after all unsure about the relative values or weightings of the various competing demands or ends of morality? Again this misdescribes the case, however, since the agent of our example is not at all unsure in the relevant sense about the relative worth of such moral qualities and attitudes as honesty, compassion and so on; if he did or could regard honesty as more important than compassion or vice versa, then he would not experience precisely the kind of dilemma which arises from a clear recognition of the equally weighty and pressing moral demands that both these virtues will make of any moral agent.

What the moral agent may, of course, be uncertain about is whether his decision to keep the knowledge of his guilt from his wife is symptomatic of the virtue of compassion or the vice of cowardice; or again, whether deciding to tell her the truth is expressive of honesty or of some callous defect of compassion, even perhaps of a certain deep psychological hostility or resentment. In that case, the moral uncertainty arises precisely at the level of determining the appropriate means to the achievement of a given moral end – or rather, perhaps, of knowing how to act virtuously as opposed to viciously – more than at the level of discerning which of the range of human dispositions we ordinarily term virtues and vices are to be regarded as having the most impeccable moral credentials.

For Aristotle, it would appear that the main problem for moral deliberation is to determine exactly what should count as, say, courage or temperance in a given circumstance, since it is clear that the forms of conduct in which such virtues might be exhibited can vary dramatically from one context to another. In the Britain of the early 1940s, for example, courage might well be appropriately expressed in the action of a not normally physically brave man who joins the army to fight the Nazis in what he reasonably considers to be a just war; in the USA of the 1960s, however, true courage might be better expressed in an agent's conscientious refusal to serve in what he considers to be an unjust war in Vietnam.

What it may appear to be rather more dubious to hold is, however, as some prescriptivists seem to have maintained,[7] that it might reasonably be doubted whether courage *is* a virtue or a generally morally commendable human characteristic. To be sure, perhaps a pacifist society might not regard *military* courage as a virtue, but it is difficult to suppose in this hard world that moral resources of persistence and endurance in the teeth of obdurate nature would not be required for the successful prosecution of at least some of the tasks of survival facing anything we should recognise as a human society; it is inevitable, moreover, that under these circumstances some moral distinction would be drawn, to the credit of the former, between those who confront and those who shirk their difficulties.

There would seem to be something profoundly suspect, therefore, about the idea that moral deliberation as expressed in the form of some process of universalisation resulting in some act of personal commendation is either necessary or sufficient to determine whether courage, honesty and so forth are rightly to be regarded as *bona fide* moral qualities or dispositions. Indeed, it would appear that moral reasoning can have real purchase or operate effectively, only against a background of fairly uncontroversial assumptions concerning the ends of moral life to the effect that whereas courage, honesty, justice, compassion and so on are conducive to those ends, cowardice, dishonesty, injustice and the like are generally subversive of them. But in that case it also seems that moral disputes and disagreements will arise not at the level of uncertainty about what qualities conduce to the ends of moral life, but at the level of determining what are to be appropriately counted as means to those ends; what counts as honesty, courage and so on in a given set of circumstances.

Now presumably, all this is why Aristotle insisted that *phronesis* or moral wisdom cannot be developed independently of a thorough initiation into the moral virtues of courage, temperance and so forth, via something like the apprenticeship model of moral education he outlines in the *Ethics*.[8] In order, as it were, to have anything to reason morally about, a young person requires a substantial grasp of or acquaintance with the basic meaning of moral life. He requires to learn from everyday experience and by trial, error and correction how right conduct needs to be understood in relation to both his own concerns and those of others; that, for example, it profits him not to act in a spoiled or self-pitying manner when things do not quite go his own way, that it is both cruel and shameful to bully or ridicule those who are weak or deformed, that stealing and general dishonesty tend to undermine such common social goods as trust and co-operation and so on.

All of this, of course, is likely to attract the familiar complaint that a serious question has been crucially begged by this account of moral education. For surely, it will be said, in the course of a moral training during which one has taught little soldiers to be brave about their grazed knees, impressed upon them that it is unkind to pull the cat's tail because it torments the beast, lectured them firmly that one shouldn't steal Sharon's pocket money because you wouldn't like it if she stole yours, one has not given children much of an opportunity to think for themselves and have thereby just largely indoctrinated them in one's own moral preferences.[9] Moreover, if the point is made by way of reply that very small children are not yet capable of thinking for themselves in relation to moral matters, it may be responded to this that whether or not this is so we are still not justified in instilling into them our own moral values and should wait until children *are* capable of thinking for themselves.

But to understand properly the Aristotelian perspective on the acquisition of moral dispositions in general and moral wisdom in particular is, I think, to recognise that all objections along these lines are quite misplaced. The idea that we are indoctrinating children by encouraging them to be brave when they fall down or not to bear false witness or to bully or extort from their peers, would after all make sense only if there was some other alternative pattern of conduct into which children might be reasonably initiated in the name of moral education. The only genuine positive alternative to encouraging children to be brave, self-controlled, honest, compassionate and so forth, however, is to instruct them in cowardice, self-indulgence, dishonesty and cruelty; but anyone who seriously held that these dispositions constitute a viable alternative moral code would, to say the very least, know the meaning of neither morality nor education.[10] To be sure, it is possible for parents and teachers to make lamentable mistakes in the initial stages of moral training. They can, for example, as some progressive educationalists have rightly insisted, manage to convey a rather bizarre or distorted picture of what moral virtue in some of its forms means – especially perhaps in the area of sexual conduct; but it borders on absurdity to maintain that when a parent urges a child to take a sanguine or stoical view of a passing mishap or a teacher rebukes a child for bullying or stealing, she is engaged in anything that might be remotely described as indoctrination. It is in this sense that the familiar virtues of courage, temperance, honesty, compassion and so on are constitutive of moral life, they are just simply what we *mean* by being moral and hence they cannot be open to question as moral values in the same way that it may be open to question whether this, that or the other item of human conduct in a given circumstance is to be taken as expressive of courage, honesty or compassion.

But if the 'positive' moral educational alternative of teaching children vices rather than virtues is not open to us, what of the 'negative' alternative of teaching them nothing at all of moral matters until they are old enough to think for themselves?[11] In order to appreciate fully what is suspect about this suggestion we need to recognise that behind Aristotle's insistence that no genuine moral wisdom or reason can be acquired in the absence of training in the moral virtues lies the more general idea that without some sort of experience or acquaintance with the practical value of certain moral dispositions, there cannot really be much for moral reason to deliberate about. Unlike some more recent moral philosophers, Aristotle does not appear to hold that moral wisdom or deliberation is distinguished from other sorts of reasoning in virtue of its form alone.

In fact, in terms of its general logical form the phronetic reasoning of Aristotle is of a relatively simple means–ends kind and as such it is hardly distinguishable from technical or prudential reasoning. Genuine practical wisdom or deliberation as expressed in the idea of *phronesis*, then, is distinguishable in Aristotelian terms from the mere cleverness exhibited in prudential calculation precisely in terms of its direction towards moral rather than narrowly personal or selfish ends. In short, practical moral wisdom is distinguished from prudential reasoning in terms not of its form but of its content; its chief purpose is to reflect upon the nature and character of the virtues or, more precisely, to deliberate with respect to questions about how the virtues in general or a given virtue in particular might receive appropriate expression in this or that set of morally problematic circumstances.

For Aristotle, though we might reasonably be reluctant to follow him strictly in this, moral deliberation is crucially concerned with determining the course of conduct which may be regarded as the proper mean between two unacceptable shortcomings of character – the Scylla of excess and the Charybdis of defect. But in any event, it would seem to follow from an Aristotelian point of view that there can be no serious question of leaving children to their own devices and untouched by any kind of instruction in moral life and conduct until they have reached some age of moral majority at which they can think for themselves; that idea is as incoherent as us supposing that we should not encourage children to learn chords and scales on a piano until they have reached an age at which they are capable of composing music for themselves. Unless children have been acquainted to a reasonable degree with certain of the fundamental features of moral life – with, for example, the moral significance for the self and others of certain attitudes and dispositions of character – they will have precious little of substance on which their moral deliberations can get to work.

244

Again, of course, this is just essentially to reaffirm that moral deliberation can operate effectively only against a background of assumptions about the nature of good and evil, virtue and vice, right and wrong which must be taken as in some sense 'given' and which moral deliberation cannot itself be required to establish. To be sure, like the adulterous agent in our example, we are often unsure what to do in certain circumstances of moral dilemma, but that is only because at the level of fundamental moral values we *are* sure, even if we have elected to betray the values in question, that the straight path to the righteous life lies in the general direction followed by the courageous, loyal, honest, compassionate and so on. In saying all of this, by the way, I should not be construed as denying that the recognition of ultimate moral ends or values is a *rational* matter; in claiming that moral deliberation concerns means rather than ends I am not subscribing to some Humean doctrine that the general direction of moral life is determined only by the passions in relation to which reason is merely the slave.

From an Aristotelian point of view, after all, the virtues which are the means to the achievement of the ends of moral life are related not merely externally to those ends but constitutively; since this is so it would be hard to deny, even if one wished to, that reason plays a crucial role in the recognition or discernment of the ends of moral life. The point here, although it is an important point, is not that honesty, courage, compassion and so on are not rationally established goals but only that they are not established as conducive to or constitutive of moral ends on the basis of any kind of moral *deliberation* since the moral credentials of these virtues are themselves presupposed to any intelligible notion of moral deliberation; the matter might be put more briefly by emphasising, as we have before, that we are not honest or compassionate in order to be morally rational but morally rational in order to be honest and compassionate.

So far, we have been concerned to reject the idea that the positive moral significance of such familiar values, principles and virtues as honesty, self-control, compassion and courage is something to be established on the basis of any of the kinds of moral deliberation that we have encountered in the works of moral theorists – Plato, Durkheim, Kant and so on – other than Aristotle. That moral life is in fact constituted by these and other familiar virtues is the bedrock of our understanding of it and it does not seem to form any part of the serious business of moral deliberation either to question or to justify this circumstance.

But how far has all of this got us? For even if it is wholly conceded that genuine disagreements are barely intelligible at the level of basic or ultimate moral values and principles – that little breath should be seriously wasted in considering whether, for example, courage and compassion are goods and cruelty and adultery are evils – it is clear enough that serious and radical disagreements *do* arise at the level of appropriate means to agreed ends and that the parties to such disagreements may appear to be totally beyond reasonable reconciliation.

With respect, then, to our earlier example of the disagreement between the G.I. who believes that he should serve his country in Vietnam and the conscientious objector who deplores his country's involvement in what he takes to be an unjust war, both men may value integrity and honour and exhibit courage, but after heated and interminable discussion with respect to the question of how honour and courage require to be expressed in the circumstances they may well be able to agree only to differ on the issue and to remain firm in their separate commitments to quite different and opposed courses of action.

Are we not, then, still faced with the problem of who is right and who is wrong in morally problematic circumstances and with the difficulty of deciding the best course of action to pursue; moreover, so long as we remain in this state of indecision and uncertainty must not the whole enterprise of moral education appear to be an uncertain and hazardous business? Well, to be sure, the entire enterprise of moral education *is* an uncertain and hazardous business, but not quite, I think, for this reason; again I suspect that the problem has not been stated quite correctly.

In order to see this, let us return again to consider the moral dilemma of the agent in our adultery example. In the mind of that man there is a genuine difficulty about what to do – he must choose between on the one hand a deceitful course of action in the name of compassion and on the other a deeply hurtful course in the name of honesty. Now first of all, is this correctly described as a choice between right and wrong? Clearly it is not, because whichever course of action the agent pursues will yield some moral benefit at the cost of some moral and emotional harm; thus, whatever the man does he cannot exactly *win* from a moral point of view.

It is possible that we are here inclined to believe in the existence of some moral algorithm or decision procedure which will provide us with a right answer in the form of the best thing to do in such circumstances because we are tempted towards a shallow cosequentialism which encourages us to weigh one amount of pain or unhappiness against another.[12] But in cases like the one under consideration, as in so many others, such reflections get us nowhere and the consequentialist turn of mind is better resisted; it is not at all clear how the immediate distress of the agent's wife at learning of her husband's infidelity might be reasonably weighed against the long term misery that might follow the strain of deceit, thus wrecking the marriage by going the long way around. It is well nigh impossible to see, then, how the agent might hope in any sense to *succeed* in these circumstances from a moral point of view.

It is possible, however, to see how the agent might *fail* from a moral point of view wholly and absolutely. For if the man chooses not to confess to his wife and to continue living with her under a cloud of deceit (telling her lies when he is questioned and so on) not because he lacks courage but because he is genuinely concerned for her welfare (perhaps she has a medical history of nervous disorder) then despite his dissemblement the man emerges with some degree of moral credit. But if, on the other hand, he chooses not to confess because he is too cowardly to do so and the matter of deceit weighs only lightly with him, then it is also clear that little moral worth is to be attributed to the man's conduct, irrespective of any amount of suffering he may have escaped inflicting. In that case rather than having compromised his moral nature and character yet further he might have done better to have steeled himself to make a clean breast of things, an action that might also have expressed a greater respect for his wife.

The general lesson to be learned from these observations is that a rather distorted view of what it is to be a moral agent has invariably been the corollary or consequence of a largely mistaken model of moral deliberation. It appears to have been the view of some famous and influential moral philosophers that the familiar moral dilemmas and predicaments that all of us encounter in life from time to time may be expressed as intellectual or practical problems or puzzles which might be susceptible of reasonable solution by means of the application of a suitable mode or style of moral reasoning; if only we can discover the right moral decision procedure we might then possess the resources whereby we can decide satisfactorily which of two competing points of view or courses of action is to be morally approved or commended. This decision procedure would enable us to tell who is right; the pro-abortionist or the anti-abortionist, the capital punisher or the abolitionist, the advocate of divorce or the person who is against it.

We may suspect immediately that something has gone rather badly wrong here as soon as we observe that this way of putting the matter is sometimes understood by the very naive as presenting us with a genuine choice between equally viable alternatives – as though it is open for people to *approve* of abortion, capital punishment and divorce as they might approve of honesty, valour and compassion, as practices which have moral worth in their own right. It is consistent with all we have so far argued, however, to observe that it is not of course open for such practices to be reasonably commended or dis-commended at anyone's pleasure; in fact no sane person could actually *approve* of abortion, capital punishment and divorce as such. Clearly, the relevant moral issue is between those who believe that these practices are always out of the question and those who hold that sometimes they constitute the lesser of two evils – it is better that the innocent teenage victim of sexual abuse should not have to bring the child of an incestuous union into the world, it is better that the multiple murderer of children should not be released after a term to claim more victims and so on.

Once again, it seems that at the root of disagreements about capital punishment, abortion and divorce there lie fundamental agreements about the shortcomings of such practices (not even the most casual attitude towards abortion would regard it as anything less than an inconvenience) and about the sanctity of birth, life and marriage; the disagreements arise rather in relation to the question of what human responses are morally appropriate to meet such shortcomings. It is also perfectly clear, moreover, that when problems and disagreements do arise at this level we are likely to be faced with a hard choice between the devil and the deep blue sea; between the Scylla of one

248

unacceptable or unpalatable conclusion and the Charybdis of another.

In fact, this is an ineradicable feature of moral life and experience which is also insufficiently acknowledged by Aristotle in his moral philosophy to the extent that it is recognised at all. Aristotle appears rather to give the impression that the life of the completely virtuous man who has acquired courage, temperance, justice and all the other moral virtues, is a life of relative ease, prosperity and peace of mind – it is that of a man who would seem to be comprehensively morally insured against all the slings and arrows of outrageous fortune and all the sins that flesh is heir to. Doubtless Aristotle's great-souled man, his paragon of moral virtue, would not have found himself in the position of the adulterer in our earlier example, but he could not be sure that he would never find himself in some other moral dilemma – like that of our American draftees – that was not of his own making. In such circumstances the great-souled man would have doubtless encountered the tragic dimension of many if not most moral dilemmas in which the choice to be made is essentially one between two competing evils and in which a man cannot serve two masters both of which have a reasonable claim on his allegiance; where, for example, in order to be honest we must fail to be compassionate, but if we are to be compassionate we must fail to be honest.

In these circumstances, moral deliberation can hardly be regarded as having as its main aim the choice of the right or the best course of action because in such circumstances there is no right or best course of action in the relevant sense. But since these are also for the most part the circumstances of ordinary moral difficulty and dilemma it would appear that the main purpose of moral deliberation in general cannot be that of discerning the right moral response to exhibit in such circumstances if by this is meant something like reaching the right solution to the problem. There is another crucially important sense, however, in which it *is* the main role or purpose of moral deliberation to help us discern the correct moral response in the circumstances of moral dilemma. That is not the sense in which moral reasoning will tell us clearly what to do to achieve, without any harmful remainder, the best possible results in terms of the least suffering for other people or whatever – if it could tell us this we would not *be* in a moral dilemma – but that in which, if we heed its voice, moral wisdom can and will tell us *how* we should act with moral propriety.

For the most part, then, moral deliberation stands in the service of the clarification of the nature of moral virtue and its main purpose is to advise us how to act with greater integrity, honesty, courage and compassion than we may naturally or ordinarily be disposed towards. In fact, it is arguable that even in the most tragic circumstances of moral dilemma, it is seldom that we require moral reason to inform us of where our duty really lies and more often that we need the services of moral wisdom to erode or undermine those familiar enough human conditions of irresolution, hypocrisy, self-deception and bad faith that so frequently disincline us to pursue that duty.

12

EDUCATION AND THE VIRTUES: OBJECTIVITY, SUBJECTIVITY AND TEACHING

To date in this section we have been concerned to construct a general account of moral virtue upon which an approach to moral education might be based. In its general form this account has been broadly Aristotelian – the moral virtues are states of character concerned with the reasonable discipline of natural human passions, sentiments and inclinations, the degree and extent of that discipline being determined by reference to the idea of practical rationality. Although some distinguished philosophers of days gone by have certainly been inclined to attempt an account of moral life in terms of either feeling or reason, then, we have followed Aristotle in taking the view that the dispositions which lie at the heart of moral life require to be understood in terms of the interplay, as it were, of both reason and feeling.

In addition, however, we have also argued that some sense requires to be made of what has often been traditionally referred to as the 'will' in human practical affairs; in short, of the idea of moral motivation. At any rate, we need to have some insight into the question of why human beings so often fail to achieve broadly moral goals and undoubtedly, as Aristotle also saw, this is a complex matter which is unsusceptible of any single easy explanation. There is a clear enough difference, for example, between the man who fails morally because he cannot see what is right (also a difference here *among* men who cannot see what is right, between those who can be held responsible and those who cannot – those who could have known and those who couldn't) and the man who fails because though he can see correctly, his moral character or nerve fails him at the crucial stage and he falls prey to weakness or temptation.

251

We may also be required to make some moral psychological sense of the conceptually problematic case of the man who sees clearly the difference between good and evil, but willingly chooses what he views as evil – the satanic personality of Milton's imagination who says 'evil be thou my good'.[1] Fortunately, it is beyond the scope of this book to attempt, were I even capable, satisfactory solutions to these vexed problems of moral psychology and I shall continue to confine my efforts to a small number of fairly limited goals.

Concerning the story so far, then, I have been concerned to argue in the chapter on virtue and passion against a fairly common view that the moral virtues are concerned exclusively with control and discipline, construed simply as the *suppression*, of entirely negative or destructive human emotions, feelings and passions. This is certainly a widespread view in conventional educational circles in which 'self-control' has fairly negative connotations and tends generally to be understood on the model of temperance. It is likely that this perspective on the development of moral qualities is based on a view of human feeling which is rather more Platonic than Kantian – upon a deeply entrenched puritanism about the natural feelings and impulses which is widespread throughout human cultures of both the east and the west.

It is certainly not an Aristotelian view, however, since as we have observed, Aristotle believed that some defects of moral character and action were to be attributed to an insufficiency rather than a surfeit of human emotion or sentiment. It is not the *absence* of fear, then, which makes a man courageous and it is precisely the absence of fellow feelings that can cause a man to fail or be defective with respect to charity or generosity. But although it is reasonable enough to characterise the moral virtues as disciplined feelings or inclinations, it is important to notice that the notions of control and discipline are ambiguous between those of suppression and proper expression.

Thus, we distinguished between two sorts of virtues according to two different kinds of human feeling that may be involved in them. Some virtues like courage and temperance would appear to be concerned with the suppression or inhibition of such potentially negative and destructive emotional states as fear, anger and greed, but others like charity and compassion appear rather more concerned with the proper expression or rational guidance of natural sentiments of a more positive, other-regarding and altruistic kind. It is important for parents, teachers and others concerned with the promotion of the virtues, to attend as much to the cultivation of a child's natural sympathies and attachments towards others as to the discipline of his selfish instincts.

In the chapter on virtue and motivation I set myself the task of indicating some of the reasons for believing that it is not possible to construct a complete account of our interest in moral life in terms of the notions of duty and obligation alone, though once again, there seems to have been some tendency among moral philosophers of modern times to suppose that this is a coherent strategy. For one thing, the realm of morality is at least partly, as we have seen, that of what is often freely given by way of care for and devotion to the good of others – not just that of what is required of us toward others by way of law or contract. We regard that man as a shining moral example to the rest of us who goes way beyond what is required of him in the direction of mercy, charity, patience and compassion. Likewise, we also consider as an admirable moral example that man who is courageous in adversity and modest in his success even when his conduct benefits no one but himself (by way, perhaps, of the regard for him which it generates among others) and though not much clear sense is to be made of the idea that he owes such conduct to himself by way of duty.

It is arguable, then, that the moral virtues are rather better construed as goals of personal aspiration inspired by some objective conception of human flourishing or of what it is to live well (not, that is, one based merely on arbitrary preference) than as systems or complexes of public duty or obligation which an individual owes, rather reluctantly, to others. In short, it is easier perhaps to understand the great motivating power that the moral virtues can have in human affairs if they are construed as representing something that a man should want to be, rather than as things he is unwillingly constrained to do.

In the chapter concerned with the role of reason with respect to moral virtue I was occupied with the fairly limited task again of trying to show that the purpose of practical wisdom in moral matters is less that of establishing what is the morally right thing to do and more that of determining the appropriate form which moral conduct should take for the effective achievement of right moral ends. It seems to have been Aristotle's view that moral wisdom operates in the service of the moral virtues rather than, as it were, *vice versa*. It is not so much, then, that courage, temperance, justice, compassion and so forth are dispositions into which human beings require to be trained for the purpose of securing moral ends which are independently established through the exercise of a neutral or disinterested moral reason, but more that the qualities of courage, temperance, justice and compassion are themselves the ends of moral life which it is the job of moral reason or wisdom to help us to clarify and achieve. It is precisely the moral dispositions called the virtues which give content and substance to moral thought and in the absence of which moral deliberation would hardly be possible.

Moral thought does not operate in a vacuum, but from some particular perspective – from within the context of some substantial conception of the virtuous life. Thus whereas the modern view sometimes appears to be that no one who has already been trained in or habituated to a particular pattern of moral conduct is in a suitable position to reflect rationally on moral matters, Aristotle's view was that no one is able to deliberate about moral life *unless* they have acquired by experience and practice some clear understanding of the nature of the virtues. I can reasonably wonder whether action A or B is the most appropriate expression of a given virtue x only if I have been acquainted in practice with what x means; if I do not have any reasonable knowledge of x because I haven't been shown or instructed, then I lack any kind of guidance in relation to deciding whether A or B is a reasonable expression of it.

In this respect, of course, things are really no different in moral matters than they are in any other realm of human enquiry or practice. Just as we should not sensibly delay with respect to instructing a child in scientific or artistic facts, knowledge and procedures until he is old enough to make neutral and independent decisions for himself, so it is absurd to delay a child's moral training in honesty, generosity, fortitude and fairness until he is old enough to choose for himself. The initial training could be objected to only on the grounds that it is indoctrinative – but in training a child to be honest, self-controlled or considerate it is absurd to speak of indoctrination when there exist no *alternative* dispositions to truthfulness and self-discipline into which we might sensibly be said to be initiating children in the name of proper socialisation or education.

Thus it seems to be a grave mistake to regard moral wisdom as centrally concerned with establishing the ultimate goals, ends or aims of moral life and education; rather it is concerned with the clarification of those ends, with establishing how in terms of precise conduct in a given set of circumstances, courage, justice or temperance might best be exhibited. We cannot reasonably doubt whether it is right here to be just or courageous, but we may well wonder whether in doing this or that (evading the draft or going to fight in Vietnam) we are being *really* just or courageous.

So in general I have taken the view that those acquired dispositions we call the moral virtues are the crucial elements in what we take to be a worthwhile and decent human life, that they conduce to the ultimate interests of all human beings individually and collectively and that no really rational being could understand fully what a quality like courage, temperance, justice or compassion is and yet fail to want to possess it. From this point of view, since the virtues are not innate but entail both proper habit-formation and the development of reason, it is clear that it is squarely within the responsibility of all concerned with the socialisation and education of children – parents, teachers and others – to ensure that such habituation and instruction takes place. It is indeed a serious dereliction of duty on the part of all those engaged in child-rearing to fail to raise children in ignorance of the value of precisely those qualities of honesty, self-control, concern for others and so on which endow human life with some degree of decency and dignity and render all achievement in some worthwhile area of human endeavour possible. The familiar moral virtues are qualities which all responsible parents must care that their children acquire and in those cases in which they do not care they are hardly to be regarded as parents in anything much more than a merely biological sense.

To argue that moral education in the form of the promotion of those dispositions we call virtues is a great human good to which children of all ages are entitled in the course of their general education and upbringing, however, seems to be to argue on behalf of something that is painfully obvious. Nevertheless, it is clear enough that many professional educationalists, especially of modern times, have viewed moral education as an essentially controversial if not suspect matter and they have often sought to avoid the appearance of any conspicuous involvement with it. It is also clear enough, moreover, why they have been chary of such involvement – because of the view that it is difficult or impossible to disassociate moral life logically from particular religious or political perspectives; the understanding is that morality is thus a subjective or at least a socially relative matter which properly belongs in the sphere of personal and private opinion more than that of rational education.

In fact I believe that all of this is essentially either false or confused despite the circumstance that it *is* intelligible enough to speak of different moral perspectives and to view these different perspectives as related inferentially to particular and diverse religious and political outlooks (for example some religious views *do* entail moral practices and some moral outlooks imply political positions). But before I attempt to spell out precisely the falsehoods and confusions about moral subjectivity and relativism, it is necessary to try to make the point as powerfully as possible that anyone who takes upon himself the responsibility of educating children, cannot logically dissociate himself from the practice of moral education.

It might be a temptation to a school teacher to believe that he can nowadays so detach himself from the responsibility for moral education precisely because morality has widely come to be regarded as a matter of mere opinion and because teachers have also come to be seen – especially in secondary schools – as transmitters of certain kinds of knowledge or information, scientific, artistic, technical, linguistic and so forth. To this extent, the schoolteacher can claim that his professionality consists just in his authority with respect to the body of knowledge he has been hired to teach and in his ability to transmit that and only that body of knowledge to children. Remaining firmly neutral on the question of whether moral life enshrines any body of epistemologically reputable truths he can insist that if it does – if there is indeed moral knowledge – then it should require an expert, not him, to teach it (and some of the recent work on cognitive moral growth countenances the idea of moral experts[2]), whereas if it does not, then neither he nor anyone else has any legitimate business teaching what is suspect or contentious to impressionable young people.

I suspect, however, that all of this reasoning is essentially fallacious and rests on certain simple but deep mistakes about the nature of education, moral life and understanding. For a start, I think that it reflects a deep mistake about the nature of education. It is widely held nowadays that the business of teaching is to be regarded as some kind of professional role (albeit a rather down-market one) which consists essentially in the delivery of a particular service to a particular clientele. The comparisons to which those who belong to the teaching profession aspire, of course, are with the medical and legal professions. But if we are truly concerned with the *education* of children as opposed simply to equipping them during their schooling with vocational or other skills, it is possible to discern an important disanalogy between the professional role of the doctor and that of the teacher which (for once) would seem to make the teacher's responsibilities of a rather more weighty concern that those of the doctor.

Suppose, for example, that my child is suffering from a case of food-poisoning which requires urgent attention. In seeking out a doctor who can make her well again I shall be concerned only with the man's reputation and skill as a competent physician – what he is like as a *person* need not be of the least concern to me. In his personal and private life the doctor may well be a drunkard, womaniser, coward, cheat and liar, but that is hardly my business so long as he is sufficiently competent and skilled as a physician to be able to cure my child.

But suppose that I am looking for a place for my child in a country village school with a single teacher and I discover that the schoolmaster possesses an impeccable knowledge of English grammar, mathematics, history, geography, science, art and so on but he is also personally known to be a profligate, coward, cheat, liar and the rest; is it quite so reasonable for me to say that I couldn't care less what he is like as a human being so long as he can teach my child all the subjects in the national curriculum? I submit that it is not at all just as reasonable because the education of a child consists of rather more than merely filling his head with so much academic and technical knowledge and skill; it is also crucially a matter of the formation of his character and attitudes and it is clear that a child's character is not going to be well served by someone who does not care highly for honesty, integrity, fairness and so on.

In fact, I believe that Socrates and Plato would have said (they did not actually say it[3] but they came close, I believe, to doing so in such dialogues as the *Gorgias*) that for this precise reason the task of the teacher is much more urgent and crucial than that of the physician, because whereas the medical man deals only with the eradication of disease from the body (the relatively un-important material aspect of human nature) the teacher or educator deals with the elimination of vice and ignorance from the soul (the all-important spiritual aspect of human nature). What a doctor performs on behalf of a sick child perhaps ensures that she will not die, but what a good teacher performs on behalf of a child at the infant, primary or secondary level of schooling may well influence significantly how that child will live and arguably a good man can perform no greater service on behalf of others than this.

The crucial point is that a good teacher is not just the technically efficient deliverer of certain curricular goods – a good teacher is also a certain kind of person. He or she is the kind of person who is to be looked up to by virtue of possessing certain admirable qualities of character upon which it is appro-priate to want to model our own lives. To be sure, weak, spiteful, vain and greedy men are also not infrequently looked up to by impressionable children but it is for this very reason that we must regard them as *bad* teachers (they should not, that is to say, be regarded as good teachers on the grounds that they are *successful* at inculcating undesirable qualities).

It is vital to grasp, then, that the professional role of the teacher cannot be as clearly disentangled from the personal qualities of the individual who occupies the role as that of the physician can be distanced from the person who occupies it; in this respect the professional role of the teacher or educator is closer to that of the priest than the doctor or lawyer. But to recognise the respects in which the professional and personal or moral lives of the teacher cannot be logically disentangled should also be to see what is wrong with the ideas that moral education is no concern of the average subject teacher and that it should be best left to those with the knowledge necessary to do the job properly.

Simply, it rests on a fundamental confusion about the basic nature of the qualities that it is the concern of moral education to transmit. It is assumed that if morality is not a body of knowledge that can be demonstrated and acquired like any other – science or history, for example – then it must be a matter of mere personal or subjective opinion or belief. But to have what is necessary to be an effective moral educator is neither to have grasped so many facts or so much information nor to be in possession of so many ungrounded opinions; rather it is to be the kind of person who values and is committed to living in a way that is more expressive of or consistent with decency, integrity and justice than otherwise.

Thus moral education and moral understanding are not appropriately construed on the model of imparting and acquiring information, but rather more on the model of seeing the point of, valuing and being favourably disposed towards certain forms of positive conduct on behalf of oneself and others. It has sometimes been alleged, by the way, that the morally beneficial value of some forms of human conduct over others is something that is likely to become clearer to children in some areas of the curriculum – literature or physical education say – than others, and that therefore such subjects have a larger claim than others to be regarded as appropriate vehicles of moral education. But without denying the moral value of literature and physical education one can safely say that such partisan views are false and the plain fact is that it is not possible to teach anything at all in any curricular context whilst remaining insulated from or neutral towards considerations of a fundamentally moral kind pertaining to the value of honesty, truthtelling, co-operation, loyalty, patience, perseverance, integrity, tolerance, fairness and so on.

The good teacher who is also by implication an effective moral educator is not the one, however, who is constantly extolling these virtues, so much as the one through whose conduct these virtues shine forth as examples to those in his charge and who is constantly concerned to encourage these qualities in others. But, in short, what follows from all these observations is that having once decided to embark upon teaching as a profession, one cannot rightly evade the task of moral educator and any account or theory of the nature of education which seems to suggest that one can is, I believe, simply mistaken.

In that case, however, we must now turn to address the various objections that moral education must be inherently indoctrinatory because moral viewpoints can only be regarded as matters of either subjective personal preference or local social custom. Once it has been grasped that the heart of moral education is concerned with the promotion of those states of character and conduct called the virtues – with general dispositions towards honesty, fairness, tolerance, compassion and so on – it is a fairly straightforward matter to deal with the objection that such education cannot be logically disengaged from particular religious and political perspectives. For of course it can. It may well be the case, to be sure, that certain religious doctrines – Christianity for example – are consistent with or even entail a certain range of familiar human virtues; but we do not *have* to be Christians to recognise the value of such qualities of character for human life in general (and I should maintain this with respect even to certain virtues which have been traditionally associated with Christianity such as faith and chastity – if these are broadly enough construed[4]).

Again, although the formation of a strong commitment to justice or fairness might well incline one towards some sort of political action, it is unlikely that it would in itself influence someone to become a Tory or a communist without the impact on his attitudes of further knowledge or information of a more factual kind about the general distribution of wealth or liberties in existing human affairs (without, say, his being outraged by reading about the oppression of the poor by the rich in some third world country). Although it is indeed to be hoped, then, that a person who has truly taken the importance of the moral virtues to heart – who aspires to be just and compassionate – would certainly be motivated towards *some* form of political action or inspired by *some* religious ideal which enjoins the believer to help the less fortunate, the virtues of justice and compassion do not incline men to any religious or political faith or creed in particular. If this were not so then we should not be able to recognise that there are good men – loyal, courageous, honest, temperate and tolerant men who are also passionately concerned about justice – of all (and no) faiths and on different sides of any given political fence (though rather less, I should say, at the extreme ends of the political spectrum).

The other objections are, I think, rather more serious, though we have already done a good deal in this work to weaken them. It still seems to be believed by many reasonably well-educated people that the principal goals of moral life and therefore any qualities of human character and conduct through which these goals might be expressed are personal and subjective and that it is consequently up to the individual to decide whether he should profess these goals or exhibit these qualities. In that case, so the story goes, since people have a right to decide for themselves what their moral goals shall be, we have absolutely no right to prejudice such decisions by encouraging or habituating children into certain forms of moral attitude and conduct in schools; such habituation can only be a matter of indoctrination.

To cut a long story short, however, whatever the plausibility of this view with respect to engaging children in debates about abortion or capital punishment (an activity which if it occurs at all is hardly going to be engaged in by any sensible teacher until children have reached the age where they are well able to think for themselves) it has hardly any at all in relation to the central enterprise of moral education in schools which properly concerns the inculcation of the moral virtues. As far as this is concerned, though I have certainly no right as a teacher to *force* rather than encourage children to be honest, fair, considerate, tolerant and resolute in their conduct (moreover, it goes without saying that nothing I can say or do is likely to make them so if they don't want to be) there can also be no doubt at all that I have a duty to insist that they *should* or *ought* to be honest, fair and tolerant, for no sense can be attached to any other educational position.

In short, the human value that the moral virtues have is not to be regarded as a subjective matter if this means something to be decided by the individual as a matter of purely personal preference. The problem here, of course, relates to an ambiguity about the notion of personal preference concerning moral choice. Since the moral virtues are certainly a matter for the free choice of the individual, he is quite free to choose a life of dishonesty, indolence, intolerance and backsliding over a life of virtue if he so wishes and, short of his breaking the law, I have no right to force him to conduct himself otherwise. This is precisely the sense in which virtue and morality are entirely a matter for his free choice or 'up to him'. But it is not at all up to him to determine whether or not the moral virtues do in fact *have* value, of course, for it is plain enough – ignoring frivolous counter-examples – that the conditions of individual and social human life in which the virtues of wisdom, justice, fortitude and self-control are exhibited are to be generally preferred to those under which ignorance, exploitation and greed prevail.

Moreover, this crucial human significance of the moral virtues is such as to render their inculcation as far as possible an absolute educational necessity and a most grave omission has occurred if children fail to be provided with genuine examples of the practice of integrity, honesty and so on in the person of the teacher or with some other acquaintance with such values through art or literature. Indeed, although it is sometimes supposed that the value of requiring children to learn science or mathematics is uncontroversial whereas inculcating habits of fairness or honesty is a rather more dubious matter – if what I have been arguing so far is correct then things would appear to be the other way about. It is *much* clearer why it is important to encourage children to be honest, tolerant or fair than it is why they should be taught mathematics or science, for although not all children will develop either an interest in or a need for science, *all* human beings require an interest in honesty or fairness.

I suspect, however, that the idea that moral goals, values and qualities are personal and subjective, though by no means uncommon – it can be found stated more or less explicitly in books on educational theory as well as in works of moral philosophy[5] – is still rather less widespread than the idea that such goals, values and qualities are relative to particular social circumstances, and we have already noticed one theoretical expression of this idea in the work of Emile Durkheim. Just as, I suppose, it is possible to regard moral subjectivism as the relativisation of the idea of a moral perspective to particular individuals, so it is also possible to think of moral relativism as a kind of group or gang subjectivism; but it is probably better still to distinguish rather more sharply between the two perspectives.

For a subjectivist such as the ancient Greek philosopher Protagoras,[6] the individual person is the sole judge of truth, moral or otherwise, and no one is epistemologically well-placed to deny what any other man asserts, on the basis of his own experience, to be true or right. It is the considered view of many philosophers that this perspective must lead the subjectivist into a hopelessly intolerable and indefensible position, since as he must also concede truth to any other individual's sincerely held belief regardless of whether it is quite contradictory to his own, he has no way of dealing with or deciding between inconsistent positions.[7]

For the moral relativist, on the other hand, truth and value are *not* merely expressions of the personal and private decisions of individuals and there are objective criteria of moral virtue and goodness. Precisely, they are what are agreed to conduce to something like human fulfilment or flourishing in *these* circumstances which, however, may differ sharply from those seen to conduce to human well-being in *those* circumstances. For the relativist, then, there *are* public criteria of moral value but what they are depends precisely on which public one is considering. You say that in your society slavery and child sacrifice are regarded as barbaric customs, but I'll show you a society in which even the slaves and the sacrificial victims justify, endorse or condone these practices.

Of course, few sane people are nowadays likely to express the differences between the moral values of different cultures quite so dramatically or by reference to quite such outrageous examples (since except at the extreme lunatic fringes of society few people are likely to regard child violation or murder in the name of religion as anything more than a disgusting obscenity) but they will point out that different social, political and religious groups within present-day western societies do hold different views of a moral character which can be clearly shown to conflict. All the same, in relation to the question of moral education it is necessary to beware of certain confusions here.

Although it is clear enough that different social groups do believe different things with respect to questions of the point and purpose of human existence, the treatment of individuals of different status within a given social hierarchy, the punishment of social deviants and outlaws and so forth, we have already pointed out that the education of children is not centrally concerned with the inculcation of such social beliefs, but rather with the promotion of certain attitudes and dispositions of honesty, integrity, self-control, tolerance and the like. It is also worth observing that different historical conditions and circumstances may have at times provided a rationale for social customs and practices which it is difficult for civilised man to condone; in the frontier towns of the American west during the last century, for example, the summary justice of the vigilante may have been the last thin line of defence against something like total civil breakdown and disorder and may to that extent have been justified in something like utilitarian terms.

That does not make lynching or any other form of capital punishment morally right, of course, only the lesser of two not simultaneously avoidable evils. And in any case, the view that in certain circumstances a lesser evil of this order may require to be accepted to avoid a greater one involves a level of rational argument or casuistry which, however suited to the later stages of education at which young people will have acquired more of a taste and a capacity for such argument and discussion, is nevertheless hardly appropriate at the earlier primary and secondary stages.

Moreover, although it would certainly seem that such open discussion and argument about different moral codes and beliefs has a definite place at the later stages of education, it would also appear that it cannot occur prior to and actually presupposes some initiation of children into moral attitudes and dispositions of a more fundamental kind. Only when children know something in practice of what courage, self-control, fairness and honesty are, are they in a position to understand or to cast a critical eye over particular or specific human social or moral codes and practices.

But it may still be objected that this does not go to the heart of the difficulty on the ground that though the range of moral attitudes and dispositions into which children do initially require to be initiated are temporally or chronologically prior to the particular social and moral codes of belief and practice fully subscribed to by the adult members of a given community, they are nevertheless not *logically* prior; in fact, it may be said, the basic moral virtues require to be defined by reference to particular social and moral codes – what *counts* as a moral virtue in a given human community simply depends upon the particular beliefs about human destiny and social structure that are entertained as true by the adult members of that community. For example, to be brought up among right-wing conservatives is to have the values of initiative, industry and paternalism instilled into one at the expense of those of co-operation and compassion – and for the child of left-wing socialists, *vice versa*. Precisely, then, the various moral dispositions acquire their value only in the context of specific systems of social and moral belief.

It is easy enough to demonstrate that this view of matters is false, however, by asking almost any conservative what he thinks of co-operation and compassion and any socialist what *he* thinks of industry, initiative and looking after people who can't look after themselves. In fact, the conservative will heartily agree with the socialist in placing a high value on all of these attitudes and dispositions and, of course, crucially on the value of justice; what they disagree over are the policies to be adopted to promote the basic ends of moral life – they disagree precisely in their practical reasoning. It is just not the case, moreover, that what counts as honesty or courage depends on particular social or political perspectives. It may be difficult for the US Republican to see the Vietnam draft evader's action as courage and likewise for the Peace Movement subscriber's view of the G.I.'s participation, but if both men stick to their principles in the face of overwhelming hostility, opposition or danger then they are *both* displaying courage; honesty, moreover, is just being truthful to others or to oneself in anyone's book.

In support of the claim that the human qualities we call moral virtues are themselves relative to social perspectives it has sometimes been argued that the moral ideal of the ancient Greeks differed markedly from that of the Christians because whereas for the Greeks the central moral virtue was pride, for Christians it is humility.[8] But this is, of course, a deplorably shallow view of matters which does not withstand the least scrutiny. For hardly anyone has been more aware than the literary figures of Greek antiquity – both the poets and the philosophers – of the important distinction to be drawn between the proper self-respect which is exhibited in an appropriate level of moral integrity and fortitude and the kind of vain and insolent arrogance to which the Greeks themselves gave the name of *hubris*.

Genuine pride or self-respect, then, consists in a reasonable estimate of one's own worth in relation to one's positive achievements and as such it is not inherently opposed to the due or proper humility by which one also recognises one's own limitations; *hubris*, on the other hand, is a defect of character which is based on a false estimate of one's worth or an unwarranted feeling of superiority over others which *is*, as such, opposed to humility. Likewise, however, the humility valued by Christians is not a grovelling or debased state but a matter of integrity, honesty and resolution – turning the other cheek demands great moral courage, a courage which is quite consistent with the Christian's proper pride and sense of self-worth in the knowledge that he is valued and loved by God.

Thus it is rather more accurate here to take the view that if the pagans valued pride and the Christians humility, these facts do not in themselves render their positions inconsistent because there was also a Greek conception of proper humility (how could there not have been?) which they did not view as opposed to pride and there is also an idea of pride or self-respect which is valued by Christians and not opposed by them to humility. On the other hand, of course, if it is insisted that Greek pride is at odds with Christian humility because the former is a concept of power, prestige and dominance, whereas the latter is a concept of doormat-like subservience, then these qualities *are* indeed opposed but they are *not* virtues – they are not what are normally valued in moral terms as self-respect and humility which are respectively an *appropriate* attitude of satisfaction regarding one's own achievements and a realistic assessment of them in the light of one's own weaknesses and limitations.

What lies behind these arguments, I suspect, is just precisely the old Greek thesis of the *unity* of the virtues – an idea dear to the hearts of Socrates and Plato. But I think that the deep truth in this thesis is not so much that, as many people appear to have thought, an individual who possesses one virtue, say wisdom or justice, must possess all the others – it seems that there is a clear enough sense in which just men are not always courageous, courageous men not always temperate and so on – it is more that if a quality of character is a *genuine* virtue it is not *logically* inconsistent with any other real virtue. Being justly proud of one's achievements, then, is not in principle inconsistent with having a modest view of oneself based on a recognition of one's own limitations, loving one's children is not inconsistent with bringing them up with a firm hand, being a true and kind friend to someone is not at all at odds with speaking one's mind to them and so on.

Viewed in this light, then, the virtues form a unity because they all stand in a certain direct relationship to the *truth* in human affairs; love, says St Paul, is not happy with evil, it is happy with the truth, and here he is speaking of the pivotal Christian *virtue*.[9] On the contrary, however, the vices exhibit a disunity or a diversity precisely because they enshrine different and conflicting forms of falsehood and failure; as Aristotle clearly pointed out, cowardice and rashness are two different ways of failing to be courageous – likewise, vanity and self-deprecation are two ways of failing to do oneself justice, neglect and spoiling are two ways of failing to love one's children and so forth.

All this, of course, is not to deny that a serious attempt to profess the moral virtues often leads to considerable difficulties. Indeed, the moral difficulties to which we are all too frequently heir and for which we require the continual exercise of practical wisdom arise precisely because it is not always possible in this hard world to satisfy simultaneously what is required of us by all the virtues – either because of the wickedness of others or because through our own weaknesses we paint ourselves into moral corners. Although it is true, then, that honesty and justice are not logically or *in principle* inconsistent and that it behoves us always where possible to be both honest *and* just, there remains the difficulty on that occasion when (to use Plato's example) returning the weapons that we have borrowed to the man who has gone mad might well lead to the murder of innocent people.[10] To be sure, it is always an offence against virtue to lie, but in this case lying may be the lesser of two considerable evils.

Again justice is of course consistent only with the protection of the innocent but practical reason may well inform us that if this innocent party is not handed over for summary execution then hundreds more of the innocent may die at the hands of the terrorists (and we cannot be sure that our own hands will remain clean if we let that happen). It is anything but the case, then, that aspiring to a virtuous life is the end of moral problems – on the contrary, there is a real enough sense in which acquiring the virtues to any degree or coming to appreciate what they mean in human life *introduces* a range of problems which creatures untroubled by reflection on questions of moral principle could not possibly have – but clearly such an aspiration must nevertheless form the basis of the proper way to proceed for all who wish to create and to contribute to a civilised and decent human society.

In that case, any process of human education which

conspicuously fails to acquaint children with the standards of character and conduct which distinguish worthwhile and decent lives from squalid and decadent ones has much to answer for. It is hardly indoctrination, then, to try to show children that it is more admirable to persist in a worthwhile enterprise in the face of failure and disappointment than otherwise, that it is a higher expression of the human spirit to seek satisfaction in the service of a cause which is of general benefit than to seek personal advantage through the shameful exploitation of others, that it is less ridiculous and more consistent with human dignity to carry oneself modestly than to delude oneself with vanity and arrogance and that a truer appreciation of life's pleasures, even the sensual and physical ones, is more readily available to the self-disciplined man of educated taste than to the coarse boor or insatiable glutton.

As we have seen, of course, how precisely a given virtue is to be expressed in a particular set of circumstances is a matter for some deliberation and experience of life, and practical reflection may sometimes lead us to change our minds – what, for example, we once regarded as patriotism now looks suspiciously like imperialism. But this should not erode our basic appreciation of the moral value of a virtue like loyalty or lead us to doubt whether, when we commend a small child for standing bravely by his best friend, we are doing the right thing. After all, we can later come to see that what we earlier saw as a brave sacrifice for our country but now see as the cold-blooded murder of defenceless peasants is not really a genuine case of patriotism or courage, only because we have some grasp of what these qualities mean in advance of learning what our country is asking us to do.

Once again, I have devoted all of the available space in this concluding chapter to trying to sort out certain conceptual problems or confusions about the nature and purpose of moral education, rather than to considerations about, say, how moral teaching in schools ought to be practically conducted or how moral education should be formalised within the curriculum, because I believe that almost everything that needs to be said concerns the former rather than the latter. For I suspect that what teachers in schools (more often) and parents at home (less often) suffer most from is not a lack of specialised technical knowledge or skill concerning how to proceed with moral education, but a failure of nerve with respect to an enterprise which modernity seems to have pronounced unlawful or hazardous.

Of course it is extremely hazardous – like any other vital enterprise in this world we may indeed fail in it. But nothing is more legitimate, indeed urgent, than for teachers and other educationalists to appreciate that the moral education of children, the job of acquainting them with those homely and familiar human excellences called the moral virtues – honesty, tolerance, fairmindedness, courage, persistence, consideration, patience and so forth – is the highest and most important task of education. The schools which best provide this firm foundation for living well are also, moreover, not especially those in which the most advanced pedagogical techniques have been adopted or the most detailed curriculum structures have been elaborated, or even those in which lessons called 'moral education' have been placed on the timetable. Rather they are those in which children are taught by teachers who are themselves clearly committed to integrity, truth and justice and who have sought to transform the school and the classroom into the kinds of communities where a love of what is right, decent and good is exhibited as often as possible in the conduct of those into whose care they have been given.

NOTES AND REFERENCES

INTRODUCTION

1 The main influence of Friedrich Nietzsche (1844–1900) has been on various forms of European mainland philosophy – especially the so-called 'existentialism' of Martin Heidegger and Jean-Paul Sartre. Similarities have often been noted, however, between the continental notions of moral choice and authenticity and the ideas of moral autonomy to be found in such forms of analytical moral philosophy as prescriptivism (see chapter 4).

2 The original source of this well-thumbed metaphor of ordinary language philosophy would appear to be G. Ryle: *Dilemmas*, Cambridge: Cambridge University Press, 1964, p. 94.

3 Neurath's analogy is frequently cited by philosophers for different purposes. See, for example W. V. O. Quine: *Word and Object*, Cambridge: MIT Press, 1960; and P. T. Geach: *Reason and Argument*, Oxford: Blackwell, 1976.

4 Moral subjectivism and relativism will be discussed more fully in the final chapter.

5 For example, Lawrence Kohlberg explicitly rejects what he calls the 'bag of virtues' approach throughout his work (see notes on chapter 7 and bibliography for references) and A. S. Neill is critical of the repressive effects of moral education throughout his own *Summerhill* (see notes on chapter 6 and bibliography for references).

6 On this matter, see my paper 'Education, professionalism and theories of teaching', *Journal of Philosophy of Education*, Vol 20, No 1, 1986.

7 N. J. H. Dent: *Rousseau*, Oxford: Blackwell, 1988.

1 VIRTUE AS KNOWLEDGE: SOCRATES AND PLATO

1 An excellent translation of the *Meno* (by W. C. K. Guthrie) has been collected together with first-rate translations of all the other dialogues of undisputed Platonic authorship in Edith Hamilton

271

and Huntington Cairns (eds): *Plato: The Collected Dialogues*, Princeton: Princeton University Press, 1961.

2   We also have evidence for and information concerning the life of Socrates, of course, from other sources – notably Aristophanes and Xenophon. See especially Xenophon: *Memoirs of Socrates and the Symposium*, translated by H. Tredennick, Harmondsworth: Penguin Classics, 1970, and Aristophanes' play 'The Clouds' translated by Alan Sommerstein in: *Aristophanes: Lysistrata, The Archanians, The Clouds*, Harmondsworth: Penguin, 1973.

3   For a helpful discussion of this matter see the introduction to Samuel Scolnicov: *Plato's Metaphysics of Education*, London: Routledge, 1988.

4   Plato discusses Protagoras' doctrine that 'man is the measure of all things' in his dialogue *Theaetetus* (translated by F. M. Cornford in the Hamilton-Cairns collection mentioned above).

5   See, for example, Friedrich Nietzsche: *Thus Spake Zarathustra*, translated by R. J. Hollingdale, Harmondsworth: Penguin, 1961; and *Beyond Good and Evil*, translated by R. J. Hollingdale, Harmondsworth: Penguin, 1973.

6   Callicles is a leading character in Plato's dialogue *Gorgias* and likewise Thrasymachus in *The Republic*.

7   This important argument against the arts of rhetoric and sophistry can be found in *Gorgias* from 462 onwards (see Hamilton-Cairns, op. cit., p. 245).

8   The four Greek virtues of wisdom, temperance, justice and courage frequently discussed by Socrates and Plato were to become the four cardinal virtues of later Scholastic philosophy. See my paper, 'The cardinal virtues and Plato's moral psychology', *Philosophical Quarterly*, Vol 38, No 151, 1988.

9   J. J. Rousseau: *The Social Contract and Discourses*, translated by G. D. H. Cole, London: Dent, Everyman's Library, 1973, p. 181.

10   I was guilty of such an incautious use of the term 'will' in relation to Plato's moral psychology in my *Philosophical Quarterly* paper mentioned above in note 8 (though, I suspect, without risk of great harm there).

11   St Augustine: *On the Free Choice of the Will*, translated by Anna Benjamin and L. H. Hackstaff, New York and Indianapolis: Bobbs-Merrill, Library of Liberal Arts, 1964.

2   VIRTUE AS CHARACTER: ARISTOTLE'S ETHICS

1   For Aristotle's ethical views I have relied entirely on the *Nicomachean Ethics* – mainly the translation by Sir David Ross for Oxford University Press, first published in 1925. The other ethical treatise attributed to Aristotle – the *Eudemian Ethics* – has traditionally been regarded as rather less representative of Aristotle's mature thought.

2   Aristotle: *Nicomachean Ethics*, translated by Sir David Ross, London: Oxford University Press, 1925, p. 1.

3 On this, see Sir David Ross: *Aristotle*, London: Methuen, 1923, pp. 190–192.

4 On this, see Georg Henrik Von Wright: *The Varieties of Goodness*, London: Routledge & Kegan Paul, 1963, chapter 7, section 2.

5 Aristotle; *Ethics*, Ross translation, p. 3.

6 Aristotle: *De Anima*, translated by Hugh Lawson-Tancred, Harmondsworth: Penguin, 1986, Book II, chapter 1, p. 157.

7 Aristotle: *Ethics*, Ross translation, p. 28.

8 ibid., pp. 28–29.

9 ibid., p. 39.

10 For a first-rate collection of highly influential articles expressing this recent interest see Joseph Raz (ed.): *Practical Reasoning*, Oxford Readings in Philosophy, Oxford: Oxford University Press, 1978, especially the extracts from Anscombe, Von Wright and Kenny.

11 The first of these points is made in Book III, section 3, of the *Nicomachean Ethics* (Ross p. 56) and the second in Book VI, section 5 (Ross p. 143).

12 ibid., Book VII. See especially section 8.

3 VIRTUE AS SELF-DETERMINATION: ROUSSEAU AND KANT

1 Thomas Hobbes: *Leviathan*, introduced by C. B. MacPherson, Harmondsworth: Penguin, 1968.

2 ibid., p. 186.

3 The main works of Rousseau I have referred to are 'The Social Contract', 'A Discourse on the Origin of Inequality' and 'A Discourse on Political Economy' collected together in the translation by G. D. H. Cole: *The Social Contract and Discourses*, London: Dent, Everyman's Library, 1973; and *Emile*, translated by Barbara Foxley, London: Dent, Everyman's Library, 1974.

4 See G. D. H. Cole: op. cit., p. 181.

5 ibid., p. 84.

6 ibid., p. 181.

7 ibid., p. 210.

8 ibid., p. 140.

9 For the views of Hume see: *A Treatise of Human Nature*, edited by E. C. Mossner, Harmondsworth: Penguin, 1969; and *Enquiries Concerning Human Understanding and Concerning the Principles of Morals* edited by L. A. Selby-Bigge, Oxford: Clarendon Press, 1966.

10 Immanuel Kant: *Critique of Pure Reason*, translated by Norman Kemp-Smith, London: Macmillan, 1929.

11 For Kant's ethical views see: *The Critique of Practical Reason*, translated by T. K. Abbott, London: Longmans, Green & Co, 1967; and *The Moral Law*, translated by H. J. Paton, London: Hutchinson, 1987. The latter – which I have mainly referred to – is a translation of the 'Groundwork of the Metaphysic of Morals', and the former also contains the Groundwork as well as the second Critique.

12 Hume's *Treatise* Book II, Part III, section iii. (Mossner: op. cit., p. 462).
13 Kant's *Groundwork* chapter 1. (Paton: op. cit., pp. 76–80.)
14 ibid., pp. 74–77.
15 ibid., pp. 63–67.

4 MODERN MORAL PHILOSOPHY: TWO CONCEPTS OF MORALITY

1 For positivist and emotivist accounts of moral language see: A. J. Ayer: *Language, Truth and Logic*, London: Victor Gollancz, 1967, especially chapter VI; and C. L. Stevenson: *Ethics and Language*, New Haven and London: Yale University Press, 1944.
2 For the prescriptivism of R. M. Hare see especially his: *The Language of Morals*, Oxford: Oxford University Press, 1952; but also *Freedom and Reason*, Oxford: Oxford University Press, 1963. The prescriptivist perspective is also endorsed by W. D. Hudson in *Modern Moral Philosophy*, London: Macmillan, 1970.
3 See generally, L. Wittgenstein: *Philosophical Investigations*, Oxford: Blackwell, 1953. It is hardly possible to overstate the extent of Wittgenstein's influence on Anglo-American analytical philosophy of recent times.
4 P. F. Strawson: 'Truth', *Analysis*, Vol 9, No 6, 1949.
5 A fair idea of what so-called naturalists or 'neo-naturalists' will and will not stand for, may be got from G. E. M. Anscombe, 'Modern moral philosophy' in *Ethics, Religion and Politics: Collected Philosophical Papers Volume III*, Oxford: Blackwell, 1981; P. T. Geach, 'Good and evil', in *Theories of Ethics* edited by P. Foot, Oxford: Oxford University Press 1967; and P. Foot: *Virtues and Vices*, Oxford: Blackwell, 1978, especially chapters 7, 8 and 9.
6 For rather more technical objections to prescriptivism see, for example, P. T. Geach: *Logic Matters*, Oxford: Blackwell, 1972, pp. 268–269; and (less directly) John Searle: *Speech Acts*, Cambridge: Cambridge University Press, 1969, Part II, chapter 8.
7 For Bentham, Mill and utilitarianism generally see: *John Stuart Mill: Utilitarianism*, edited by Mary Warnock, London and Glasgow: Collins-Fontana, 1962.
8 See especially, M. Warnock: *Schools of Thought*, London: Faber & Faber, 1977, chapter 4.
9 For John McDowell see especially, 'Virtue and reason', in *Monist*, 62, 1979; 'Are moral requirements hypothetical imperatives?' in *Proceedings of the Aristotelian Society*, Supp Vol 52, 1978; and 'Non-cognitivism and rule-following' in Holtzman and Leich (eds): *Wittgenstein: To Follow a Rule*, London: Routledge & Kegan Paul, 1981.
10 See especially, Alasdair MacIntyre: *After Virtue: A study in Moral Theory*, Duckworth, 1981; and *Whose Justice? Which Rationality?*, London: Duckworth, 1988.
11 G. E. M. Anscombe 'Modern moral philosophy' in *Collected Philosophical Papers Volume III*, Oxford: Blackwell, 1981.

12 See H. O. Mounce and D. Z. Phillips: *Moral Practices*, London: Routledge & Kegan Paul, 1969.
13 Concerning my own views on disagreements between modern virtue theorists: first, I am inclined to the view that the differences between MacIntyre and earlier naturalists are more apparent than real and thus very probably reconcilable: second I am still not entirely clear about the implications of McDowell's arguments for the problem of moral weakness. If like Socrates and Plato (at certain stages) he is disposed to regard moral wisdom or knowledge as entirely *sufficient* for right action, then I could not follow him; but it may well be that his position on motivation is more like the more modest one I have taken in chapter ten. (But in *that* case I am still not clear about the nature of his quarrel with the 'non-cognitivists'.)

5 MORAL EDUCATION AS SOCIALISATION: EMILE DURKHEIM

1 Karl Marx: 'Preface to a contribution to the critique of political economy' in *Karl Marx and Frederick Engels: Selected Works*, London: Lawrence & Wishart, 1968, p. 181.
2 The works of Durkheim to which I shall chiefly refer are: *Suicide: A Study in Sociology*, London: Routledge & Kegan Paul, 1952; *Moral Education: A Study in the Theory and Application of the Sociology of Education*, New York: Collier-Macmillan, 1961; *Rules of Sociological Method*, New York: Free Press, 1964; and *The Division of Labour in Society*, New York: Collier-Macmillan, 1964.
3 See, Jeremy Bentham: 'Introduction to the principles of morals and legislation', in *Utilitarianism*, edited by Mary Warnock, London and Glasgow: Collins-Fontana, 1962; and Herbert Spencer: *First Principles*, New York and London: D. Appleton and Co, 1900.
4 Emile Durkheim: *Moral Education*, p. 23.
5 ibid., p. 51.
6 Emile Durkheim: *Division of Labour*, pp. 429–431.
7 *Moral Education*, p. 86.
8 On this see, P. T. Geach 'Plato's Euthyphro' in *Logic Matters*, Oxford: Blackwell, 1972, I.4; also his *God and the Soul*, London: Routledge & Kegan Paul, 1969, chapter 9.
9 In Shakespeare's play, Hamlet is given to say 'there is nothing either good or bad but thinking makes it so' (Hamlet: 2.2.225).
10 See my 'Three approaches to moral education' in *Educational Philosophy and Theory*, Vol 15, No 2, 1983.

6 PSYCHOANALYSIS AND MORAL CHARACTER: FREUD, LANE AND NEILL

1   R. F. Mackenzie was a quite charismatic Scottish educationalist who attempted to introduce progressive ideas into the state system in the sixties and seventies, especially as the headmaster of the ill-starred Summerhill Academy, Aberdeen (not to be confused with A. S. Neill's famous school of the same name). He was the author of several books including: *The Unbowed Head*, Edinburgh University Student Publications, undated; and *State School*, Harmondsworth: Penguin Education, 1970.

2   I have drawn much of the material for this chapter from my own previously published articles on progressive education, especially: 'Moral philosophy and psychology in progressive and traditional educational thought' in *Journal of Philosophy of Education*, Vol 18, No 1, 1984; and 'The free child and the spoiled child: anatomy of a progressive distinction in *Journal of Philosophy of Education*, Vol 19, No 1, 1985; but see also 'Education and the promotion of human freedom' in *Educational Philosophy and Theory*, Vol 13, No 1, 1982; and 'Freud and sexual ethics' in *Philosophy*, Vol 62, No 241, 1987.

3   A useful introduction to the ideas of Arthur Schopenhauer can be found in: Patrick Gardiner: *Schopenhauer*, Harmondsworth: Penguin Books, 1963.

4   For the ideas of Freud see generally the Pelican Freud Library, especially Vol 4, *The Interpretation of Dreams*, Harmondsworth: Penguin, 1976; and Vol 5, *The Psychopathology of Everyday Life*, Harmondsworth: Penguin, 1975. I have also drawn quite heavily, however, on Freud's essays in Vol 7, *On Sexuality*, Harmondsworth: Penguin, 1977.

5   See Freud's 'Three essays on the theory of sexuality' and the other essays in *On Sexuality*, Harmondsworth: Penguin, 1977.

6   See, for example, David Will's excellent: *Homer Lane: A Biography*, London: Allen & Unwin, 1964.

7   Homer Lane: *Talks to Parents and Teachers*, London: Allen & Unwin, 1954.

8   For an account of the Little Commonwealth see, E. T. Bazely: *Homer Lane and the Little Commonwealth*, London: Allen & Unwin, 1948.

9   Lane, op. cit., p. 82.

10   Lane, ibid., p. 51.

10   ibid., pp. 31–32.

11   A. S. Neill: *Summerhill: A Radical Approach to Education*, London: Gollancz, 1965, p. 105.

12   Neill's widely read *Summerhill* was in fact drawn from previous works of Neill's published by Herbert Jenkins, London, over something like half a century. They included *A Dominie in Doubt* (1920), *The Problem Child* (1926), *The Problem Parent* (1932), *The Problem Teacher* (1939), *That Dreadful School* (1948) and *The Free Child* (1953).

276

13 Neill, *Summerhill*, p. 268.
14 For a sensitive and sympathetic account of Homer Lane's tragic demise see Wills, op. cit., 1964.
15 For a fairly unsympathetic appraisal of Neill's educational thought and practice see, Robin Barrow: *Radical Education*, London: Martin Robertson, 1978, chapter 4.

7 COGNITIVE GROWTH AND MORAL DEVELOPMENT: PIAGET AND KOHLBERG

1 For a useful and accessible introduction to behaviourist learning theories in connection with education see, Winifred F. Hill: *Learning*, London: Methuen & Co. Ltd, 1963.
2 The great American pragmatist philosopher John Dewey was profoundly influenced by the work of such pioneers of behaviourism as Watson and Thorndyke, and perhaps the greatest living American philosopher W. V. O. Quine has acknowledged the influence of B. F. Skinner in his celebrated *Word and Object*, Cambridge, Mass.: MIT Press, 1960.
3 See, for example, John Dewey: *Experience and Education*, New York: Collier, 1938; and W. H. Kilpatrick: *Foundations of Method*, New York: Macmillan, 1925.
4 For an account of Thorndyke's 'instrumental' and Skinner's 'operant' conditioning see, W. Hill: op. cit., chapter 4.
5 In his: *Beyond Freedom and Dignity*, Harmondsworth: Penguin, 1973, B. F. Skinner denies the necessity for a 'mentalistic' vocabulary of thoughts, intentions, plans and purposes in the explanation of human behaviour.
6 On this, see my paper: 'Dance education, skill and behavioural objectives' in *Journal of Aesthetic Education*, Vol 18, No 4, 1984.
7 For an account of behaviourist (and other) approaches to the understanding of learning as applied to moral life see, Derek Wright: *The Psychology of Moral Behaviour*, Harmondsworth, Penguin, 1971.
8 The so-called 'Gestalt' psychologists such as K. Koffka, W. Kohler and M. Wertheimer are notable for having observed the structural or interpretive nature of human perception. For a critical discussion of Gestalt theory see D. W. Hamlyn: *The Psychology of Perception*, London: Routledge & Kegan Paul, 1957, especially chapter 4.
9 See, Jean Piaget: *The Moral Judgement of the Child*, London: Routledge & Kegan Paul, 1932.
10 For the ideas of Lawrence Kohlberg see his: *The Philosophy of Moral Development*, San Francisco: Harper & Row, 1981, Vols I–III.
11 ibid., Vol I, chapter 2.

8 MORAL DEVELOPMENT IN PROGRESSIVE AND TRADITIONAL EDUCATIONAL THOUGHT

1 The most celebrated attack on the so-called analytic–synthetic distinction in mainstream philosophy was by W. V. O. Quine in 'Two dogmas of empiricism'. See chapter 2 of his *From a Logical Point of View*, New York: Harper & Row, 1953.

2 See, for example, John Darling 'Progressive, traditional, radical: a re-alignment' in *Journal of Philosophy of Education*, Vol 12, 1978; and my own, 'On understanding educational theory' in *Educational Philosophy and Theory*, Vol 17, No 2, 1985.

3 See, Paul H. Hirst and Richard S. Peters: *The Logic of Education*, London: Routledge & Kegan Paul, 1970.

4 ibid., p. 32. There is, however, a good deal of looseness about Hirst and Peters' uses of 'progressive', 'traditional', 'child-centred', 'authoritarian' and other key terms in this chapter (which may well be excused in the light of the fairly pioneering nature of this work).

5 See, for example, G. H. Bantock's 'Towards a theory of popular education' and John White's 'The curriculum mongers: education in reverse' both included in: *The Curriculum: Context, Design and Development*, edited by Richard Hooper, Edinburgh: Oliver and Boyd, 1971.

6 Matthew Arnold: 'Preface to *Literature and Dogma*' in *Matthew Arnold*, edited by James Gribble, London: Collier-Macmillan Educational Thinkers Series, 1967, p. 150.

7 See, R. S. Peters: *Authority, Responsibility and Education*, London: Allen & Unwin, 1959, Part III, chapter 8, p. 104.

8 Generally speaking, for example, A. S. Neill is very reminiscent of Rousseau in his own 'anti-social' bias and with respect to his own brand of non-interventionism.

9 R. S. Peters: *Hobbes*, Harmondsworth: Penguin, 1956.

10 For Bertrand Russell's 'progressive' educational ideas see his: *On Education*, London: Allen & Unwin, 1964; and *Education and the Social Order*, London: Allen & Unwin, 1961. See also, Leslie R. Perry (ed.): *Four Progressive Educators*, London: Collier-Macmillan Educational Thinkers Series, 1967.

11 A. S. Neill: *The Free Child*, London: Herbert Jenkins, 1953, p. 64.

12 See especially, Homer Lane: *Talks to Parents and Teachers*, London: Allen & Unwin, 1954, p. 51.

13 R. S. Peters' important collection *Moral Development and Moral Education*, London: Allen & Unwin, 1981, contains several essays related to Kohlberg's theory (see, especially chapters 5 and 8). Whilst, however, these essays are undoubtedly critical in nature they are also generally sympathetic to Kohlberg.

14 See my 'Moral philosophy and psychology in progressive and traditional educational thought' in *Journal of Philosophy of Education*, Vol 18, No 1, 1984.

9 VIRTUE AND PASSION:
SELF-CONTROL AND EXPRESSION

1 The source of the modern idea of *natural* evolution is, of course, to be found in such works of Charles Darwin as *Origin of Species* and *Descent of Man*. The concept of *social* evolution is perhaps especially associated with the ideas of the nineteenth-century philosopher Herbert Spencer in such works as *First Principles* and *System of Synthetic Philosophy*. More recent attempts to explain social and moral concepts in natural-evolutionary terms have been made by the so-called 'sociobiologists'; see, for example, E. O. Wilson: *Sociobiology*, Cambridge, Mass.: Harvard University Press, 1975.

2 Georg Henrik Von Wright: *The Varieties of Goodness*, London: Routledge & Kegan Paul, 1963, chapter 7.

3 Aristotle: *Nicomachean Ethics*, translated by Sir David Ross, Oxford: Oxford University Press, 1925, p. 39.

4 G. H. Von Wright: op. cit., p. 146.

5 ibid., p. 147.

6 ibid., p. 147.

7 Phillippa Foot: 'Virtues and vices' in *Virtues and Vices*, Oxford: Blackwell, 1978, p. 7.

8 ibid., p. 10.

9 P. T. Geach: *The Virtues*, Cambridge: Cambridge University Press, 1977, p. 17.

10 Here, I refer to the notorious experiments on isolation conducted by Harlow and others and described in H. F. Harlow and M. K. Harlow, 'Social deprivation in monkeys' in *Scientific American*, Vol 207, No 5, pp. 136–146.

11 Aristotle: op. cit., p. 28.

12 But recall, however, my attempt to give a charitable interpretation of the doctrine of the mean in chapter 2.

13 See C. S. Lewis: *The Great Divorce*, London and Glasgow: Collins-Fontana, 1972.

10 VIRTUE AND MOTIVATION:
OBLIGATION AND ASPIRATION

1 See Aristotle: *Nicomachean Ethics*, Book II, section 1.

2 Some telling criticisms of classical contract theory were made by David Hume; see, *Essays, Moral, Political and Literary*, edited by T. H. Green and T. H. Grose, London: Longmans, Green & Co, 1875. See also J. D. Mabbott: *The State and the Citizen*, London: Hutchinson University Library, 1970, chapter 2.

3 Immanuel Kant: *Groundwork*, translated as *The Moral Law*, by H. J. Paton, pp. 84–86.

4 See Plato: *The Republic*, translated by Paul Shorey in: Hamilton-Cairns (eds) *The Collected Dialogues*, Princeton: Princeton University Press, 1961, p. 580.

5   See Durkheim: *Moral Education*, p. 57; and *Division of Labour* pp. 427–431.

6   There is a strong inclination on the part of many moral theorists and historians of ideas to regard the idea of reciprocity in general and the Kantian version in particular as rooted in the fundamental principle of Christian ethics; but I am not so sure. In the form 'do as you would be done by', the idea was, of course, popularised by Charles Kingsley in *The Water Babies*.

7   See J. S. Mill's essay 'On Liberty' in *Utilitarianism* edited by Mary Warnock, London and Glasgow: Collins-Fontana, 1962.

8   See Plato: *Gorgias* translated by W. D. Woodhead in Hamilton-Cairns (eds): *Collected Dialogues*, especially pp. 255–263.

9   For Socrates' rather controversial defence of filial piety see Plato: *Euthyphro*, translated by Lane Cooper in: Hamilton-Cairns (eds) *Collected Dialogues*. See also P. T. Geach's criticism of Socrates in 'Plato's *Euthyphro*', in his *Logic Matters*, Oxford: Blackwell, 1972.

10 By, for example, Richard Taylor in *Ethics, Faith and Reason*, Englewood Cliffs, NJ: Prentice-Hall, 1985. Taylor's influence on the arguments of this chapter has been quite considerable, but in the final chapter of this work I take great exception to some of the conclusions which Taylor believes, mistakenly I think, to follow from his anti-deontological arguments.

11 Again, I am indebted to Taylor op. cit., 1985, for this precise perspective on the moral dubiety of such human attitudes and conduct as betrayal, dishonesty, vanity and so on.

12 The problem of teleology in Greek ethical and other thought is discussed by Alasdair MacIntyre in *After Virtue*.

13 Aristotle: *Nicomachean Ethics*, Ross translation p. 1. For a discussion of Aristotle's reasoning here, however, see P. T. Geach, 'History of a fallacy' in his: *Logic Matters*, Oxford: Blackwell, 1972.

14 This point was frequently made by C. S. Lewis in his works of popular theology. See, for example, *Mere Christianity*, London: Collins, Fount Paperbacks, 1977, Book I, chapter 1.

11   VIRTUE AND REASON: PROBLEM-SOLVING AND CLARIFICATION

1   See, for example, David McNaughton: *Moral Vision*, Oxford: Blackwell, 1988, chapter 1.

2   In several dialogues, but see especially the curious discussion in: *Lesser Hippias*, translated by Benjamin Jowett, in Hamilton-Cairns (eds) *Collected Dialogues*, pp. 200–214.

3   See, for example, Aristotle: *Nicomachean Ethics*, Book III, sections 1–5; and Book VI, sections 3–8 (as well as elsewhere in Aristotle's writings).

4   Aristotle: *Nicomachean Ethics*, Ross translation, p. 10.

5   This warning is given, for example, by David Wiggins in 'Delibera-

tion and practical reason', *Proceedings of the Aristotelian Society*, Vol 75, 1975–76.

6   The example and discussion which follow are drawn from my US Department of Education paper 'Aristotle and Durkheim on moral education' presented at a conference on moral education and character in Washington, 1987.

7   For a critical discussion of R. M. Hare's views on this matter see, P. T. Geach: *The Virtues*, Cambridge: Cambridge University Press, 1977, chapter 9, pp. 152–153.

8   See Aristotle: *Nicomachean Ethics*, Book VI, section 13, Ross translation pp. 156–158.

9   On this it is interesting to see, Scottish Education Department: *Moral and Religious Education in Scottish Schools* (The Millar Report) London: HMSO, 1972, 4.28, p. 62: 'The sensible educator will neither take up the extreme authoritarian thesis nor the extreme liberal thesis. He will not use "indoctrination" procedures more than is necessary (and he will always respect the personality of the pupil) but he will not feel guilty about using them when they are necessary.'

10   On this point see my 'Education, professionalism and theories of teaching', *Journal of Philosophy of Education*, Vol 20, No 1, 1986.

11   This 'negative' strategy has indeed been proposed by some modern progressive educationalists; see A. S. Neill's, *Summerhill* and also my own discussion in 'Moral philosophy and psychology in progressive and traditional educational thought', *Journal of Philosophy of Education*, Vol 18, No 1, 1984.

12   This 'shallow consequentialism' is, of course, largely due to the powerful influence on modern moral thought of utilitarianism. For an important recent debate on utilitarianism see, J. J. C. Smart and Bernard Williams: *Utilitarianism: For and Against*, Cambridge: Cambridge University Press, 1973.

12   EDUCATION AND THE VIRTUES: OBJECTIVITY, SUBJECTIVITY AND TEACHING

1   See John Milton: *Paradise Lost*, Book IV, 108, in: *Paradise Lost and Other Poems*, New York and Toronto: Mentor, New American Library, 1961, p. 118.

2   For a guide to 'practical' attempts to develop specific curricular programmes and teaching strategies for moral education see, John Wilson: *A Teachers Guide to Moral Education*, London: Geoffrey Chapman, 1975. Although I do not believe that these pedagogical and curricular strategies are *entirely* without value, it will be clear from this work that I regard them as predicated on a fundamentally mistaken and incoherent conception of moral life and moral education. See also, Mary Warnock: *Schools of Thought*, London: Faber & Faber, 1977, chapter 4.

3   In fact, I have written for him the Socratic dialogue that Plato

should have composed on this topic. I presented 'The Pedagogue: A lost dialogue of Plato', to the national conference of the Philosophy of Education Society in the spring of 1987. Although it is one of the few pieces I am fairly fond of I have unfortunately been unable to interest any publisher in it so far.

4   For a defence of chastity as a virtue see my, 'Chastity and adultery' in *American Philosophical Quarterly*, Vol 23, No 4, 1986.

5   This confusion between deciding for oneself in moral matters – making one's own choices – and determining for oneself what should *count* as having moral value, runs through much recent educational discussion of these topics. It seems to be especially prevalent in official educational reports and policy statements.

6   For the subjectivism of Protagoras see, Plato: *Theaetetus* translated by F. M. Cornford in: *Collected Dialogues* ed. Hamilton-Cairns.

7   Essentially this was Plato's own criticism of Protagoras.

8   This idea of a fundamental conflict between Pagan Greek and Christian ethics and the (to my mind) concomitant confusion about the basic nature of moral virtue is a cornerstone of Richard Taylor's: *Ethics, Faith and Reason*, Englewood Cliffs, NJ: Prentice-Hall, 1985, to which I am in other respects much indebted. Taylor's quite passionate defence of what he takes to be the Greek ideal and his vehement denunciation of Christian values is, of course, rather reminiscent of Nietzsche.

9   St Paul: *First Letter to the Corinthians*, chapter 13, especially verse 4.

10 Again, see Plato: *The Republic* in Hamilton-Cairns (eds): *Collected Dialogues*.

BIBLIOGRAPHY

Anscombe, G. E. M.: *Ethics, Religion and Politics: Collected Philosophical Papers Volume III*, Oxford: Blackwell, 1981

Aristophanes: *Lysistrata, The Acharnians, The Clouds*, translated by Alan Sommerstein, Harmondsworth: Penguin Classics, 1973

Aristotle: *The Nicomachean Ethics*, translated by Sir David Ross, Oxford: Oxford University Press, 1925

—— *The Politics*, translated by T. A. Sinclair, Harmondsworth: Penguin, 1962

—— *De Anima*, translated by Hugh Lawson-Tancred, Harmondsworth: Penguin, 1986

Ayer, A. J.: *Language, Truth and Logic*, London: Victor Gollancz, 1967

Bazely, E. T.: *Homer Lane and the Little Commonwealth*, London: Allen & Unwin, 1948

Barrow, R.: *Radical Education*, Martin Robertson, 1978

Bourke, V. J.: *The Essential Augustine*, Indianapolis: Hackett Publishing Company, 1964

Carr, D.: 'Education and the promotion of human freedom', *Educational Philosophy and Theory*, Vol 13, No 1, 1982

—— 'Three Approaches to moral education', *Educational Philosophy and Theory*, Vol 15, No 2, 1983

—— 'Dance education, skill and behavioural objectives', *Journal of Aesthetic Education*, Vol 18, No 4, 1984

—— 'Moral philosophy and psychology in progressive and traditional educational thought', *Journal of Philosophy of Education*, Vol 18, No 1, 1984

—— 'Two kinds of virtue', *Proceedings of the Aristotelian Society*, Vol 84, 1984/5

—— 'The free child and the spoiled child: anatomy of a progressive distinction, *Journal of Philosophy of Education*, Vol 19, No 1, 1985

—— 'On understanding educational theory', *Educational Philosophy and Theory*, Vol 17, No 2, 1985

—— 'Education, professionalism and theories of teaching, *Journal of Philosophy of Education*, Vol 20, No 1, 1986

—— 'Chastity and adultery', *American Philosophical Quarterly*, Vol 23, No 4, 1986

—— 'Freud and sexual ethics', *Philosophy*, Vol 62, No 241, 1987

—— 'Aristotle and Durkheim on moral education', Conference paper for US Department of Education, Washington, September 1987

—— 'The cardinal virtues and Plato's moral psychology, *Philosophical Quarterly*, Vol 38, No 151, 1988

Darling, J.: 'Progressive, traditional, radical: a re-alignment', *Journal of Philosophy of Education*, Vol 12, 1978

Dent, N. J. H.: *The Moral Psychology of the Virtues*, Cambridge: Cambridge University Press, 1984; *Rousseau*, Oxford: Blackwell, 1988

Dewey, J.: *Experience and Education*, New York: Collier, 1938

Durkheim, E.: *Suicide: A Study in Sociology*, London: Routledge & Kegan Paul, 1952

—— *Moral Education: A Study in the Theory and Application of the Sociology of Education*, New York: Collier-Macmillan, 1961

—— *The Division of Labour in Society*, New York: Collier-Macmillan, 1964

—— *Rules of Sociological Method*, New York: Free Press, 1964

Foot, P.: *Virtues and Vices*, Oxford: Blackwell, 1978

Foot, P. (ed.): *Theories of Ethics*, Oxford: Oxford University Press, 1967

Freud, S.: *The Interpretation of Dreams*, Pelican Freud Library Volume 4, Harmondsworth: Penguin, 1976

—— *The Psychopathology of Everyday Life*, Pelican Freud Library Volume 5, Harmondsworth: Penguin, 1975

—— *On Sexuality*, Pelican Freud Library Volume 7, Harmondsworth: Penguin, 1977

Gardiner, P.: *Schopenhauer*, Harmondsworth: Penguin, 1963

Geach, P. T.: *God and the Soul*, London: Routledge & Kegan Paul, 1969

—— *Logic Matters*, Oxford: Blackwell, 1972;

—— *Reason and Argument*, Oxford: Blackwell, 1976

—— *The Virtues*, Cambridge: Cambridge University Press, 1977

Green, T. H. and Grose, T. H. (eds): *Essays, Moral, Political and Literary*, London: Longmans, Green and Co, 1875

Gribble, J. (ed.): *Matthew Arnold*, London: Collier-Macmillan Educational Thinkers Series, 1967

Hamlyn, D. W.: *The Psychology of Perception*, London: Routledge & Kegan Paul, 1957

Hare, R. M.: *The Language of Morals*, Oxford: Oxford University Press, 1952; *Freedom and Reason*, Oxford: Oxford University Press, 1963

Harlow, H. F. and Harlow, M. K.: 'Social deprivation in monkeys', *Scientific American*, 207, 5, pp. 136–146

Hill, W.: *Learning*, London: Methuen & Co. Ltd, 1963

Hirst, P. H. & Peters, R. S.: *The Logic of Education* London: Routledge & Kegan Paul, 1970

Hobbes, T.: *Leviathan*, edited by C. B. MacPherson: Harmondsworth: Penguin, 1968

Holtzman and Leich (eds): *Wittgenstein: To Follow a Rule*, London: Routledge & Kegan Paul, 1981

Hooper, R. (ed.): *The Curriculum: Context, Design and Development*, Edinburgh: Oliver & Boyd, 1971

Hudson, W. D.: *Modern Moral Philosophy*, London: Macmillan, 1970

Hume, D.: *A Treatise of Human Nature*, edited by E. C. Mossner, Harmondsworth: Penguin, 1969

—— *Enquiries Concerning Human Understanding and Concerning the Principles of Morals*, edited by L. A. Selby-Bigge, Oxford: Clarendon, 1966

Kant, I.: *The Critique of Pure Reason*, translated by Norman Kemp-Smith, London: Macmillan, 1929

—— *The Critique of Practical Reason*, translated by T. K. Abbott, London: Longmans, Green & Co., 1967

—— *The Moral Law*, translated by H. J. Paton, London: Hutchinson, 1987

Kilpatrick, W. H.: *Foundations of Method*, New York: Macmillan, 1925

Kohlberg, L.: *The Philosophy of Moral Development* Volumes I–III, San Francisco: Harper & Row, 1981

Lane, H.: *Talks to Parents and Teachers*, London: Allen & Unwin, 1954

Lewis, C. S.: *The Great Divorce*, London and Glasgow: Collins-Fontana, 1972; *Mere Christianity*, London and Glasgow: Collins: Fount Paperbacks, 1977

Mabbot, J. D.: *The State and the Citizen*, London: Hutchinson University Library, 1970

McDowell, J.: 'Are moral requirements hypothetical imperatives?' *Proceedings of the Aristotelian Society* Supplement Volume 52, 1978

—— 'Virtue and reason', *Monist*, Vol 62, 1979

—— 'Non-cognitivism and rule-following' in Holtzman and Leich (eds): *Wittgenstein: To Follow a Rule*, London: Routledge & Kegan Paul, 1981

MacIntyre, A.: *After Virtue: A Study in Moral Theory*, London: Duckworth, 1981

—— *Whose Justice? Which Rationality?*, London: Duckworth, 1988

MacKenzie, R. F.: *The Unbowed Head*, Edinburgh University Student Publications, undated

—— *State School*, Harmondsworth: Penguin, 1970

McNaughton, D.: *Moral Vision*, Oxford: Blackwell, 1988

Marx, K. and Engels, F.: *Selected Writings*, London: Lawrence and Wishart, 1968

Milton, J.: *Paradise Lost and Other Poems*, Mentor: New American Library, 1961

Mounce, H. O. and Phillips, D. Z.: *Moral Practices* London: Routledge & Kegan Paul, 1969

Neill, A. S.: *A Dominie in Doubt*, London: Herbert Jenkins, 1920

—— *The Problem Child*, London: Herbert Jenkins, 1926

—— *The Problem Parent*, London, Herbert Jenkins, 1932

—— *The Problem Teacher*, London: Herbert Jenkins, 1939

—— *That Dreadful School*, London: Herbert Jenkins, 1948

—— *The Free Child*, London: Herbert Jenkins, 1953

—— *Summerhill: A Radical Approach to Education*, London: Gollancz, 1965 (published Harmondsworth: Penguin after 1968)

Nietzsche, F.: *Thus Spake Zarathustra*, translated by R. J. Hollingdale, Harmondsworth: Penguin, 1961

—— *Beyond Good and Evil*, translated by R. J. Hollingdale, Harmondsworth: Penguin, 1973

Perry, L. (ed.): *Four Progressive Educators*, London: Collier-Macmillan Educational Thinkers Series, 1967

Peters, R. S.: *Ethics and Education*, London: Allen & Unwin, 1966

—— *Moral Development and Moral Education*, London: Allen & Unwin, 1981

Piaget, J.: *The Moral Judgement of the Child*, London: Routledge & Kegan Paul, 1932

Plato: *The Collected Dialogues* edited by Edith Hamilton and Huntington Cairns, Princeton: Princeton University Press, 1961

Quine, W. V. O.: *From a Logical Point of View*, New York: Harper & Row, 1953

—— *Word and Object*, Cambridge, Mass.: MIT Press, 1960

Ross, W. D.: *Aristotle*, London: Methuen, 1923

Rousseau, J. J.: *The Social Contract and Discourses* translated by G. D. H. Cole, London: Dent, Everyman's Library, 1973

—— *Emile*, translated by B. Foxley, London: Dent, Everyman's Library, 1974

Russell, B.: *Education and the Social Order*, London: Allen & Unwin, 1961

—— *On Education*, London: Allen & Unwin, 1964

Ryle, G.: *Dilemmas*, Cambridge: Cambridge University Press, 1964

St Augustine: *On the Free Choice of the Will*, translated by Anna Benjamin and L. H. Hackstaff, New York and Indianapolis: Bobbs–Merrill, Library of the Liberal Arts, 1964

Scolnicov, S.: *Plato's Metaphysics of Education* London: Routledge, 1988

Searle, J.: *Speech Acts*, Cambridge: Cambridge University Press, 1969

Sigmund, P. E. (ed.): *St Thomas Aquinas on Politics and Ethics*, New York: Norton & Co., 1988

Skinner, B. F.: *Beyond Freedom and Dignity*, Harmondsworth: Penguin, 1973

Smart, J. J. C. and Williams, B.: *Utilitarianism: For and Against*, Cambridge: Cambridge University Press, 1973

Spencer, H.: *First Principles*, New York and London: D. Appleton & Co, 1900 Scottish Education Department

—— *Moral and Religious Education in Scottish Schools*, (The Millar Report) London: HMSO, 1972, 4.28

Spiecker, B. and Straughan, R. (eds.): *Philosophical Issues in Moral Education and Development*, Milton Keynes: Open University Press, 1988

Stevenson, C. L.: *Ethics and Language*, New Haven and London, 1944

Strawson, P. F.: 'Truth' *Analysis*, Vol 9, No 6, 1949

Taylor, R.: *Ethics, Faith and Reason*, Englewood Cliffs, NJ: Prentice-Hall, 1985

Von Wright, G. H.: *The Varieties of Goodness*, London: Routledge & Kegan Paul, 1963

Wallace, J. D.: *Virtues and Vices*, Ithaca and London: Cornell University Press, 1978

Warnock, M.: *Utilitarianism*, London and Glasgow: Collins-Fontana, 1962

—— *Schools of Thought*, London: Faber & Faber, 1977

Wiggins, D.: 'Deliberation and practical reason' *Proceedings of the Aristotelian Society*, Vol 75, 1975–76

Wills, D.: *Homer Lane: A Biography*, London: Allen & Unwin, 1964

Wilson, E. O.: *Sociobiology*, Cambridge, Mass.: Harvard University Press, 1975

Wilson, J.: *A Teachers Guide to Moral Education*, London: Geoffrey Chapman, 1975

Wittgenstein, L.: *Philosophical Investigations*, Oxford: Blackwell, 1953

Wright, D.: *The Psychology of Moral Behaviour*, Harmondsworth: Penguin, 1971

Xenophon: *Memoirs of Socrates and the Symposium*, translated by H. Tredennick, Harmondsworth: Penguin Classics, 1970

INDEX

teaching methods 171
techne (craft reasoning) 57
teleological (purposive)
    conceptions of morality
    99–100, 101–7, 228
Thorndike, E.L. 130, 150,
    152
thumos (spirit) 36–7, 43
totalitarianism 43
traditionalism, and progressivism
    17–18, 170–87
transcendental ('nuomenal') self
    79–80
tyranny 64–5

unconscious mind 133–4
universalisation 81–3, 94–5, 102,
    212, 213, 235
utilitarianism 100, 114, 116, 123,
    172, 220

verification of moral law 74–5,
    234
vice, and ignorance 33–5
vices of excess 205–7
virtue 48; acquisition of 50–2,
    195–6, 253–5; and choice
    68–9, 70, 195–6; classification

of 197–8, 200, 252–3; defining
4–5, 18; and duty 19, 253; in
education *see* moral education;
ethics of 87, 97–107; 'genus'
52–3; intellectual 48; and justice
35–7; as knowledge 23–41,
58–61; and passion 18–19,
31–5, 232–50, 253–4; and
reason 19, 31–5, 232–50,
253–4; relationship to human
nature 17–19; and self-control
53–5; and social influences
17–19, 221–31; Socratic view
31–3; and suppression of
desires 28–32, 53, 69–70, 252;
unity of 266–7
Von Wright, G.H., *The Varieties of
Goodness* 195–9, 200, 201, 202,
205

Warnock, Mary 101
Watson, J.B. 130, 150
White, John 172
will, *see* motivation
Wittgenstein, Ludwig,
    Philosophical Investigations 92–3

Zeno 25